# West Texas

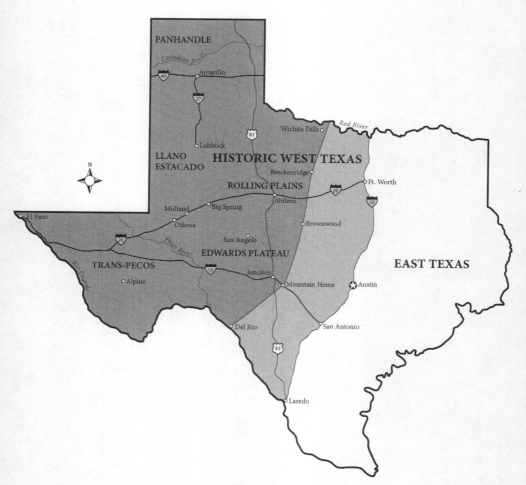

PANHANDLE

*Canadian River*

40

Amarillo

27

Wichita Falls

*Red River*

Lubbock

LLANO
ESTACADO

HISTORIC WEST TEXAS

Breckenridge

ROLLING PLAINS

Abilene

20

Ft. Worth

35

Midland

Big Spring

Odessa

Brownwood

El Paso

20

*Pecos River*

San Angelo

EDWARDS PLATEAU

EAST TEXAS

10

TRANS-PECOS

Junction

*Rio Grande*

Alpine

Mountain Home

Austin

Del Rio

San Antonio

83

Laredo

N

*Courtesy Curtis Peoples, Southwest Collection, Texas Tech University*

# West Texas

A HISTORY OF THE GIANT SIDE OF THE STATE

*Edited by*

Paul H. Carlson and Bruce A. Glasrud

University of Oklahoma Press : Norman

ALSO BY PAUL H. CARLSON AND BRUCE A. GLASRUD
(co-edited with Tai D. Kreidler) *Slavery to Integration: Black Americans in West Texas* (Abilene, Texas, 2007)

Library of Congress Cataloging-in-Publication Data

West Texas : a history of the giant side of the state / edited by Paul H. Carlson and Bruce A. Glasrud.
     pages cm
Includes bibliographical references and index.
ISBN 978–0–8061–4444–3 (pbk. : alk. paper) 1. Texas, West—History. 2. Texas, West—Travel and description. 3. Texas, West—Population. I. Carlson, Paul Howard, editor of compilation. II. Glasrud, Bruce A., editor of compilation.
F386.W46 2014
976.4'9—dc23

2013042690

# Contents

# Illustrations

## FIGURES

## MAPS

# Preface

This book grew from a series of discussions among historians after a special session on West Texas history at the 2009 annual meeting of the West Texas Historical Association. Although most attendees conceded that many aspects of the region's rich past have been explored, everyone recognized that no comprehensive survey of West Texas history has yet been published. Many superb studies have already appeared that treat a great variety of aspects of West Texas history. In book or article form they examine its people; its institutions; its social, cultural, and economic life; its environmental issues; and its general background. Until now, however, there has been no synthesis, no broadly based narrative attempting to establish meaning and provide an overarching description and analysis that might explain the growth and development of the "giant side of Texas" from its geological beginnings to its dynamic present.

Our discussions at the conference thus centered on the need for a broad, general history of the large region, and from those conversations grew the present volume, *West Texas: A History of the Giant Side of the State*. The book examines the long history of West Texas and by extension the area's relationship over time to Texas and the Southwest. Its eighteen chapters are arranged in four parts. Chapters that make up part I, "The Place," focus on major geographical and environmental subregions of West Texas.

Chapters of part II, "The People," treat gender and local ethnic groups and their contributions to West Texas history. Chapters of part III, "Political and Economic Life," consider some of the larger cities of West Texas as well as the region's political heritage and economic activities, including oil and gas production. Chapters of part IV, "Society and Culture," view the region's music heritage, its educational heritage, its parks and recreation areas, and intellectual notions that have given the region a sense of itself.

The nonlinear organization of the book is intentional, and the separate chapters, each on its own topic, may be read in any order. Each chapter includes a list of suggested items for further reading, and near the end of the book a selected bibliography lists important works that review many aspects of West Texas history. In short, the book covers both a wide-ranging history and significant historiography of a very large territory.

For help in putting the book together, we are indebted to many people. Leland K. Turner of Midwestern State University organized the special session from which the book grew. Presenters at the important 2009 session included Bruce A. Glasrud, Glenn Ely, M. Scott Sosebee, Diana Davids Hinton, and Ty Cashion.

For the subtitle of our book, we acknowledge with gratitude Eddie McBride, Phil Price, and the Lubbock Chamber of Commerce. For several years, "The Giant Side of Texas" has been a marketing slogan for the Lubbock Chamber, and McBride, who is with the chamber, agreed to our use of the idea.

Additional help came from Curtis Peoples of Texas Tech University's Southwest Collection. He drew the maps presented in this book. Others at the Southwest Collection, particularly Freedonia Paschal; Jennifer Spurrier; John Holmes; and Randy Vance and his student assistants, Nicci Hester, Glennisha Elliott, and Austin Allison, aided our research. Vance also, with Monte L. Monroe, was especially helpful in locating photographs and providing ideas and information. Colleagues associated with the West Texas Historical Association, including Tai Kreidler, Robert Weaver, and Laura Horner, also provided assistance. In addition, Ty Cashion, Gene Preuss, Diana Davids Hinton, H. Allan Anderson, David J. Murrah, Monte Monroe, Tom Crum, the late Frederick W. Rathjen, and others suggested topics to cover, debated with us about what constitutes West Texas, or read portions of the manuscript.

Because the book covers a lot of ground, the cooperation of its constituent authors was vital. The results have been rewarding. The contributors, all of whom have built reputations as competent historians of the region, range in background from such established writers as Arnoldo De León, James Smallwood, and Thomas Britten to emerging scholars, including Scott Sosebee, Richard Wright, and Sean Cunningham. All are familiar with the historical and geographical sweep of West Texas as well as the diverse peoples of the region.

In addition, we are indebted to editors of the region's historical journals—*West Texas Historical Association Year Book*, *Panhandle Plains Historical Review*, *Permian Historical Annual*, *Password*, and *Journal of Big Bend Studies*—who have published numerous thoughtfully written, solidly researched articles treating new and important aspects of West Texas history. We likewise express our thanks to the many younger scholars of West Texas history who have energized the profession with recent works on music, family, women, and sports. They have demonstrated clearly that West Texas has a vital past, a history in need of wide dissemination.

We especially acknowledge the contribution of our reviewers at the University of Oklahoma Press, Michael Collins and an anonymous reader. We took their suggestions to heart, made the most of them, and our work is a better book because of their advice. We are also grateful to the acquisitions editor at Oklahoma, Jay Dew. He was always an encouraging and helpful advocate as the book grew into its present form.

Finally, we especially thank our wives, Ellen Carlson and Pearlene Glasrud, for their patience and understanding. To them and to all those who have helped with the book we are grateful for encouragement and support.

Paul H. Carlson, Lubbock
Bruce A. Glasrud, San Antonio

## WEST TEXAS FEATURES

Perryton

Dalhart

*Canadian River*

Amarillo

Palo Duro Canyon
State Park

*Prairie Dog Town Fork*

Caprock Canyon
State Park

*Pease River*

LLANO
ESTACADO

Red River

Wichita Falls

*Brazos River*

Lubbock

Breckenridge

Ft. Worth     Dallas

## HISTORIC WEST TEXAS

Abilene

Big Spring

Stephenville

Midland

*North Concho River*

Odessa

*Colorado River*

El Paso

Guadalupe Mountain
National Park

Brownwood

*Pecos River*

San Angelo

EAST TEXAS

Balmorhea
State Park

*Rio Grande*

Alpine

Junction

Mountain Home

Fredricksburg

Austin

Houston

Presidio

Big Bend Ranch
State Park

Big Bend
National Park

Del Rio     Uvalde

San Antonio

Corpus Christi

Laredo

*Courtesy Curtis Peoples, Southwest Collection, Texas Tech University*

# Introduction

## WEST TEXAS, AN OVERVIEW

West Texas is huge, larger than many states and some countries, but it is not always easy to define, at least geographically. In a broad, general sense the region is defined as the western part of the state of Texas as constituted after the Civil War. Under such a definition, West Texas in the late nineteenth century included Fort Worth, "the city where the West begins," and represented most of the state west of a line that ran south from Fort Worth following the long curve of the Balcones Escarpment. In the twenty-first century one is hard pressed to include Fort Worth in West Texas, and the line, such as it is, has shifted. In 2014, vague and amorphous, it ran roughly from just east of Wichita Falls southward in a sweeping curve through Breckinridge in Stephens County, Brownwood in Brown County, and Mountain Home in Kerr County to Del Rio.

This book has adopted the older, nineteenth-century view and broader definition of what constitutes West Texas. Nonetheless, it gives Fort Worth and other cities located along the Balcones Escarpment, or approximately the 98th meridian as Walter Prescott Webb suggested, only minor consideration.[1] For present purposes, then, West Texas as a region includes the Panhandle; the Rolling Plains and Llano Estacado; the Edwards Plateau, western Hill Country, and Permian Basin; and the Big Bend–Trans-Pecos country—the "Giant Side of Texas."[2]

A geographic definition aside, West Texas is a land of big sky, of little rain, of nearly ceaseless winds, and of ever-changing clouds. It is a semiarid, sometimes rough and broken country, but one that supports agricultural enterprises both rich in history and important to the state's contemporary economy. It is a region blessed with state and national parks remarkable for their size and breadth and beauty. It is a land of contrasts, with rugged, desert mountains; deep, enormous canyons; and immense, high plateaus as flat as tabletops. It is a place diverse in its population and growing ever more so.

West Texas is culturally diverse as well—a phenomenon not unexpected over such a large geographic area. The Rolling Plains west of Abilene, for example, and the Llano Estacado above the Caprock Escarpment are southern in background, settled by adherents of Southern Protestant Christianity with conservative traditions. Many people here can trace their cotton-based agricultural societies across generations back through East Texas and ultimately to the American South. The Panhandle, by contrast, is in many ways midwestern, settled by people from Iowa, Illinois, and Wisconsin who brought with them a northern brand of Protestantism. They looked north to Kansas City and Chicago as their marketplace, and in fact Amarillo, the major city of the Texas Panhandle, lies closer to capitals in New Mexico, Colorado, Oklahoma, and Kansas than to the state capital in Austin. The Trans-Pecos–Big Bend region, including El Paso, is bi-cultural: many of its early settlers came from Mexico, bringing with them their Catholic Christianity and Hispano-Indian cultural traditions. It is basin and range country and contains the state's highest mountain peaks and most extensive deserts.

Modern interstate highways cross these culturally and geographically diverse areas of West Texas. Toward the north, they connect some of the region's busiest cities with Dallas and Fort Worth, and in its southern stretches they link other cities of West Texas to Houston and San Antonio. Interstate 27 reaches from below Lubbock north to Amarillo, where it connects to Interstate 40 along the old path of U.S. Route 66, the iconic Mother Road in the popular culture of the Panhandle. In addition, U.S. 83, the "Main Street" of the Great Plains, slices north and south through much of the West Texas heartland.

*Lohn, northern McCulloch County, in the 1920s, just as trucks, automobiles, and rural telephones and electric power were entering the region. (Courtesy David Murrah and Southwest Collection, Texas Tech University)*

The immense West Texas heartland is a part of the state that in many ways remains rural and often isolated. Through much of this area there is what might be called an emptiness, an unending vastness about the place. Roberts County in the Panhandle in 2014, for example, held fewer than 900 people, less than one person per square mile. More than one hundred years before, at the end of the nineteenth century, the federal government classified a county with fewer than two persons per square mile a "frontier."

Under such a definition the Texas Panhandle in fact contains several counties—Roberts, Briscoe, and Oldham, for example—that today would still qualify as frontier, and several others—Collingsworth, Hartley, Hemphill, Lipscomb, and Sherman—that remain barely removed from frontier status. In the Trans-Pecos–Big Bend country at least seven counties in 2014 held fewer than two people per square mile, and in the bordering region east of there, several additional counties registered populations just above that threshold. Elsewhere in West Texas wide stretches of sparse rangeland appear empty and deserted of human habitation.

It has been suggested that the vastness of this terrain scares people "because the land is too much, too empty, claustrophobic in its immensity."

Some people may in fact feel a bit threatened by the huge, open expanse "because," as one writer put it, "they feel lost, with nothing to cling to, disoriented. Not a tree, anywhere. Not a slice of shade." That may be so for someone fresh from Manhattan, Brooklyn, or Chicago, but such is not the case for a cowboy or roughneck or schoolteacher who has grown up with the country.[3]

Indeed, people who have spent their lives in the broad, expansive sections of West Texas welcome the openness, the freedom, and the independence that come with the emptiness. Stand, for example, in the southwest corner of Hemphill County in the Texas Panhandle, where Tom Hanks stood while filming the closing scenes of *Cast Away*, the popular Hollywood movie from 2000, and one sees lonely, empty roads stretching in four directions straight to the vanishing horizon and a sweeping, beautiful panorama of space and sky and clouds. Both the movie scene and the same view in 2014 suggest wonderful possibilities.

Likewise, before movies, before whites intruded, the lands of West Texas gave American Indians in the region a feeling of personal freedom and well-being. The land had an enchantment, a mysterious quality, that few of them could explain, but they were an inseparable part of it, together with the animals, the winds, and the rocks. They saw in the open, sweeping landscape a life-giving woman—a Mother Earth—who provided them with what they needed, offered them opportunities for a livelihood, and brought intangible benefits as well: "I love the land and the buffalo," said Satanta, a Kiowa leader, in 1867. "I love to roam over the wide prairie, . . . and when I do, I feel free and happy."[4]

In 2014, as we write, the emptiness, the openness, still conveys an elusive sense of freedom. And the big sky with its majestic, sweeping sunsets of shifting hues and dramatic colors still mirrors the wide, expansive nature of West Texas. There is beauty in the place, and it is not hard to find, but there is also utility. West Texas in 2014 produced most of the state's oil and gas. Cotton-based agriculture, vital to the state's economy, continued to increase in the region even as it declined elsewhere in Texas, and the region's production of food crops remains essential to the state and nation. Farmers and ranchers across the large territory raise enormous numbers of livestock, especially sheep and cattle, with West Texas among the world's leaders in the production of Angora goats and mohair.

*A big sky and oil pump jacks, characteristic of much of West Texas. (Courtesy Gene B. Preuss)*

Yet, West Texas represents more than agriculture and petroleum products. The region has several major universities, as well as many community colleges, technical schools, and private or parochial institutions of higher education. It contains several large and busy museums, such as the Panhandle–Plains Historical Museum in Canyon and the Petroleum Museum in Midland, and many superb but smaller ones, such as the Carson County Square House Museum in Panhandle and the Museum of the Big Bend in Alpine.

West Texas is also a place of modern, dynamic cities. El Paso in 2014 was the largest, with a metropolitan population of nearly 800,000 inhabitants. The metropolitan areas of Lubbock, Amarillo, and Midland and Odessa likewise were expanding in population, and Abilene, San Angelo, and Wichita Falls, the other large cities, enjoyed stable populations. Between the scattered cities, however, the region's rural population in 2012 was in decline, even as the total population of West Texas increased. Most towns slowed in economic and social activity and declined in population, and many of them disappeared. Ghost towns, such as Texon in Reagan County and Bronco in Yoakum County, were seemingly everywhere. Local economic activity, which had created them in the first place, was now in decline; local schools had consolidated; and perhaps other local factors had deteriorated as well.

The massive consolidation of schools in the 1930s clearly played a significant role in the disappearance of these towns. Local schools provided community identity, were a consumer of local business products and services,
and offered housing for teachers and administrators. As two, three, or four
small school districts became consolidated at one location, the communities whose schools had closed declined. Additional consolidation in the
twenty years following passage of the 1949 Gilmer-Aikin laws reduced the
number of school districts in Texas from 6,409 to 1,539.

Another state law that contributed to the phenomenon of disappearing
towns and communities was the 1949 Colson-Briscoe Act. This legislation
created the Texas Farm to Market Roads, a system that extended paved
roads through much of West Texas. The subsequently improved roadways,
intended to facilitate efforts to convey crops and livestock to local markets,
had an important if unforeseen result: the enhanced travel conditions
allowed farm and ranch owners to move off their rural, isolated properties
to houses in nearby towns or neighboring cities. Good roads and modern
pickup trucks continued over time to enable people to commute to farm or
ranch land from towns farther and farther away from their old home place.

Lifestyles in rural regions of West Texas—and in fact much of the
state—have thus shifted over the years since the sweeping legislative innovations in the 1930s and 1940s. One might argue that there has always
been change. But in the twentieth century such innovations as high-speed
automobiles and improving highways, inventive home appliances, and
in general rapidly advancing technological developments accelerated
the pace of change. In the 1930s and afterward, for example, the federal
government's Rural Electrification Administration at long last brought
for the first time electricity to many rural areas. The positive results of
this initiative were enormous, particularly in terms of making life easier
and more convenient. And for farmers and ranchers, the development of
modern tractors, of improved irrigation equipment and techniques, and
of hybrid seeds and feeds added to the changing rural portrait of West
Texas, the state, and the nation at large.

Human societies have been present in West Texas for nearly 12,000
years, perhaps since not long after people first entered the Western
Hemisphere. Archaeological sites in scattered places of West Texas, but

particularly on the Llano Estacado, reveal that Clovis, Folsom, and other early Native American societies and cultures included the Texas High Plains in their annual migration routes. For food supplies, they sought many animals—such as ducks and other birds, turtles, pronghorns, deer, and elk—that are still present in West Texas, but they also hunted some dramatically larger game animals, such as Columbian mammoths and giant, straight-horned bison, which are now extinct.

Over time, the early American societies and cultures evolved. Some ceased to exist. Some groups disappeared as they merged into others, and some perhaps await modern archaeological discovery. By the time Europeans arrived in West Texas in the sixteenth century, American Indian societies there had developed a wide variety of life-ways, religious practices, living arrangements, and political organizations. Their craftsmen and women were skilled, their traders covered long distances, their medical practitioners employed sophisticated plant-based healing techniques, and their leaders guided and protected a wide variety of peoples in complex networks of affiliations and alliances.

In contrast to its very long American Indian presence, West Texas in the twenty-first century in other ways remains a young place, with many communities just beginning to celebrate the centennial of their incorporation, as can be seen in the many books published as part of such celebrations. But historians and other scholars from the time of Spanish colonization in the seventeenth century at present-day Presidio and El Paso have produced reports and documents that describe parts of the region and represent early efforts at a history of West Texas. Over time, but especially in the late nineteenth century, Anglo, Hispanic, and African American soldiers, ranchers, farmers, townspeople, entrepreneurs, preachers, and settlers, women as well as men, left journals, diaries, letters, personal or business records, and other documents from which histories of the region have been written. As the bibliography at the back of this book attests, the works and sources for historiography of West Texas are abundant and of high quality.

One of the more influential books relating to the region is Walter Prescott Webb's *The Great Plains* (1931). Although the scope of the book extends well beyond West Texas, Webb often uses the region's natural history and human experience to validate his theses, and he defines the large territory, as we do in this volume, as the state's land west of the 98th meridian, essentially west of the Balcones Escarpment. Following some of his topics and ideas, but not his environmentally deterministic point of view, contributors to this survey history of West Texas treat such subjects as the environment, American Indian studies, European exploration and settlement, and the area's multicultural heritage in agriculture, military activities, literature, and music. But as they explain anew the human experience in West Texas, they also cover material Webb neglected or died too soon to witness: topics such as the arrival of the area's wealth of parks and recreational opportunities, modern urban issues, developments in petroleum mining, more recent politics, and the greater inclusion of women and other minorities in the region's affairs and its contemporary history. Webb's superb study tackles a huge part of the continent, but like him, if over a smaller territory, the contributing authors of *West Texas: A History of the Giant Side of the State* examine the deep anatomy of a massive subject.

Clearly, the giant side of Texas is a land of contrasts with mountains, deserts, and plains. Just as clearly, it is a place that won't go away. Its physical hugeness and the wide variety of human experience in that landscape over time speak to the region's enduring vitality.

## NOTES

1. See Walter Prescott Webb, *The Great Plains: A Study in Institutions and Environment* (New York: Grosset & Dunlap, 1931; reprinted, Lincoln: University of Nebraska Press, 1981).

2. As acknowledged in detail in our preface, the phrase "the Giant Side of Texas" originated with the Lubbock Chamber of Commerce and is used with the chamber's permission.

3. Timothy Egan, *The Worst Hard Time: The Untold Story of Those Who Survived the Great American Dust Bowl* (New York: Houghton Mifflin, 2007), 1.

4. *New York Times*, October 30, 1867, as cited in Charles M. Robinson III, *Satanta: The Life and Death of a War Chief* (Austin: State House Press, 1997), 70.

# Part I

# THE PLACE

W est Texas can be and has been defined in different ways. As explained in the introduction, the region is defined here in a broad sense to include first, the Texas Panhandle; second, the Rolling Plains and the Texas portion of the Llano Estacado; third, the Hill Country, the Edwards Plateau, and the Permian Basin; and fourth, Far West Texas. It is a common, traditional definition that places an enormous part of the state and its subregions all to the west of modern Interstate 35.

Part I surveys this "giant side of Texas." After an opening chapter that sweeps through the environmental history of the region from its deep past to its relative present, four subsequent chapters explore the major subregions of West Texas, their history, and their economic and social life.

Collectively, the authors examine natural and economic forces and influential or notable people that contributed to each subregion's historic development, pursuing themes that continue from prehistory through the nineteenth and twentieth centuries to the present. They often show, as well, how events in the larger state, the greater Southwest, and the United States in general impacted West Texas and the people who have lived there.

WEST TEXAS SUBREGIONS

PANHANDLE

*Canadian River*
○ Pampa
Amarillo ○
*Prairie Dog Town Fork*
*Pease River*

WEST TEXAS PLAINS
Wichita Falls ○
*Red River*

Lubbock ○
HISTORIC WEST TEXAS
*Brazos River*
Breckenridge ○
○ Snyder    ○ Albany    Ft. Worth ○
Sweetwater ○ ○ Abilene
○ Colorado City
Big Spring ○
*Colorado River*
Midland ○
○ Odessa    ○ Brownwood
PERMIAN BASIN
N
San Angelo ○
TRANS-PECOS &
BIG BEND
*Pecos River*
EDWARDS PLATEAU
EAST TEXAS
Fort Stockton ○
Junction ○
○ Fort Davis
○ Alpine
Rocksprings ○ ○ Mountain Home    ☆ Austin
*Rio Grande*
Presidio ○
○ Del Rio    ○ Uvalde

El Paso ○

*Courtesy Curtis Peoples, Southwest Collection, Texas Tech University*

# CHAPTER 1

# The West Texas Environment

*Monte L. Monroe*

West Texas is a land of contrast. It holds the state's highest mountains and driest deserts. It contains rich farmland, dusty plains, and hard-scrabble country seemingly empty of human habitation. It is largely rural country, its rivers and streams dry in their upper reaches, its lakes often reservoirs. This chapter reaches back through deep geological time to explore the origins of the West Texas environment we see today.

Defining the environmental, cultural, and geographical boundaries of West Texas is like trying to catch the whirling tail of a spring dust devil—twisting, turning, and dodging across the plains. The environment is always moving. International, national, state, and political boundary contrivances imposed upon the natural region have changed much since Spanish officials first designated the terrain northeast of the Rio Grande, south of the Red, and west of the Sabine rivers as "Tejas." Historically and in 2014, as of this writing, West Texas comprises the Permian Basin and Edwards Plateau, the Rolling Plains and the Southern High Plains, the Texas Panhandle, and the Trans-Pecos country. Unique environmental characteristics have distinguished this area from the neighboring regions, East Texas and the Coastal Plains.

West Texas is arid and geographically diverse. Historians remind us that before the introduction of modern irrigation techniques, lack of water discouraged nonaboriginal migration into the western part of the state. Stark terrain, large bison herds, the threat of Native American resistance to incoming settlers, and a lack of extensive timber and other natural resources prevalent in the East made the area unappealing to all but the hardiest of Spanish, Mexican, and, later, European and Anglo-American pioneers. In addition, the region's environmental incompatibility with the economic system of plantation agriculture and slavery stymied extensive settlement until after the Civil War. The ecology of the place has not always been as it appears today.

In fact, through "deep time," the several billions of years since Earth began, the human construct that we call West Texas has undergone unimaginable environmental transformations. During the first 3.5 billion years of geologic history the Earth's crust and oceans formed. Over deep time continental plates emerged. Convection within the Earth's mantle moved the plates, causing them to shift, collide, fold, or slide one beneath another (subduction). This tectonic movement along with volcanic action created the land, atmosphere, and chemical makeup of the Earth and the creatures that gradually evolved and became extinct upon it. The concomitant, ongoing power of compression and folding of the Earth over great periods of time reformed its landscapes, while rain, wind, ice, and heat eroded them and redeposited their broken sediments.

Such titanic forces affected the environment of West Texas. Along the vast time continuum of the Cambrian and Ordovician periods (600 million–500 million years ago) shallow, warm seas, teeming with marine plant and nonskeletal animal life—trilobites, other brachiopods, and corals—submerged the region, creating the sedimentary limestone formations that encase the large oil, gas, and mineral reservoirs found today in the Permian Basin and elsewhere in the area. During the Silurian and Devonian periods (400 million–300 million years ago) bony fishes filled that sea, while primitive ferns, leafy plants, shrubs, and insects emerged onshore.

As time passed, additional environmental transformations occurred. In the Carboniferous period primeval rivers, flowing from higher elevations in what is today East Texas, deposited sedimentary sand, gravel, and mud layers in deltas that emptied into the sea that covered what became

West Texas, while limestone barriers grew offshore. Larger plants, ferns, giant insects, and the first reptiles emerged on land and flew in the air. Over what seem today to be incomprehensible periods of time, heat and pressure compressed the decaying organic materials rotting in bogs and swamps near the sea into substantial coal deposits in the area around modern-day Thurber, ultimately mined by the Texas and Pacific Coal Company during the late nineteenth and early twentieth centuries.

Some 300 million years before such human activity, however, during the Permian period, the small inland Delaware Sea, as it is called, covered the West Texas region, which then lay near the western equatorial zone of what was then the supercontinent Pangaea—that is, no oceans separated the globe's single huge landmass. Off the coastline of the inland Delaware Sea the extensive Capitan Reef built up over the eons from the invertebrate carcasses of trillions of dead marine creatures and plants. It now composes the largest fossilized barrier reef exposed on Earth, located in Guadalupe Mountains National Park in West Texas, a place thousands of people visit each year. Today at the park hikers can ascend mountain peaks covered with Douglas Fir trees of monumental size that grow upon the skeletal remains of innumerable creatures that once inhabited the bottom of a shallow sea—all in what is now the Trans-Pecos Chihuahuan Desert. Somewhat recently, about 1.8 million years ago, glacial melting would form a shallow lake in the basin of the former Delaware Sea. As the lake evaporated, salt deposits remained, and during the nineteenth century these would become the focus of the infamous "Salt Wars" in modern Hudspeth County.

In contrast, during most of the Mesozoic era (286 million–65 million years ago), dry land dominated what is now Texas. Then, in the Cretaceous period (about 180 million years ago), which came at the end of the Mesozoic era, seas again immersed most of area, dumping the marl and mud sediments found in the shale and limestone deposits that are conspicuous in the geologic record of the Llano Basin, Edwards Plateau, and Trans-Pecos regions.

Dinosaurs reached their zenith during the Cretaceous period. They ranged across most portions of West Texas. Their footprints, laid down millions of years ago by four-legged herbivorous sauropods

(*Paluxysaurus*) and bipedal carnivorous theropods (*Acrocanthosaurus*), are remarkably preserved along the Paluxy River in limestone formations in Dinosaur Valley State Park near Glen Rose, their presence suggesting that ancient megaflora and fauna once thrived in the region. In the Big Bend, sea monsters like the ichthyosaur and plesiosaur swam in the Mesozoic sea. Early forms of modern animals, conifers, mosses, ferns, canes, and flowering plants also evolved.

During the Cretaceous period, faulting and warping west of today's Balcones Escarpment created the Llano-Burnet Uplift. Volcanic action raised mountains in the Trans-Pecos, covering the region in lava flows and ash. Evidence of such volcanism is easily seen today along the roadways from Fort Davis to Marfa and from Alpine south through the Big Bend country.

Through many millions of years during the Cretaceous period dramatic environmental changes occurred in West Texas. The various forces that gradually created the Rocky Mountains also served to uplift the Trans-Pecos highlands, thus splitting, folding, and penetrating older sediments. Eroded gravel, clay, and sand materials from the southern Rockies flowed eastward down ancient rivers, forming succeeding alluvial blankets beyond the eastern slopes of the mountains and ultimately creating the High Plains and Llano Estacado. Eroded materials also arrived via the wind, as seen at the present-day Monahans Sandhills State Park. By the end of the Tertiary period (80 million to 3 million years ago) the landscape of the region increasingly started to resemble the topographic character that marks it today.

Even so, environmental transformations continued. The glaciers of the Quaternary period (3 million–ca. 20 thousand years ago) did not reach West Texas, but when huge ice sheets in the high Rocky Mountains melted, the runoff deposited sedimentary materials along the valleys of the ancient predecessors of the Canadian, Brazos, Colorado, and Rio Grande rivers. During the same time, the earliest ancestors of modern humans emerged on the African Continent and over hundreds of millennia evolved and spread across the planet.

Between 12,000 and 10,000 years ago, toward the end of the Pleistocene epoch, as global warming caused the last of what is termed the Wisconsin glaciation to slowly retreat from North America, Paleo-Indians of the

Clovis and Folsom cultures arrived in what is today West Texas. Migrating along water routes, such as the Running Water, Blackwater, and Yellowhouse draws on the Llano Estacado, they pursued and hunted Columbian mammoths, mastodons, giant straight-horned bison, ground sloths, short-faced bears, and smaller mammals that dominated the regional biosphere of the time. For thousands of years, working in small familial bands, Paleo-Indians hunted across the region, killing some animals in great numbers at such sites as Bonfire Shelter near modern-day Langtry. Eventually the creatures succumbed to global warming, more arid environmental conditions, and increasingly more sophisticated human hunting techniques. The success of the Paleo-Indians and their heirs in slaughtering the megafauna at the beginning of the Archaic period provides early evidence of human impacts on the natural environment.

Archaic peoples occupied West Texas from approximately 8,500 to 2,000 years ago. Unlike the Pleistocene epoch, when a cooler and wetter climate prevailed, Archaic times included the Altithermal, a period of severe drought extending from about 6,000 to 2,500 years ago. In addition, for several thousand years, a regional Mild Pacific, drier air mass dominated atmospheric wind patterns, causing further environmental changes. On the West Texas plains tall coarse grass vegetation gave way to shorter grasses, and in the Trans-Pecos shrub-like plants prevailed. As the tall coarse grasses diminished, large mammal species, such as ancient bison (*Bison antiquus*), suffered. Their populations declined, they migrated away from the drought, and over time they changed. The once enormous beasts—up to 7.5 feet (2.3 meters) tall—became smaller and able to thrive on shorter grasses. They developed curved horns and evolved into the postglacial, modern species, the current plains variety of bison (*Bison bison*).

During the Altithermal, Archaic peoples lived along canyons and river valleys that provided fresh water in dry times and where trees gave comfort and protection. They hunted bison on the plains but diversified their diet by foraging for shellfish, seasonal fruits and berries, nuts, and sunflowers and by hunting deer, rabbits, coyotes, gophers, ducks, frogs, salamanders, turtles, and snakes. Two thousand years ago, in the boundary interval between the end of the Archaic period and the dawn of the Modern era, damper and cooler conditions returned. Post-Archaic Indians and eventually European Americans invaded the area in this new age, exerting greater control over the environment and changing the trajectory of ecological transformation.

The Modern era has encompassed three subperiods: the Ceramic, the Protohistoric, and the Historic. The Ceramic period occurred from about 2,000 years ago until 1450 C.E. Indian peoples during this time became more sedentary, planted crops, and used bow and pottery technology. They relied less on hunting bison and depended more on foraging for plants and hunting smaller game. They mined Alibates flints near modern-day Borger and constructed pueblo-type houses. The Protohistoric subperiod occurred between 1450 and 1650. The Apache people dominated the era. They reestablished a nomadic and bison-hunting culture in West Texas, scattering most of the sedentary village-dwellers of the previous age. They lived in tepees and used dogs to carry their possessions.

During this period, beginning about 1530, Europeans and a few Africans entered the area. The literate people among these new arrivals created our first documentary snapshot of aboriginal cultures in West Texas and published what can be seen today as an ecological baseline of the Rio Grande and Pecos River regions. Álvar Núñez Cabeza de Vaca and three other shipwrecked survivors of the failed Pánfilo de Narváez expedition became the first Europeans to traverse West Texas. They lived briefly among Jumanos in the La Junta de los Rios villages along the Rio Grande near modern-day Presidio. Some Jumanos engaged in horticulture, irrigating crops and shaping their environment. Other Jumanos near modern-day Menard and San Angelo hunted bison.

In 1541 Francisco Vásquez de Coronado, following information in Cabeza de Vaca's report, mounted an *entrada* that in due course marched across the Llano Estacado in search of the Gran Quivira (a fabulous, promised city) and gold. He camped among the Teyas in Blanco Canyon near modern-day Crosbyton. Coronado noted that the Teyas were nomadic bison hunters. He also described the Llano Estacado environment as a vast, flat tableland covered by a sea of grass and great bison herds. Nuts, grapes, mulberries, cactus fruit, hackberries, plums, sunflowers, onions, mesquite pods, and other plants existed in enough abundance to feed not only the Teyas but also the expedition, which comprised about 1,800 souls. Coronado arrived during a period of global cooling—today often called the Little Ice Age. Thus early Spanish chroniclers of the region depicted the various upper Brazos River canyons as verdant, with adequate water supplies.

During the Historic period that spanned the years from 1650 to 1875 tremendous ecological and cultural changes came to the area. Following the first explorers, Spanish and later Mexican governments for two hundred years advanced European civilization into West Texas. They introduced nonnative species and altered the landscape with mining, roads, missions, towns, and presidios. Strayed or abandoned European cattle and horses eventually bred feral herds, infringing upon bison grasslands, and the Spaniards introduced more environmentally disruptive irrigation and farming methods. Early mission life inadvertently introduced European diseases to human, plant, and animal populations. Indians lacked resistance to such diseases as smallpox, and died in shocking numbers. The surviving Jumanos, though once prosperous, comingled with Apaches in the Trans-Pecos and disappeared as a distinct people, an apparent casualty of the environmental holocaust now called the Columbian Exchange.

Following the Pueblo Revolt of 1680, Spaniards retreated from what is now New Mexico into West Texas and established missions and presidios at Ysleta near present-day El Paso. An unintended consequence of the revolt occurred when Apaches acquired more than 10,000 horses and other livestock that Spanish ranchers had abandoned and for which the Pueblo farmers had found little use. This windfall accelerated cultural and ecological change. Apaches, Tonkawas, Wichitas, Comanches, and other tribal groups rapidly developed mobile, bison-dependent cultures that dominated the bioregion and for two hundred years blocked European and Anglo-American settlement. The cultural and environmental shift put pressure on such plains grasses as big bluestem, Indian grass, switch grass, and buffalo grass. The swelling herds of horse and cattle, domestic and feral, competed with bison for native plains grasses.

From the 1700s until the 1870s Comanches with their Kiowa and Southern Cheyenne allies dominated much of West Texas. The Comancheria, as their hunting territory was called, encompassed the High Plains, the Central Plains, and the Edwards Plateau, and over it Comanches ruled. Not long before the Civil War, Comanche life began to change; then, after the infamous Salt Creek Massacre near Jacksboro in 1871, General William T. Sherman, the father of the concept of "total war," adopted an aggressive military approach to Indian depredations. He called for an offensive campaign, ordering troops at various western forts to mount constant attacks. The U.S. Cavalry under Colonel Ranald S. Mackenzie and others attacked Comanche, Kiowa, and Cheyenne camps. During what came to be called the Red River War, 1874–75, operations in Palo Duro Canyon in September 1874 included scattering the Indians, shooting their horses and mules, and destroying food stores.

Concomitant with this new approach to fighting Indians, the U.S. forces, who viewed bison as Indian commissary, encouraged bison hunters to operate in areas heretofore restricted. Hunters quickly entered the Texas Panhandle at places like Adobe Walls or moved to Fort Griffin near Albany, where herds were abundant. The subsequent killing of bison dovetailed with federal plans to confine Indians to reservations.

*Cattle, Matador Ranch, 1880. Note the absence of mesquite and juniper, woody plants that in 2012 choked many parts of West Texas. (Courtesy Southwest Collection, Texas Tech University)*

The story is a familiar one. By the early 1870s, bison hides had become a valuable commodity, and the lively market that emerged contributed to a storm of ecological destruction. Between 1873 and 1880, hunters slaughtered hundreds of thousands, if not millions, of bison on the plains of West Texas. Ultimately, settlers collected bison bones and sold them to manufacturers of fertilizer.

Environmental historian Dan Flores has argued that even if the army and the hide hunters had never appeared, bison were doomed. Indians hunting bison, now on horseback, also hastened the demise of the beasts through overkilling. Flores theorizes that Indians themselves, if left to their own devices, eventually would have wiped out the herds, partly because of their preference for taking five-year-old females—the breeding stock.

The near-obliteration of bison and the concomitant settlement of Indian tribes on reservations opened the region's lush grasslands for grazing domesticated animals. At the same time, new demands for fresh beef, the westward extension of railroads, and the advent of refrigerated rail cars contributed to the emergence of a large-scale cattle industry and an open-range culture, further altering the biodiversity of West Texas. By 1890 large corporate operations like the XIT Ranch (3 million acres) had moved onto the High Plains and adopted stock farming and scientific breeding of their herds.

But the range cattle industry or Cattle Kingdom, as it came to be called, in its turn did not last. Indeed, even as cattlemen dominated West Texas agriculture, other complicated but environment-altering events changed western ranching. Barbed-wire fencing closed off the open range, for example, and new meat packing operations in Fort Worth ended the need for long trail drives to northern railheads.

Railroads brought additional changes. In 1870, Texas ranked twenty-eighth among states in the amount of railroad mileage constructed. By 1900 the state had leapt to first place. In Texas, railroad companies with their rapidly expanding networks of tracks were granted sixteen sections of land for each mile of track they laid. Through this system of acquisition, by 1900 they owned approximately half of the state's surface land. In turn, the railroads, portraying West Texas as an ideal place for settlement, sold their land to pioneers. Most of the new settlers were farmers, and their agriculture put great pressure on available lands. To exacerbate the situation, through the "Fifty Cent Law" of 1879, the state sold more than 2 million acres of public lands to extinguish public debts. Mere construction sites, such as Abilene, sprang up quickly and became thriving towns on land that previously had been bison commons.

State and railroad land sales and subsequent pioneer settlement in West Texas helped to transform the state's essentially subsistence farming economy into a commercial one. As part of the transition, many farmers focused on planting cotton. Between 1870 and 1900 cotton production increased from 500,000 bales to approximately 3.5 million bales annually. Farming, including the wide adoption of cotton agriculture, became economically more important than raising cattle.

Windmills likewise helped to alter the agrarian ecology. They provided water to an arid land and allowed farmers to expand cotton agriculture to places once too dry to support the crop. By the mid-twentieth century, cotton production had transformed parts of West Texas into an agricultural monoculture.

The emergence of a huge cotton agribusiness industry on the Llano Estacado and elsewhere decimated traditional grassland habitats. In addition, plows and related equipment used for cotton growing scarred and denuded the land of vegetation for several months of each year. Eventually, severe droughts, such as the Dust Bowl of 1930s and the long dry spell of the 1950s, as well as the relentless southwest winds of spring, resulted in the erosion and dispersion of millions of tons of topsoil in sometimes blinding dust storms. Nonetheless, in 2012 High Plains farmers grew approximately 20 percent of the world's cotton.

There were problems. The High Plains is a semiarid, subtropical steppe environment, but it is also a place where farmers grow crops, including cotton, that rely on irrigation. Growing water-dependent crops in a semiarid environment is potentially unsustainable over the long haul. In the near term, however, electrically operated center-pivot systems and water-intensive underground drip irrigation techniques have increased cotton crop yields to as much as five bales per acre. Unfortunately, heavy use of irrigation has drawn down the slow-to-recharge Ogallala Aquifer, which is vital to life on the Llano Estacado.

And other uses for Ogallala water remain. The growing cultivation of various grain sorghums led in the Panhandle to the development of the largest cattle feeding operations in the world. A related rise in dairy farming on the High Plains has encouraged greater production of water-dependent corn crops. As a result, in 2014 some water conservation districts in the region were estimating that by 2020 only a 40 percent water reserve in the Ogallala will remain.

Other environmental challenges persist. Farm chemicals in the form of pesticides, fertilizers, and fuel trickle into groundwater and pollute rivers, creeks, surface reservoirs, and playas frequented by animals and migrating waterfowl, such as Canada geese. Often the stench and methane produced by swine farms and thousands of feeder cattle at stockyards in Hereford, Lubbock, and other West Texas towns pollute the air and contribute to toxic runoff. In places like Montague County, Mediterranean-style fruit farming has taken root, invading native grasslands and competing with trees in the Cross Timbers zone, such as the post oak. The region's Mediterranean climatological characteristics encouraged expansion of *vinti* (grape and wine) cultures in the late twentieth century, thus introducing further competition with native vegetation and for water resources.

Farming and ranching have wrought other environmental changes. Native animals, such as the prairie dog, ground squirrels, various lizards, horned frogs, turkeys, quail, and snakes, fall prey each year to habitat disruption. Topsoil erosion and overgrazing of pasturage are constant threats to wildlife and native vegetation. In the Trans-Pecos, stock farming and ranching have left many areas overgrazed, thus increasing soil depletion and erosion. Similar conditions exist in the Edwards Plateau, where extensive overgrazing of sheep, Angora goats, and other domestic animals denudes fragile grasslands and deprives native species of food and water resources. Since the beginning of the twentieth century, irrigation and drought have diminished water tables in some areas of the Edwards Plateau and Rolling Plains, thus depriving native fauna of vital watering holes.

Oil and gas production has likewise greatly affected the environment. The Spindletop oil discovery in East Texas in 1901 led the way, but soon after that famous well came online, oil and natural gas exploration moved into West Texas. Wildcatters explored all over the western part of the state. Between 1917 and 1920 Ranger became a notorious boomtown. Searchers found oil under the Edwards Plateau at places like W. R. McEntire's historic U Ranch near Sterling City. Massive discoveries took place in the Panhandle near present-day Borger and in the Permian Basin. In 1923 the rail towns of Midland and Odessa boomed as oil wells opened in the basin, including the famous Santa Rita well drilled in Reagan County on University of Texas lands. The Yates Field near Iraan became significant.

Oil made Texas a prosperous state while wreaking significant ecological damage. Drilling spilled oil, sometimes generated fires, and polluted water sources that defiled wildlife habitats and areas of human occupation. Derricks, tank farms, refineries, and oil pipelines increasingly marred and straddled the natural landscapes, as did electrical plants and telephone poles, as grids emerged to power the industries and towns. In 2011 "fracking" technology renewed oil and gas production in West Texas. This new activity apparently threatened the habitat of the dunes sagebrush lizard, leading to political disputes between environmentalists and petroleum producers.

Oil and automobiles, at least after the development of mass-produced motor vehicles, further challenged the environment. Oil-covered dirt roads soon replaced long-used trails created by bison, Indians, cattle, and horses. Asphalt and concrete roadways followed. When the Good Roads Movement emerged in Texas in the 1910s, private enterprise thoroughfares, such as the Bankhead Highway and William "Coin" Harvey's Ozark Trails Association highways, connected numerous counties in West Texas along byways intended eventually to reach from coast to coast. Ultimately, most such private roads were wrapped into the federal road network. Road building increased through the Great Depression and World War II, providing jobs and supporting defense installations that sprouted up throughout West Texas.

After the war, federal legislation created the Eisenhower Interstate Highway system, a vast, defense-related, German Autobahn–style, four-lane, high-speed road network that expanded quickly across the United States. Interstate 20 was constructed along the old Texas and Pacific Railway route; Interstate 10 parallels the former Southern Pacific Railway course across West Texas. Interstates 27 and 40 also cut huge swaths through the landscape. Interstate highways increased traffic into the region at a phenomenal rate, and they accelerated urbanization.

Cars, tractor-trailer rigs, agricultural tractors, harvesters, module-makers, gas stations, truck stops, and petrochemical plants all came to West Texas in the twentieth century, polluting the air to some extent and often disfiguring the visual beauty of the area. Rusting automobiles, discarded tire casings, dilapidated filling stations, and junked farm equipment have littered the environment despite federal highway beautification legislation during the 1960s.

Urban and industrial expansion have played a massive role in altering the environment. In 2014, six cities in West Texas had populations exceeding 100,000 inhabitants: El Paso, Lubbock, Amarillo, Abilene, Midland, and Odessa (in descending order by size). Smaller cities—San Angelo, Alpine, Fort Stockton, Snyder, and others—are numerous. Into these urban landscapes, people have imported nonnative traditional and ornamental trees, grasses, and garden plants for their homes and yards. These cultivated species and varieties have supplanted regional flora. Birds and animals transfer seeds from such plants sometimes far beyond their places of origin and, as a result, alter the native ecology of rural and natural landscapes. Domestic and exotic birds, mammals, reptiles, and amphibians imported into the region for human purposes pose other problems, often hunting native birds, ground squirrels, and traditional reptiles and amphibians of various species; some become naturalized, creating permanent environmental threats. Domestic animals and pets often escape or stray from owners and compete with indigenous species for resources as well.

Military and industrial operations provide important jobs near the cities, but they also have changed the environment. Military installations have appeared and disappeared over the centuries of Spanish, Texan, and federal military activity in the region. In some places their deserted quarters stand as silent specters of human intrusion upon the land. In the post–World War II era nuclear weapons have been produced at the Pantex facility near Amarillo, posing potential hazards to all life in the region. Decommissioned military bases, such as Reese Air Force Base near Lubbock, have sometimes left significant ecological damage. In Lubbock, for example, chlorinated aircraft engine cleaning solvents seeped underground, poisoning water in wells surrounding the base.

During the 1980s fierce political battles occurred over a proposed federal nuclear waste site on the High Plains in Deaf Smith County. Detractors believed it would contaminate the Ogallala Aquifer or cause worse havoc. At about the same time, the Texas Low-Level Radioactive Waste Authority approved disposal sites near Fort Hancock in Hudspeth County. Both projects were thwarted. In 2010, however, the Texas Commission on Environmental Quality licensed Waste Control Specialists, a Dallas corporation, to store millions of cubic feet of low-level material near Andrews.

Adequate water reserves are critical to the economic and cultural viability of West Texas cities and towns. The various urban centers work in conjunction with smaller surrounding communities to pipe water supplies from reservoirs, water farms, or underground aquifers. On the High Plains, for example, the Canadian River Municipal Water Authority (CRMWA) supplies water to approximately 500,000 people in eleven member communities via what was once the longest aqueduct system in the world. Faced with a severe drawdown of the Lake Meredith reservoir, however, CRMWA policymakers now depend on the John C. Williams Aqueduct and Wellfield in Roberts and Hutchinson counties to supplement and blend well water from the Ogallala with increasingly chloride-laden water from Lake Meredith.

Other environmental problems have appeared in recent decades. Depletion of underground water resources, such as the Hueco-Bolson Aquifer under El Paso, has led to hazardous ground subsidence. As water is withdrawn from underground reservoirs, rock sediments collapse, causing fissures or cracks in the land that can destroy manmade structures and impede the possibility of recharging the water. Citizens dependent on water from the Edwards Aquifer compete with approximately 2 million people along the eastern perimeter of the Edwards Plateau for ownership and control of that resource. Also, legal and illegal landfills blemish the urban landscapes and in some locales cause groundwater and underground water contamination. West Texas cities serve as hubs for rail, highway, and air transportation. Because drainage is inadequate in many communities, rainfall runoff contaminated with transportation byproducts seeps into local water supplies.

Fortunately, during the last few decades positive changes have also appeared, including successful experiments in the use of solar energy. Near where Francisco Coronado encountered the Teyas Indians in Blanco Canyon in 1541, the Crosbyton Solar Project, funded by federal grants to Texas Tech University in the 1980s, has contributed much to the research database on solar electric power, a potentially limitless energy resource. More significantly, power companies, including Central and South West Corporation and Kenetech's Delaware Mountains Project, prompted by concerns about carbon emissions and global warming, have turned to alternative forms of energy, specifically wind power.

Since 2000, wind farms have begun to dot the high ridges, escarpments, and flatlands of West Texas. Although most of these farms' turbines are not yet, as of 2014, connected to statewide power grids, the promise of connection is on the horizon. Historian Robert Righter of Southern Methodist University and wind energy expert Andy Swift of Texas Tech University have estimated that the new wind-based technology could someday generate most of the state's power needs.

Presently, in 2014, electrical utilities in the region are powered by coal-fired plants that spew carbon dioxide and other pollutants into the atmosphere, which makes "clean" alternatives such as solar and wind power very appealing. Accordingly, the 79th Legislature passed Senate Bill 20 of 2005 to develop renewable energy resources, identify Competitive Renewable Energy Zones, and position Texas as the national leader in wind energy. This action has not created a perfect solution. Critics complain that the massive turbines disrupt wind flows in the lower atmosphere and disturb the seasonal patterns of migratory birds. Others decry what they see as a form of visual pollution that the huge machines bring to a once open landscape. Ultimately the potential of this new technology, as well as its problems, promise yet another significant ecological change in this seemingly timeless corner of the world.

The narrative of the West Texas environment from deep time to the twenty-first century is a tale of incredible transformations. Clearly, millions of years of dramatic change and extinctions occurred long before humans arrived on the scene. Over eons seas emerged and waned, mountains rose and eroded or collapsed, and rivers deposited layers of sediments across the region. Sea creatures, dinosaurs, giant mammals, ancient bison, and archaic birds and insects have all lived and fallen extinct in West Texas. Aboriginal peoples from Paleo-Indians to early modern, mounted Comanches with guns have hunted, ruled, and nearly disappeared from the region, today comprising about one percent of the population (U.S. Census, 2012). And though native groups greatly affected the environment they occupied, especially after the arrival of the horse, far greater alterations came later, with the era of European and Anglo-American settlement and the arrival of modern-day commerce, transportation, and industry. As vast waves of people moved into West Texas during the dramatic period after 1850, biological shifts took place at an exponential pace. For example, most settlers entering the area believed that the native fauna and flora were an infinite resource. This "myth of superabundance"—the term is Stuart Udall's, from *The Quiet Crisis* (1964)—led to the destruction of many native species. Settlers introduced their own domestic species to the area as well, and over the ensuing decades exotic plant and animal species were also introduced from Africa, Europe, and Asia, further taxing native ecosystems. Before 1850 only a few natural historians, game hunters, and informed travelers realized that European and Anglo-American settlement would cause massive declines in wild animal and plant populations. Those who catalogued the natural history of West Texas left written accounts that establish benchmarks by which scientists today can measure ecological transformations in native biota. Yet railroad promotional tracts, newspapers, and other immigration materials from that era often promoted the inexhaustibility of natural resources, encouraging the taking of animals for food, trade skins, trophies, and protection. Increasingly more powerful, accurate, and repeating firearms magnified the animal slaughter on a scale unimaginable to generations of aboriginal hunters. Some species of snakes, deer, antelope, coyotes, foxes, turkeys, panthers, mountain lions, bears, bighorn sheep, wolves, and bison disappeared through unregulated killing by Indians, pioneers, and later immigrants to West Texas. Then domesticated and culturally acceptable animals, such as hogs, horses, mules, sheep, goats, certain fish, and cattle, invaded the region. It was a massive onslaught: the *Biological Survey of Texas* (1905) delineates the great transformations that had come to the environment in a very short time.

Positive changes have also been part of the region's environmental past. A state conservation movement led to fish and game laws passed in the state as early as the 1860s and again in 1925, thus helping to preserve wildlife. Water and soil conservation districts, first defined in 1916, have helped conserve precious natural resources from unregulated exploitation. Beginning in the 1920s and 1930s state and federal parks became established, preserving the environment even as they provided recreation for the region's residents. Over time, further legislation has worked to preserve flora, fauna, and unique landscapes in approximately seventy-seven state parks and historic sites in the area. Because no federal public domain lands exist in Texas, grassroots advocates like J. Evetts Haley and Glenn Biggs and legislators such as Ralph W. Yarborough have encouraged the federal government to purchase lands to create national parks. The Guadalupe Mountains and Big Bend national parks, acquired through such efforts, today preserve singular environments and wilderness habitats for future generations.

Present-day West Texans are gaining an increasing pride of tenure and stewardship in the expansive and dramatic landscapes in which they live. Importantly, most understand that if they are to prosper in the region, humans must learn to conserve the environment and native biota that feed their bodies, pockets, and souls.

## FOR FURTHER READING

Carlson, Paul H. *Deep Time and the Texas High Plains: History and Geology.* Grover E. Murray Studies in the American Southwest Series. Lubbock: Texas Tech University Press, 2005.

Cruse, J. Brett, et al. *The Battles of the Red River War: Archeological Perspectives on the Indian Campaign of 1874.* College Station: Texas A&M Press, 2008.

Doughty, Robin W., and Barbara M. Parmenter. *Endangered Species: Disappearing Animals and Plants in the Lone Star State.* Austin: Texas Monthly Press, 1989.

Flores, Dan L. *Horizontal Yellow: Nature and History in the Near Southwest.* Albuquerque: University of New Mexico Press, 1999.

Hickerson, Nancy Parrot. *The Jumanos: Hunters and Traders of the South Plains.* Austin: University of Texas Press, 1994.

Jasinski, Laurie E. *Dinosaur Highway: A History of Dinosaur Valley State Park.* Fort Worth: TCU Press, 2008.

Johnson, Eileen, ed. *Ancient Peoples and Landscapes.* Lubbock: Museum of Texas Tech University, 1995.

Perttula, Timothy K., ed. *The Prehistory of Texas.* College Station: Texas A&M University Press, 2004.

Righter, Robert W. *Wind Energy in America: A History.* Norman: University of Oklahoma Press, 1996.

Schmidly, David J. *Texas Natural History: A Century of Change.* Lubbock: Texas Tech University Press, 2002.

CHAPTER 2

# The Texas Panhandle

*John T. "Jack" Becker*

The Texas Panhandle is a lot of ground to cover in one chapter, but discussion here concentrates on factors that consistently have characterized the area: raising wheat and cattle, and the production of oil and gas. Becker also reviews new economic developments in the Panhandle, describes early settlement and town building, and explores the history of education and of social, political, and cultural trends that have marked life in the state's far northwest.

The Texas Panhandle is here defined as the northernmost thirty-two counties of Texas. It is bounded on the west by New Mexico, on the north by the Oklahoma Panhandle, and on the east by Oklahoma proper. The southern boundary is more difficult to define, but leading historians of the Panhandle often cite an east–west line along the southern boundaries of Bailey, Lamb, Hale, Floyd, Motley, and Cottle counties. The Panhandle totals approximately 31,300 square miles and has the distinction of being one of the last large regions of the continental United States that Anglo-Americans settled.

Two physiographic regions, the High Plains (or Llano Estacado) and the Rolling Plains, make up the Texas Panhandle, but both of these spill over into states and counties adjacent to the Panhandle. The High Plains, which makes up the western two-thirds of the area and extends into New Mexico, is noted for its almost table-top flatness, its aridity (less than 22 inches of moisture a year), and for the Ogallala Aquifer, which lies beneath it. The Rolling Plains is a gently undulating land in the eastern one-third of the region and stretching along the banks of the Canadian River, which crosses the Panhandle west to east.

Archaeological evidence suggests human habitation of the Southern High Plains and Texas Panhandle began 12,000 to 14,000 years ago. For thousands of years after the last, or Wisconsin, ice age, early humans hunted the large region, living off its abundant animals and such plants as roots, berries, seeds, and nuts. Eventually, some plains people began living in permanent villages, especially along the Canadian River and its tributaries. Rich, alluvial soil and Alibates flint quarries attracted them. One group, the Antelope Creek people, flourished until about 1350 C.E., when their society went into decline and disappeared.

Thus, two centuries later in 1541, when they crossed the Llano Estacado just below the Panhandle, members of Francisco Vásquez de Coronado's *entrada* did not meet villagers at Antelope Creek. Nor did they meet other people living in permanent villages. Rather, the expedition, perhaps 1,800 members strong, met Querechos and Teyas, who, Coronado's chroniclers reported, lived by hunting large herds of migrating bison. The identity of the Teyas is unknown, but the Querechos are believed to be Athapaskan-speaking people who were ancestors of modern-day eastern Apaches, including Lipan, Mescalero, and Jicarilla tribes. Eventually, the Lipans dominated the Panhandle country.

About 1700, Comanches and shortly afterward Kiowas from the west and north moved into the Texas Panhandle. In 1790 the two tribes negotiated an alliance. Then, together they pushed the various Apache groups from the Panhandle and for a century or more controlled the region, sometimes called the Comancheria.

Meanwhile Spanish exploration did not stop with the Coronado entrada in 1541. Don Juan de Oñate in 1601 crossed the Texas Panhandle along the Canadian River. Like Coronado, Oñate was looking for mineral riches and a lost empire, known as the Gran Quivira, with its Seven Cities of Cibola. His failure to find this fabled, elusive wealth ended the first phase of Spanish exploration in the Panhandle. Subsequent Spanish explorers primarily concerned themselves with finding a direct route between Santa Fe and Spanish settlements in Texas, particularly San Antonio and Nacogdoches.

Travel to and through the Texas Panhandle continued. Various people from New Mexico visited the region to hunt and trade with Indian groups. Pueblo villagers, for example, traded corn, pottery, turkey feathers, and possibly turquoise for bison meat, hides, and Alibates flint. Later, Hispanic–New Mexican bison hunters known as *ciboleros* traveled to the plains to hunt and trade. *Comancheros,* traders from New Mexico, also entered the Panhandle. They began operating shortly after a Comanche–Spanish treaty in 1786 allowed such activities, and they concentrated almost exclusively on exchanging agricultural products, iron tools, and alcohol for bison products, horses, mules, and cattle. Beginning in the 1840s, the trade increasingly included stolen horses, cattle, Indian slaves, and kidnapped Texans and Spaniards. Trading took place annually, often at familiar sites far out on the High Plains. Locations at Tecovas Springs (west of Amarillo), Sweetwater Creek (Mobeetie), Atascosa Creek (Old Tascosa), and Los Lingas Creek near Quitaque were common comanchero trading places.

The Red River War (1874–75) put an end to the comanchero trade and the Panhandle's century-long focus toward New Mexico. Fought between Comanches, Kiowas, and Cheyennes on one side and U.S. troops on the other, the war resulted from a number of factors, one of which was an Indian desire to obtain at the conflict's conclusion better annuity terms from the government. The spark that set the war ablaze, however, was the illegal presence of bison hunters in territory reserved for Indians. In response, Indian warriors, led by Quanah of the Comanches, attacked the white hunters at a placed called Adobe Walls in the Canadian River valley. The army struck back. More than 3,000 troops under Colonel Nelson A. Miles entered the Panhandle from five directions in the summer and fall of 1874. Through fourteen pitched battles they kept heavy pressure on the warriors and their families, burning camps, destroying food supplies, and forcing families to return to reservations in Indian Territory (Oklahoma). Colonel Ranald S. Mackenzie of the Fourth Cavalry delivered a critical blow when in Palo Duro Canyon with 500 troops he defeated warriors from five villages before burning tepees, destroying large quantities of supplies, and capturing more than 1,400 horses.

After the Red River War, American cattlemen with large herds entered the Panhandle. The first operator, A. G. Springer, opened a store and saloon near Fort Elliott and trailed a herd of longhorns to his ranch in Hemphill County. Shortly afterward, Charles Goodnight established the first permanent cattle operation in the area when he trailed 1,600 animals from Colorado to Palo Duro Canyon in 1876 and formed the JA Ranch with his partner, Irish businessman John Adair.

After establishment of the JA, as it was called, ranchmen poured into the area. Three years later more than 100,000 head of cattle grazed in the Texas Panhandle. The lure of easy profits and the myth of a romantic lifestyle led many wealthy investors into cattle ranching. Several of them came from the East or from Europe. Less than ten years later, about 1888, thirty-three large ranches controlled more than 14 million acres in the region. One of these, the Prairie Cattle Company, founded in 1880 in Edinburgh, Scotland, enjoyed spectacular early success.

Other ranches were also successful. They included the 250,000-acre Frying Pan Ranch, owned by Joseph F. Glidden and Henry B. Sanborn; the Francklyn Land and Cattle Company, which owned land in Hutchinson, Gray, Carson, and Roberts counties; and the T-Anchor and LS ranches. In 1882 the Texas legislature gave 3 million acres of land to owners of the XIT Ranch, led by a group of Illinois investors. In exchange for the land the investors built the state of Texas a new capitol building in Austin. The huge ranch stretched for more than 200 miles along the New Mexico border in Dallam, Hartley, Deaf Smith, Bailey, and Cochran counties.

About the time cattle ranching made its appearance in the Texas Panhandle, sheepherders from New Mexico, known as *pastores,* entered the region. They centered their activities around Tascosa and along the Canadian River. In 1880, 400 pastores called the Panhandle home. They grazed more than 60,000 sheep, but barbed wire, a devastating drought in the late 1880s, and antagonism from cattlemen reduced sheep herds to only 10,000 head by 1890.

Problems plagued cattlemen as well. In their eagerness to control grass and water on their home ranges many cattlemen fenced in public land owned by the state of Texas. Sensing an opportunity to make money, real estate companies moved into the Panhandle promoting and selling fenced-in but publicly owned land to potential farmers or farmer-stockmen. One company, the New York and Texas Land Company, bought up millions of acres of public and railroad land and sold it for $1.25 to $1.75 per acre.

Moreover, in an attempt to sell land for schools and thus attract additional people to the state, the Texas legislature passed the Land Act of 1879. It sold certain lands for as little as $1.00 an acre. Seeing the writing on the wall, several large cattle companies began selling off their land to farmers and farmer-stockmen. The XIT was one of the first ranches to sell off its holdings to potential farmers, dispersing of 1.35 million acres of land by 1901. Most of it sold for $2.00 or more an acre.

Railroads also promoted land sales. Two railroads, which had built tracks into the Texas Panhandle in the late 1880s, owned large sections of land. The Fort Worth & Denver City Railroad (FW&DC) had crossed the Panhandle along a northwest–southeast route. It reached Amarillo in 1887 and built farther westward until it reached New Mexico Territory near Clayton. It continued to lay tracks all the way to Denver, which it reached by April 1888, thus making it possible for the first time to travel by rail between the large Texas and Colorado cities.

Following close behind the FW&DC, the Kansas & Southern line, a subsidiary of the Santa Fe Railway, laid tracks in a southwesterly route through Amarillo to Clovis, New Mexico. Soon afterward the Santa Fe built a trunk line through Canyon and Plainview to Lubbock. The Rock Island Railroad built a line running east–west across the Panhandle along approximately the course of present-day Interstate Highway 40. All three lines met in Amarillo. After completion of the railroads, the Panhandle population jumped from about 1,600 in 1880 to approximately 9,000 in 1890.

But Anglo settlement of the Texas Panhandle had begun more than forty years before the appearance of the railroads. In 1843 traders William Bent and Ceran St. Vrain had built a short-lived trading post on what is now Bent's Creek in Hutchinson County, later known as Adobe Walls. By 1846 the partners had left their post, forced out because of Indian depredations.

More permanent settlements started in the mid 1870s. Mobeetie, established in 1875 in Wheeler County; Tascosa, laid out in 1876 in Oldham

County; and Clarendon, founded in 1878 in Donley County, were the first. Each was located near water, and wagon trails connected the small towns to each other and to Dodge City, Kansas.

Mobeetie is the oldest continually inhabited community in the Texas Panhandle. Charles Rath and Bob Wright, bison hide traders, founded Mobeetie in 1875, when they opened a store and trading center for bison hunters on Sweetwater Creek. Later the establishment of Fort Elliott in the vicinity assured the town's survival, and shortly afterward the small village boasted about its population of 150. Although the army closed Fort Elliott in 1890, Mobeetie in 2012 still boasted a population of more than 100.

Tascosa started life as a small Hispano plaza that Casimero Romero, a pastore from New Mexico and former comanchero, established. Built on a natural but boggy ford of the Canadian River about 1876, it became the county seat. But, after the Fort Worth & Denver City Railroad bypassed the town, it declined in population until 1939, when Cal Farley established his Boys' Ranch, for boys needing a second chance in their lives, on the location of the nearly abandoned community.

Clarendon, on the other hand, prospered from its beginning. Careful planning by its founders, Methodist minister L. H. Carhart and his brother-in-law Alfred Sully, was responsible. Located on Carroll Creek on the headwaters of the Salt Fork of the Red River, it became the county seat of Donley County in 1882. Five years later, when the railroad bypassed the community, town leaders wisely moved their businesses and homes to the railroad. For years Clarendon was disparaged by some as "Saints Roost" because Reverend Carhart forbade the sale of alcohol within the city limits.

About this time, 1887, Amarillo came into existence. After a brief period of competition between several town promoters over the proper site for a community, the group that supported a site near the head of Palo Duro Creek, just south of Wild Horse Lake, won out. Amarillo grew rapidly after the Fort Worth & Denver City Railroad arrived. In July 1888 it boasted eleven stores, several saloons, a hotel, a restaurant, and a population of 200. Because of its location, with stockyards, water, and railroad connections, it became a regional cattle shipping center. In 1895 Amarillo stockyards shipped 2,500 train car loads of cattle to points north. Henry B. Sanborn, known as the father of Amarillo, encouraged several community improvements, including a large and modern hotel—painted bright yellow, in honor of the town's Spanish name. His efforts in part pushed the community's population to 482 in 1890.

The number and diversity of Amarillo businesses grew. The most common business, general merchandise stores, sold a wide variety of goods, including harnesses, tools, dishes, sewing supplies, and patent medicines. Grocers such as Henry and Millard Noble sold food staples by the pound or the barrel. Lawyers, real estate agents, and cattle brokers also set up businesses, and of course there were several blacksmith shops and livery stables. The first bank opened in 1889. As in many other small Texas towns, local merchants had functioned as bankers until the community could support an independent financial institution. The merchants Burns & Walker served as a bank in the early days until the First National Bank of Amarillo opened for business. Nine years later it had deposits of $500,000. Amarillo National Bank opened in 1893.

Education was also important to pioneers, and the first settlers established schools soon after they arrived in the Panhandle. Students in Amarillo met in a variety of places until 1900, when a three-story building on Twelfth Avenue and Polk Street became the school. The town's citizens established Amarillo College in 1897. It remained open until 1910, when lack of funds forced its closure. In 1929 another Amarillo College, a two-year community college, opened; by 2014 it enrolled several thousand students. West Texas State Normal College opened for classes in Canyon, about the time the first Amarillo College closed its doors. In 1963 this important school became West Texas State University, and in 2014, as West Texas A&M University, it is part of the Texas A&M system and enrolls nearly 7,000 students.

Two other institutions of higher learning, both two-year schools, serve Panhandle citizens. One, Clarendon College, has the distinction of being the oldest continually operated college in the Texas Panhandle. Opened in 1898, in its early years it was affiliated with the Methodist Episcopal Church. Frank Phillips College in Borger started life as Borger City Junior College. In 1948 it changed its name to honor oilman Frank Phillips, a long-time benefactor.

*Wheat harvest, Texas Panhandle, 1920s. (Courtesy Southwest Collection, Texas Tech University)*

Many of the Texas Panhandle's first Anglo-American citizens trace their roots to the Midwest. Other early settlers came to the region from American communities with large European ethnic populations, and as a result after 1900 a small number of Germans, Russians, Norwegians, and Czechs moved to the Panhandle. In addition, Quakers from Indiana, Catholics from the Midwest, and some temperance advocates established agricultural communities in the region and helped push the population past 90,000 by 1910.

Such modern pioneers helped to change Panhandle agriculture. Wheat became the principal product, but growers, farmer-stockmen, and ranchers increasingly diversified their crop and livestock operations. The farmer-stockmen among them raised a mixture of various crops and livestock, including hogs, sheep, poultry, and eggs. By 1920, in many counties the number of acres in corn and grain sorghum followed close behind the acres of wheat. Alfalfa, soybeans, and other small grains also appeared on Panhandle farms.

The economic depression and dust storms of the 1930s halted agricultural expansion for a time, and the number of farms and ranches decreased between 1935 and 1940. People moved away to seek opportunities elsewhere.

But World War II brought changes. The area's population and agriculture-based economy rebounded. Wartime prices, technological innovations (especially irrigation), and improved crops and livestock all had a hand in reversing the area's declining population and making agriculture profitable once more.

Until the beginning of World War II, despite a greatly diminished but still present Indian population and a large number of foreign-born people, the Texas Panhandle remained a region of mainly white Anglo-Saxon Protestants. With the improving wartime economy, the population's ethnic makeup changed. African Americans and Hispanics, attracted by agricultural and manufacturing jobs, moved to the region. The Hispanic population continued to increase; in 2014 Hispanic residents outnumbered Anglos in some Panhandle counties. With more than 240,000 people in its metropolitan statistical area in 2014, Amarillo enjoyed the highest Panhandle population, and the city itself boasted of being home to more than 40,000 Hispanic residents. Outside of the larger cities, the farther north and west one travels in the Panhandle, the larger the Hispanic population—both in real numbers and as a percentage of the total population.

The African American population in the Panhandle remained small in 2014. Potter County has the largest number of black citizens—about 12,000. Some black Americans had been in the region since its earliest settlement, but in the frontier years and into the early twentieth century, more moved into the region and to the city of Amarillo in increasing numbers, attracted by jobs in the meat packing industry. After World War II, employment opportunities for African Americans continued to improve.

Census figures reveal that in 2009 minority populations represented the only ethnic part of the population growing at a sizable rate. In fact in some counties minority populations represented the only growth. But in 2014, although Anglos still accounted for almost 60 percent of the total Panhandle population, an emerging demographic dynamic showed many rural Panhandle counties composed of an aging Anglo minority, while the younger population, households likely to have school-aged children, was almost exclusively of Hispanic background.

Socially, politically, and in its religious affiliations the Panhandle is conservative in its outlook. Except for Lyndon Baines Johnson, elected in 1964, no

Democratic president has carried the region since 1948. Republican strength in the region grew after the middle 1950s, as Panhandle voters switched in large numbers to the GOP. They moved for many reasons, the chief of these perhaps the personal popularity of Dwight D. Eisenhower in the 1950s; and also his party's support of state regulation of gas and oil, as opposed to Democratic support for federal controls. The Republican Party's more conservative philosophy was also important, of course, as it reflected ideas of most Panhandle's citizens.

Other changes took place in the late 1950s and early 1960s. Because the Panhandle sits in a semiarid region, water has always been a major concern for people living there. To provide a source of dependable water to the area, the Texas legislature established the Canadian River Municipal Water Authority in 1950. In 1962 it completed construction of Sanford Dam, which impounded Canadian River water to form Lake Meredith ten miles west of Borger. The lake covered parts of Hutchinson, Moore, and Potter counties and provided water to eleven West Texas cities including Borger, Amarillo, and Lubbock. At one time the lake contained more than 1.4 million acre-feet of water, but in 2014 it was in danger of going dry.

By the mid-1980s ongoing improvements in irrigation technology had transformed Panhandle agriculture. Irrigated acres under cultivation, as an example, outnumbered the dry land acres, allowing some farmers to plant corn, grain sorghum, and peanuts. When irrigated, cotton also produced well. Because of expanded grain production, especially corn and sorghum, Amarillo became a major center of the feed grain industry. In the late twentieth century Cargill Corporation built in Amarillo one of the largest grain elevators in the world. At capacity it holds 3.6 million bushels.

After World War II grain sorghum production expanded as new varieties, improved mechanization, increased irrigation, and cuts occurred in cotton and wheat acreage. A ready-made market for the grain existed in the feed cattle industry, which started in the Texas Panhandle in the early 1960s. Nebraska cattle buyer Paul Engler opened the Hereford Feedyard in Amarillo. He foresaw potential in the Texas Panhandle as a cattle feeding location because of the area's mild climate, open spaces, abundant cattle, and proximity to large amounts of corn and grain sorghum. Retired Texas Tech University professor W. L. Stangel also helped the fledgling feed cattle industry. Traveling through the region on a trip to Arizona and California, he had noted the large number of West Texas cattle being fed West Texas grain, and, thinking logically, he promoted the development of a feed cattle industry for the Panhandle.

Such efforts from Stangel, Engler, and others increased the number of cattle on feed in the Panhandle from 220,000 in 1966 to 1.3 million in 1980. At one time nine giant feedyards fattened cattle near Amarillo. Some yards held up to 100,000 head. Cactus Feeders, founded in 1975, became in 1985 the largest custom feeder in the world and today contributes $1 billion annually to the area's economy. In 2014, Panhandle livestock men raised 3.7 million beef cattle or about a one-fourth of all cattle in Texas.

In the late 1990s an unexpected problem emerged for Panhandle feed-yard operators. Moreover, it came from a surprising direction and drew international attention to Amarillo and the larger cattle feeding industry. During an April 1996 airing of her popular daytime television show, Oprah Winfrey stated that she would not eat another hamburger. The context of her remark was her topic for that day's show, public concern regarding a possible threat of Mad Cow disease in the United States. Panhandle cattle feeders were furious, especially Paul Engler. He and other cattle feeders sued Winfrey and her company, Harpo Productions, for libel. In 1998, after a highly publicized trial in Amarillo, the court found Winfrey innocent of all charges. In the meantime she had moved the production of her show to Amarillo and led a highly visible public relations campaign in the city, an effort at restoring goodwill that met with a measure of success.

Like cattle feeding, wheat growing has remained an important part of the Panhandle economy. In 1980 the region produced more than half of all wheat grown in Texas, and in 1987 area growers harvested more than 3.6 million bushels. The ten largest wheat-producing counties in Texas are located in the Panhandle, and those counties produce 42 percent of the state's crop. Farmers in Hansford County, the top producer, planted 234,000 acres of wheat in 1987.

Over the two decades immediately before 2014, swine production and dairying expanded in the Panhandle. The area's climate, open space, busi-ness-friendly attitude, availability of feed grains, and the ability to build and profitably run large production facilities have all led to this expansion. In

1990, for example, the Panhandle held 5,000 milk cows that daily produced about 150,000 pounds of milk. By 2014, more than 205,000 cows produced in excess of 4.4 million pounds of milk per day. Many of the region's largest dairies, especially those with more than 1,000 cows, had moved in from California, where an expanding human population and environmental concerns made dairy farming unprofitable. In the Panhandle, Dallam County contained at least eleven giant dairies. Part of the attractiveness of milking in that rural county was the construction of a Hilmar Cheese Company processing plant in Dalhart. The $190 million Hilmar facility has the capacity to process daily 11 million pounds of milk.

The Panhandle swine industry remained small as late as 1990, but thereafter hog numbers boomed, the totals nearly doubling every three years. In 2008, pork producers raised more than 1 million animals for market. As with the dairy industry, large corporate producers accounted for the big gains. Premium Stock Farms, with operations in Dallam and Sherman Counties, in the 1990s produced annually more than 1 million pigs.

Petroleum, of course, plays a substantial role in Panhandle life. The industry began in the Panhandle in 1910, when oil was found in Wheeler County, and in 1918 in Potter County the Amarillo Oil Company successfully drilled the first gas well: Masterson No. 1. The well came in at 2,269 feet and almost immediately began producing daily 10 million cubic feet of gas. Other wells soon followed and confirmed a gas field of an estimated 25 trillion cubic feet. Because of the Panhandle's remoteness from major markets, several gas companies in 1925 had combined resources to build storage facilities and pipelines to distant markets. By 1931, fifty-three processing plants refined natural gas for customers. By 1994 Panhandle natural gas fields produced 165 billion cubic feet of gas annually.

Oil production lagged in the area until 1921, when J. C. Whittington's No. 1 Sanford well in Hutchinson County came online. By 1926 the Texas Panhandle had become a major oil producing area, with much of the production coming from near the boomtown of Borger, located in Hutchinson County. Production climbed when wells in Gray, Potter, Moore, and Carson counties came online, and in 1917 production reached more than 39 million barrels annually. By 1940 the area had produced a total of 346.8 million barrels of oil, with annual totals climbing to 5 million barrels in

1994. With its gigantic yields of both gas and oil, Panhandle oil patches represented one of the largest petroleum fields in Texas.

Petroleum-related businesses grew astride the gas and oil production. Carbon black companies opened facilities that refined carbon from natural gas. The Western Carbon Company operated a plant in Carson County that produced carbon for the tire industry. In addition, the Texas Panhandle soon became the world's largest producer of helium and a major area for smelting zinc, which requires a steady supply of natural gas.

A cheap and available supply of gasoline, together with the increasing use of automobiles, brought a demand for better roads all across the United States, including Texas and the Panhandle. Indeed, in the 1920s the region led Texas in the development of highways, including the famous U.S. Route 66 (popularly called the Mother Road) and its predecessor, the Ozark Trail. Farm to market roads followed the building of federal and state highways.

Paved roads helped strengthen Amarillo's position as a tri-state trade center. With the passage of the Interstate Highway and Defense Act of 1956, the construction of Interstate Highway 40 soon followed. It crossed the Panhandle near the old path of Route 66 and connected Amarillo to the expanding interstate highway system. Later the construction of Interstate 27 connected Amarillo to Lubbock.

Improved transportation, including railroads, increased tourism in the Texas Panhandle. With improved roads, Palo Duro Canyon and Caprock Canyon became tourist destinations—even before they became state parks, in 1934 and 1982 respectively. To a lesser extent Lake Meredith National Recreation Area, Alibates Flint Quarries National Monument, Buffalo Lake Wildlife Refuge, and Paul Green's outdoor musical *TEXAS* staged in Palo Duro Canyon beginning in 1966 also became tourist attractions. In addition, throughout the year, the Cowgirl Hall of Fame in Hereford, although it eventually moved to Fort Worth, and the Muleshoe Wildlife Refuge in Bailey County attracted visitors.

Several regional museums are popular tourist destinations. The Panhandle–Plains Museum on the campus of West Texas A&M University in Canyon has become noted for its collection of artifacts relating to the area's history, petroleum industry, and ranching. The American Quarter Horse Association Hall of Fame, museum, and national headquarters, in Amarillo, attracts thousands of visitors annually. Other museums in Amarillo include Kwahadi Kiva Indian Museum, which features a replica of a Native American underground ceremonial chamber, the Amarillo Museum of Art, and the U.S. Route 66 Historic District.

Federally funded defense spending has added to the Panhandle mosaic. Because of the area's mild weather, the Army Air Corps during World War II built several training centers in the region, including facilities in Dalhart, Pampa, and Amarillo. In 1942 the federal government built the Pantex Army Ordnance Plant in Carson County not far from Amarillo. It produced bombs and artillery shells, and after the war it became an assembly plant for nuclear warheads.

Also during the war, the federal military built several prisoner of war camps in the Texas Panhandle. The camps held thousands of captured German and Italian soldiers. Many of the prisoners, especially the Italians, found work on local ranches and farms and built close relationships with local people.

The almost constant winds of the Texas Panhandle have led to the construction of wind turbines to produce electricity. Turbines dot the Panhandle. Amarillo native T. Boone Pickens announced late in 2008 that he planned to spend $2 billion on a wind farm in Carson, Gray, Hemphill, Roberts, and Wheeler counties. His Pampa Wind Project, as it was called, planned to build 667 wind turbines, but a year later Pickens put his plans on hold. Nonetheless, others before and since have erected hundreds of wind turbines across the region.

The wind turbines suggest that the Texas Panhandle, like much of the American West, is a unique blend of old and new. The region has been favored by human sojourners and inhabitants for a greater period than most parts of the United States, yet it remained sparsely settled until early in the twentieth century. But by the end of the century, it had become a place where old technology blended with recent innovations, where cattle ranching could be found across the fence from the Pantex Ordinance Plant and its latest nuclear weapons, and where farmers and ranchers followed age-old customs beneath modern wind turbines. And, at the beginning of the twenty-first century, it remains diverse in its population, society, and culture.

In a state that is considered both southern and western in terrain and culture, the Texas Panhandle in 2014 continues to present a distinctively Midwestern feel and outlook. Historically its citizens and interests have often faced northeast, toward Kansas City, Saint Louis, and Chicago, places tied to the region by prosperous business and beneficial cultural contacts. It remains a place where tradition counts for something, but where modern technology is always welcome.

## FOR FURTHER READING

Carlson, Paul H. *Empire Builder in the Texas Panhandle: William Henry Bush.* College Station: Texas A&M University Press, 1996.

———, and John T. Becker. *Georgia O'Keeffe in Texas: A Guide.* Abilene, Tex.: State House Press, 2012.

Egan, Timothy. *The Worst Hard Time: The Untold Story of Those Who Survived the Great American Dust Bowl.* New York: Houghton Mifflin, 2006.

Fairchild, Louis. *The Lonesome Plains: The Death and Revival of an American Frontier.* College Station: Texas A&M University Press, 2002.

Kenner, Charles L. *The Commanchero Frontier: A History of New Mexico–Plains Indian Relations.* Norman: University of Oklahoma Press, 1994.

Meinig, D. W. *Imperial Texas: An Interpretive Essay in Cultural Geography.* 6th paperback edition. Austin: University of Texas Press, 1993.

Murrah, David J. *"And Are We Yet Alive?" A History of the Northwest Conference of the United Methodist Church.* Buffalo Gap, Tex.: State House Press, 2009.

Paul, Rodman W. *The Far West and the Great Plains in Transition, 1859–1900.* Norman: University of Oklahoma Press, 1998.

Price, B. Byron, and Frederick W. Rathjen. *The Golden Spread: An Illustrated History of Amarillo and the Texas Panhandle.* Northridge, Calif.: Windsor, 1986.

Rathjen, Frederick W. *The Texas Panhandle Frontier.* Rev. ed. Lubbock: Texas Tech University Press, 1998.

Weaver, Bobby, ed. *Panhandle Petroleum.* Canyon, Tex.: Panhandle–Plains Historical Society, 1982.

CHAPTER 3

# The West Texas Plains

*Leland K. Turner*

The West Texas Plains is here broadly defined as the Llano Estacado and the Rolling Plains country. It is a region characterized by farming and ranching but dominated by its cities, especially Lubbock, Abilene, and Wichita Falls. Using the region's strong winds and the ideas of change and transformation as unifying dynamics, Turner describes the landscape and its people, their ways of making a living, and their social and cultural activities from the time of the Comancheria, when Native peoples dominated the area, into the twenty-first century.

Wind is a near constant across the West Texas Plains, an agricultural and ranching land stretching from the northeastern limits of West Texas westward to New Mexico. Essentially, the prairie lands west of Fort Worth, the Rolling Plains beyond them, and the southern Llano Estacado make up the West Texas Plains. Westward from Fort Worth, the heavily used and busy Interstate 20, before turning south near Sweetwater, cuts like a knife through the center of an extensive portion of the large subregion of West Texas.

Two centuries ago, likewise, the wind was a near constant across the Comancheria, the land of the Comanches, which covered much of the modern West Texas Plains. Indeed, certain oral traditions suggest that generations ago and far to the north Comanches were swept up on the wings of the wind and borne southward to their new domain. Although the Comanches employed the wind in various ways, over time, utilization of the wind evolved, and never, of course, was it simply a mystic force. But today, in 2014, the wind has become a sustainable source of electric energy, as demonstrated by the thousands of gyrating wind turbines that now rise from the West Texas Plains, leisurely but relentlessly generating power necessary to modern living.

The West Texas Plains region is not defined by wind alone. The place contains rolling prairies; vast, semi-arid grasslands; and rich agricultural land on which farmers raise cotton, wheat, grain sorghum, corn, peanuts, and other crops. Moreover, as a significant component of the southern Great Plains, the area is often dominated by its important cities, especially Abilene, Wichita Falls, and Lubbock—cities that grew in response to a vibrant agricultural economy that took root in the second half of the nineteenth century. Subsequently, livestock producers and agrarian settlers transformed the region from one that was home to a horse-mounted, mobile hunting society dominated by Comanches to one that is technologically advanced, machine driven, and agriculture-based.

Long before the ancestors of most modern-day occupants arrived in the late nineteenth century, the region was home to a long series of Native peoples whose societies stretched back perhaps 12,000 years. Among them were Comanches, whose power, reach, and influence after the middle of the eighteenth century increased manifold. Comanches, who had replaced Apaches in the area, traded with Pueblos to the west and Wichitas and others to the east. They met with Spanish authorities in San Antonio and New Mexico, and they maintained a large trading center in what today is eastern Colorado. As a result of the Treaty of Pecos in 1786, Comanches allowed *comancheros* (traders) from New Mexican villages to carry goods to the plains, and they usually met these traders in the well-watered canyons that cut deep into the Llano Estacado's eastern escarpment. They also allowed *ciboleros* (bison hunters) from New Mexico to come to the plains to hunt.

In addition, Spanish explorers were active in the West Texas Plains. Francisco Vásquez de Coronado in 1541 was the first, but others would follow. From 1785 to 1787, Pedro Vial, a Frenchman in the service of Spain, made several trips to the area with a view to connecting by road such far-flung outposts as Santa Fe, Nacogdoches, and San Antonio. In 1787 José Mares, an experienced Spanish soldier from Santa Fe, traveled from New Mexico to San Antonio and back, seeking to shorten the route Vial had explored. In 1808, sixty-nine-year-old Francisco Amangual, another military veteran, led 200 troops from San Antonio to Santa Fe. He moved his men through West Texas, climbed the caprock, and crossed the Llano Estacado.

Anglo-American settlers also entered the Rolling Plains, reaching the region from both the east and west. After 1803—that is, after the United States had purchased the vast Louisiana Territory from France—several entrepreneurs and daring traders followed the Red River westward plying their trade among the Wichitas and Comanches but also among native groups who bordered the Comancheria. Beaver trappers from Santa Fe, including Albert Pike, in 1832 crossed the Llano Estacado to the Rolling Plains along Blackwater Draw and Yellowhouse Canyon. Once they emerged from the canyon, they turned north to search for beaver in the Pease River country.

A different Anglo incursion onto the West Texas Plains began when Texas secured its independence from Mexico. A growing Anglo population in the new republic led Texans, especially those who had recently arrived from the United States, to challenge Comanches for the grasslands and farming country north and west of Austin. After Germans and other European immigrants settled among these first Anglo pioneers, there followed an enormous assault on Comanche lands in the West Texas Plains.

Fighting resulted. For about fifty years, approximately 1825 to 1875, warfare across West Texas was bloody and bitter, with neither side willing to understand its foe. Although white pressure, except during the Civil War years, was relentless, the Comanches, especially, but also their allies the Kiowas, Cheyennes, and Arapahoes, resisted with much success until the late 1860s. Final defeat came as a result of declining bison populations, restricted hunting territory, and the arrival of federal troops. After the Civil War, the United States Army, with an aristocracy of talent in its field officers and a seemingly unlimited number of soldiers, built forts and roads throughout the area, fought Indian warriors, protected the white settlers, and with the aid of Texas Rangers and local militia groups attacked Indian villages. The half-century of warfare ended at long last in 1874–75 with the Red River War in the Texas Panhandle, after which the government forced Comanches to settle on reservations in Indian Territory or modern-day Oklahoma.

As U.S.–Indian warfare neared its end in the 1870s, Anglo bison hunters entered the West Texas Plains. From bases at Fort Griffin in Shackelford County, Rath City in Stonewall County, and Mobeetie in the Panhandle, the hunters, who wanted only the bison hides and preferred younger females, killed hundreds of thousands of animals. For good hunters, such as J. Wright Mooar and John Wesley Mooar, Billy Dixon, George Causey, and John Cook, it was a lucrative business. Hides sold for $3.00 to $4.00 each, and the West Texas Plains held a few million bison. Hide buyers, such as Charles Rath, W. M. D. Lee, and the Beverley interests in Dodge City, Kansas, also enjoyed healthy profits during the mid- to late 1870s, when the bison hunt was at its peak.

In the late 1870s, with Comanches and their allies resettled on reservations and bison gone from the grasslands, the way was open for farmers and ranchers to enter West Texas. The Clear Fork country, the area between present-day Abilene and Jacksboro, served as a gateway for the Anglo settlement that followed. Prior to the American Civil War the federal government had established several forts in the region. In fact, as early as 1851 a line of posts west and southwest of Fort Worth included Forts Belknap, Phantom Hill, and Chadbourne. In later years Fort Richardson, east of Belknap and near Jacksboro, and Fort Griffin northeast of Abilene solidified civilian access to the region.

The West Texas Plains was cattle country at first. The Chisholm Trail pushed through Fort Worth and skirted the northeastern edges of the plains. Eventually cattle and their herders moved cattle trails westward, in response to complaints from Kansas farmers about the tick-borne disease known as Texas fever (babesiosis). The Western Cattle Trail pressed due north through the heart of the Clear Fork country. The Goodnight-Loving trail originated in that region and proceeded to the southwest in its long trek toward Colorado. As a result, by the late 1870s ranching was the dominant economic activity on the verdant grasslands.

Farming and ranching boomed in the early 1880s. Along with agricultural settlement came towns and cities, which facilitated transportation and trade. Wichita Falls was established in 1876. Various small villages, such as Albany and Fort Griffin, sprang up along the Western Cattle Trail. In the 1870s ranchers began to graze their herds in the area that became Taylor County, which was organized in 1878. In 1881, as the result of a deal between several ranchers and the Texas and Pacific Railroad, Abilene was founded. The construction of the Fort Worth & Denver City Railroad (FW&DC) in the 1870s and 1880s attracted town builders along its tracks on the northern edge of the Rolling Plains.

The railroads, especially, but town building as well, attracted large ranching operations. C. C. Slaughter, for example, formed the Long S Ranch in 1877 and took cattle onto the South Plains of the Llano Estacado near present-day Lamesa. At the time it was the largest ranch in the West Texas Plains. Two years later, Hank Campbell established the Matador Ranch along the Pease River in Motley County. He purchased half a section of land and, like most other plains cattlemen, ran his animals on the open range. The Matador Land and Cattle Company became one of the largest such operations on the Great Plains. Burk Burnett established his first ranch in the vicinity of present-day Wichita Falls and eventually leased more than 300,000 acres on the Oklahoma side of the Red River. Around 1900, when drought and the federal government drove him back upon the Rolling Plains of West Texas, he anchored his famous Four Sixes Ranch (6666) in King County.

Prior to the 1880s, economic and environmental concerns favored expansion of the open range cattle business. Reports in 1877 described free West Texas land abounding with lush grass. Soon a rush of foreign and eastern capital descended on the plains. By 1882, cattle that once sold for $7.00 a head brought $25.00 each. Investors sank millions of dollars into cattle operations. A "beef bonanza" ensued.

The bonanza did not last. Overgrazing, overproduction, inflated stock prices, and a nasty spate of weather all combined to deal the open range a fatal blow. With the closing of the range and the financial disaster of the late 1880s, ranchers made radical changes in their operations. As a result of such alterations, the cattle business on the West Texas Plains modernized and diversified, and the cattle industry shifted significantly from what essentially was an adventure to a settled, business-oriented agricultural economy. Business reverses, railroads, barbed wire fencing, improved breeding, and hydraulic technology in the form of windmills all played a part in transforming the industry from the open range adventure it was to the closely managed system it became.

The use of windmills was an important part of the transformation. In a 1932 editorial in *The Cattleman*, windmill salesman F. W. Axtell said, "The rapid development of the great western country would not have taken place had it not been for the windmill."[1] Another *Cattleman* correspondent agreed that the windmill was responsible for the settlement of the vast West Texas Plains. It enabled stockmen, he said, "to push out beyond the streams and ponds and depend upon wells for watering their cattle. This made available for grazing purposes vast tracts of land which otherwise would have been useless" to stock raisers.[2]

The windmill was essential to the development and subsequent maintenance of the cattle industry. Moreover, with the introduction of barbed wire, windmills became integral to range management. First introduced to Texas ranches in the 1870s, the individual windmill was relatively inexpensive, but when introduced into management of the open pastures of the larger ranches, hydraulic technology became a costly ledger entry in the new business of livestock production. Following the incorporation of the range in the late 1880s and early 1890s, large ranch corporations pursued windmill technology with vigor. In 1886, for example, such large ranches as the Franklyn Land and Cattle Company, the Magnolia Cattle and Land Company, and the Matador Land and Cattle Company utilized windmills extensively in efforts to obtain adequate water.

Murdo Mackenzie, appointed general manager of the Matador in 1891, transformed the megaranch from an open range operation to a closely managed enterprise. In doing so he developed an elaborate water management scheme in which Matador ranges took water from various branches of the Pease River and nearby tributaries and springs. Mackenzie's plan utilized dams, canals, and reservoirs. Nonetheless, his ultimate goal of no more than four miles between watering holes could not have been accomplished without the additional use of windmills.

Because the Anglo version of the West Texas Plains economy was initially dependent on livestock operations, underground water reserves became essential to the survival of settlers and their livestock. Windmills wrangled much of that water from the earth. By 1900, the windmill was a common element of the landscape and vital to the success of a livestock economy. Yet windmill technology at the time was insufficient for significant irrigation projects. Small orchard and garden patches were viable with windmill-pumped wells, but not large fields and commercial crops.

Nonetheless, agrarian encroachment increased and presented stock raisers with yet another challenge. Encouraged by government policy, farmers laid claim to the most productive and well-watered regions of the West Texas Plains. Stock raisers were thus relegated to the marginal lands not suited to crop farming. One cause of this development was the Four-Section Act. The law, passed on April 4, 1895, allowed an individual to purchase or lease four sections of public land. Ostensibly meant to help ranchers, the law in practice enabled farmers to homestead Texas land much as the Homestead Act of 1862 had enabled agrarian settlement throughout much of the Great Plains. In effect, the Four-Section Act and the various laws associated with it facilitated a transformation of the West Texas Plains agricultural economy.

The appearance of the farmer-stockman, something of a hybrid agriculturalist, was a result. Farmer-stockmen laid claim to numerous sections of West Texas grasslands. They raised a few head of livestock, including pigs and sheep, as well as the traditional cattle and horses. They also raised crops of small grains, particularly wheat, grain sorghum, and corn, and relied on the railroads to carry any surplus to market.

Among the first of the farmer-stockmen was Hank Smith, who settled in Blanco Canyon about 1878. A former teamster and hotel manager, Smith raised cattle, hay, and vegetables. He was the first permanent non-Indian resident of the area, and he boasted of its good water and excellent potential for hay as a crop for cattle. "I do not exaggerate," he wrote, "when I say 5,000 tons of hay could be cut within one mile of our place."[3] Smith's enthusiasm brought farmers and ranchers alike to the area.

Eventually the encroachment of farmer-stockmen upon large cattle-raising operations resulted in the sale of much of the original open range ranch land. The huge XIT Ranch sold portions of its several divisions to smaller, but still large, ranching enterprises. The George W. Littlefield interests, for

*A Bailey County farmer pauses while plowing across a cow trail, 1915, as if to symbolize the transformation from cattle raising to farming then occurring on the West Texas Plains. (Courtesy Southwest Collection, Texas Tech University)*

example, in 1901 bought XIT's 312,000-acre Yellowhouse division centered at Casas Amarillas west of Lubbock. And, not many years later, Littlefield established Littlefield Lands Company to sell some 64,000-acres in what is now Lamb County to farmer-stockmen. About 1912, he established the town of Littlefield along a mainline of the Atchison, Topeka & Santa Fe Railway that extended from southeast of Coleman through much of the Rolling Plains and Lubbock to Clovis, New Mexico.

Many other large ranchers "colonized" their land. Partly as a result, farmers and town builders poured into the West Texas Plains, lured there by land speculators and the promise of cheap and productive land. From about 1890 to about 1930, they created something of a farming frontier on the Rolling Plains and the Llano Estacado. Land colonizers and farmers turned the livestock pastures of the Llano into farmlands for cotton, grains, and other farm products. Land booms, technological advancements, and population growth characterized the period.

During this period, farmers turned more and more to the cultivation of cotton. In 1889 Rollie Burns of Lubbock, a founding participant and prominent area ranch manager, planted the first cotton on the High Plains. Notwithstanding his efforts, it was later, between 1905 and 1915, that cotton growing developed as a major economic activity. Cotton cultivation also stimulated ginning operations and related businesses. Still, until the 1920s the production of hay and grain sorghums plus wheat and Sudan grass represented crops that many farmers cultivated. For most of this period farmers on the Llano Estacado raised a variety of crops. Those crops tended to be forage crops to support the region's livestock economy but, significantly, included some cotton.

Conditions changed with World War I. As demand for cotton increased during and immediately after the war, prices soared—sometimes, as in 1919, dramatically. Farmers on the South Plains of the Llano Estacado were quick to take advantage of the inflated prices and turned more and more of their land over to the white fiber. Cotton production rose as dramatically as the price. In Lubbock County, for example, the amount of farmland devoted to cotton reached 136,518 acres near the end of the 1920s. When other counties witnessed a similar expansion of cotton-based agriculture, diversified farming began a slow demise and would not revive until the end of the century. By the 1930s the South Plains, centered at Lubbock, had been transformed from livestock to a cotton economy.

Mechanization of farming was another trend that characterized the years from World War I through the 1920s. Technology was much improved, and the use of machines to replace horses and mules seemed an attractive proposition. Huge coal-fired, steam-driven "traction engines" had appeared even before the war, but in the 1920s, as the technology continued to advance, gasoline-powered tractors and more effective equipment for plowing, planting, and harvesting came into use. In 1925 some 1,773 tractors, which worked efficiently with cotton, were employed in cultivation on the South Plains.

Irrigation marked a third agricultural innovation effecting High Plains farming. While it was not as widespread as it would become in the 1930s or in the 1950s and afterward, irrigation practices nonetheless had a noteworthy beginning before World War I. As noted earlier, windmills could not raise enough water from the rich Ogallala Aquifer to irrigate extensive commercial crops. A dependable water supply was needed.

Among the first people to drill a successful well for irrigation was J. J. Slaton. In 1910, he and his assistants produced a well in Running Water Draw five miles east of Plainview. Others followed. At Muleshoe the Coldron Land Company of Chicago drilled a well on company lands. In the Lubbock area Don H. Biggers (who would write at least two books on West Texas) drilled a well on his farm, as did B. O. McWhorter in 1911, W. A. Bacon in 1911, and George W. Boles in 1912. All of these tapped into the Ogallala Aquifer, deep beneath the farm properties.

Other efforts at well drilling for irrigation purposes occurred to the east, off the caprock escarpment of the Llano Estacado and into the Rolling Plains country. C. W. Post, the Battle Creek, Michigan, cereal king, established a utopian community at Post City in Garza County in the early years of the century, before the war. He divided his holdings, some of which were below the caprock, into 160-acre farms. On each he planned for a house, barn, and various outbuildings. He wanted to place a well with a windmill on each farmstead and offer the property for sale. Eventually, Post owned some 250,000 acres of land, and hundreds of West Texas pioneers took advantage of Post's instant farms.

Irrigation also helped to expand cotton agriculture into the Rolling Plains. Farmers near Snyder and Roscoe, in Scurry County, planted extensive acres to cotton. Farmers in some areas in the northern reaches of the Rolling Plains likewise turned to cotton production. Growers in Archer, Baylor, and Haskell counties, for example, raised cotton, and eventually there were many producers in Shackelford, Stephens, Stone-wall, Jones, and Taylor counties as well. In effect, cotton growing and marketing became a major industry in the early decades of the twentieth century.

Changes occurred. Drought and drastically low prices during the Great Depression and Dust Bowl years of the 1930s affected both cotton rais-ing and large-scale irrigation. Cotton prices, which had reached as high as 40 cents per pound around 1920, plunged to 10 cents per pound in 1927—even before the onset of the depression. To counter the falling prices, farmers planted more cotton. The long years of below-average rainfall—severe drought, really—in the 1930s encouraged growers, when they could afford it, to invest in massive irrigation projects with deep wells and large pumping plants to bring water to the surface and spread it across their fields.

Even greater efforts at extensive irrigation transpired in the 1950s, after World War II. Another long drought, especially during the years from 1950 to 1956, encouraged this development, and now, as a result of wartime profits in the 1940s, growers could marshal financial assets large enough to invest in technologically superior pumping equipment, tubular goods, and deep wells. Such investments allowed farmers to abandon most crops other than cotton and become commercial monocrop operators on a large scale. As Donald Green explains it in *The Land of Underground Rain*, these irrigation plants with large-volume, deep-well pumps are an essential criterion for making the transition from subsistence farming to commercial agriculture. The irrigation pumping plant and centrifugal pump, which had become available in the 1930s had promised and now at last delivered such a solution. By the 1950s cotton producers on the High Plains ran highly mechanized operations with high-impact irrigation, large tractors, complex planting and harvesting equipment, and sophisticated marketing strategies. They used specialized and hybrid seeds, liquid fertilizers, and powerful weed killers to increase production. The notion that irrigation should facilitate capacity crop production began to replace earlier ideas that had defined irrigation as a rainfall subsidy.

Thus after the 1950s cotton growing and cattle raising as commercial operations dominated agricultural enterprises throughout the West Texas Plains. Today the counties around Lubbock lead in cotton production. King County with its Four Sixes Ranch, Dickens County with its Pitchfork Ranch, and Shackelford County with its Lambshead Ranch dominate livestock raising. Wheat production, some of it very large-scale in the Rolling Plains, is also a major part of West Texas Plains commercial agriculture.

Petroleum, including oil and gas production, has also played a key role in the West Texas economy since the industry developed in the early decades of the twentieth century. Major oil fields exist on the Llano Estacado in Hockley, Yoakum, Cochran, and Terry counties, and oil and gas are important in many counties of the Rolling Plains. Wichita and Kent counties, for example, have produced more than 1 billion barrels of oil, and Archer, Garza, Stonewall, Stephens, Wilbarger, and Young counties have each produced between 250 million and 500 million barrels. Oil has provided jobs, created wealth, subsidized schools, and brought enormous benefits to people involved in its production, refining, transporting, and marketing.

Oil and gas added significantly to the development of several modern cities in the West Texas Plains. Wichita Falls, Abilene, and Snyder have particularly benefited from petroleum operations. Lubbock, too, owes some of its wealth to oil and to the great incomes that have derived from its production. Many smaller cities dependent upon oil and its production have boomed and declined with oil's fortunes in the area

Petroleum and large cities aside, the West Texas Plains remains rural and agricultural in character. Most towns are small, and many are in a state of decline. On the Llano Estacado's High Plains, especially, communities are losing population and vitality. Indeed, many of them no longer serve as a marketing and trade center for their surrounding area. Some have lost their identity as their schools closed, hospitals or clinics disappeared, and main street shops became vacant. Wide roadways and modern trucks and automobiles have allowed citizens in small towns to reach quickly and in relative comfort larger cities with their ostensibly lower prices and wider range of shopping, eating, and entertainment choices.

Lubbock, Abilene, and Wichita Falls, the only true metropolitan areas on the West Texas Plains, have grown significantly in the post–World War II era and continue to grow as rural residents migrate to urban centers. Douglas Hurt, in *The Big Empty*, has described how young adults across the Great Plains are leaving rural communities for better economic, educational, and social opportunities in urban centers. The plains population, he says, is becoming essentially urban. Many people leave the plains altogether, but some migrate to regional urban centers. Today, in 2014, both Abilene and Wichita Falls host populations above 100,000, and Lubbock, with more than 220,000 residents, is the largest city on the Great Plains.

The story of decline and growth is represented well by a comparison of Lubbock County, on the western edge of the West Texas Plains, and Baylor County, on the eastern fringes. Baylor County supports a diverse farming, ranching, and oil economy. In 1900 its population stood at 3,052 people, and it was growing because of the Northwest Texas oil boom and the increase in cotton production. The population peaked in 1910 at 8,411 people but has declined since. In 2000, only 4,092 people called Baylor County home. Conversely, the Lubbock County population has grown exponentially. The county boasted a meager population of 293 citizens in 1900. Cotton agriculture, education, medicine, and some oil production with peripheral industries created jobs and social opportunities that brought the Lubbock County population to 242,628 by 2000. In 2014 the city of Lubbock served as the retail, industrial, and service center for much of West Texas and eastern New Mexico.

The larger West Texas Plains continued in 2014 to play a significant role in the state's and indeed in the nation's economy. Its agricultural enterprises and oil and gas production have been vital to the United States, and they will continue to remain important for the foreseeable future. During and after World War II the region with its several military bases was important for national defense, and with Dyess Air Force Base in Abilene and Sheppard Air Force Base near Wichita Falls the region retains a strong military presence in the present era.

West Texas has been describe as a region with a "distinct environment, diverse cultures, and a traditional dependence on the federal economy."[4] This assertions holds especially true for the West Texas Plains. Extractive industries of the region are supported through various federal subsidy programs. Defense spending is an important element of the region's economy. Federal dollars invigorate research spending at the area universities and medical schools. Various federal aid programs enable many students to attend regional colleges and universities. Ironically, it is a culture that by and large disdains federal interference but is heavily dependent, economically, on federal spending. Generally, West Texans are culturally conservative and identify themselves as among the "rugged individualists" rather than as economic collectivists. Nonetheless, these same farmers, ranchers, independent oilmen, and urban dwellers adjunct to those industries become politically active through various agrarian, livestock, and oil and gas associations in efforts to preserve federal funding or influence federal policy in favor of their work and their society.

Clearly, the West Texas Plains landscape of the early twenty-first century is a distinct one. What were once vast grasslands are now cotton fields, oil patches, and, in too many cases, rangelands choked by mesquite. And, of course, there are the wind turbines. The first wind wheels on the West Texas Plains were not an attempt to satiate the human need for artificial energy, but to slake the thirst of valuable livestock. Over time, and given environmental realities, wind-driven profits came to make perfect sense in West Texas. Wind energy may well become the engine that propels profitability in the rural region. In the short term wind farms are not likely to replace pump jacks, cotton fields, or rangeland livestock operations. Essentially, wind energy promises to supplement and maybe even sustain agricultural profitability in twenty-first century West Texas.

## NOTES

1. F. W. Axtell, "Windmill Efficiency," *The Cattleman* 19 (October 1932), 14–15.

2. F. L. Dole, "West Made Habitable By Windmills," *The Cattleman* 19 (October 1932), 14.

3. Scott Sosebee, "Henry C. 'Hank' Smith: A Westering Man." Ph.D. dissertation (Texas Tech University, 2004), 137.

4. Glen Ely, *Where the West Begins: Debating Texas Identity* (Lubbock: Texas Tech University Press, 2010.)

## FOR FURTHER READING

Baker, T. Lindsay. *Blades in the Sky: Windmilling through the Eyes of B. H. "Tex" Burdick.* Lubbock: Texas Tech University Press, 1992.

Betty, Gerald. *Comanche Society: Before the Reservation.* College Station: Texas A&M University Press, 2002.

Carlson, Paul H. *The Centennial History of Lubbock: Hub City of the Plains.* Virginia Beach, Va.: Donning, 2008.

Cashion, Ty. *A Texas Frontier: The Clear Fork Country and Fort Griffin, 1849–1887.* Norman: University of Oklahoma Press, 1996.

Cunfer, Geoff. *On the Great Plains: Agriculture and Environment.* College Station: Texas A&M University Press, 2005.

Ely, Glen. *Where the West Begins: Debating West Texas Identity.* Lubbock: Texas Tech University Press, 2010.

Green, Donald E. *Land of the Underground Rain: Irrigation on the Texas High Plains, 1910–1970.* Austin: University of Texas Press, 1973.

Hamalainen, Pekka. *The Comanche Empire.* New Haven: Yale University Press, 2008.

Hurt, R. Douglas. *The Big Empty: The Great Plains in the Twentieth Century.* Tucson: University of Arizona Press, 2011.

Morris, John Miller. *El Llano Estacado: Exploration and Imagination on the High Plains of Texas and New Mexico, 1536–1860.* Austin: Texas State Historical Association, 1997.

Murrah, David J. *C. C. Slaughter: Rancher, Banker, Baptist.* Austin: University of Texas Press 1981.

Pace, Robert F., and Donald S. Frazier. *Frontier Texas: History of a Borderland to 1880.* Abilene: State House Press, 2004.

Pearce, William M. *The Matador Land and Cattle Company.* Norman: University of Oklahoma Press, 1964.

Sledge, Robert W. *A People, a Place: The Story of Abilene.* Vol. 1, *The Future Great City, 1881–1940.* Abilene: State House Press, 2008.

Smith, Sherry L., ed. *The Future of the Southern Plains.* Norman: University of Oklahoma Press, 2003.

Wilson, Steve. *Wichita Falls: A Pictorial History.* Norfolk, Va.: Donning, 1982.

CHAPTER 4

# The Edwards Plateau and Permian Basin

*James T. Matthews*

Like much of the rest of West Texas, the Edwards Plateau and Permian Basin are rural farming and ranch country, with cattle, sheep, and goats forming significant portions of their economies. Oil, its production and distribution, is also a dominant characteristic of these areas, especially around Midland and Odessa. This chapter carefully reviews the history of these areas with attention to agriculture and petroleum and also considers the vital role played by military installations.

The Edwards Plateau and Permian Basin lie in the southwestern part of West Texas. Their combined subregion is bounded on the east by the Balcones Escarpment, on the south by the Rio Grande, and on the west, at least geographically, by the Pecos River. The northern boundary is more difficult to determine, but it melts into the Llano Estacado in the northwest and the Rolling Plains toward the northeast. The major cities in this southwestern sector include San Angelo, Midland, Odessa, and Del Rio.

The Edwards Plateau, rising with the South Texas Hill Country and extending west over some twenty-five counties, is an area of thin soils, limestone hills, and savanna grasslands. Its mid-height to short grasses provide poor farming territory but good grazing land, with a scattering of such trees as ash, juniper, post oak, shin oak, and mesquite. The rough, timbered basin of the Llano and Colorado rivers crosses the region.

The Permian Basin, which geologically extends into southeastern New Mexico, is also a grassland environment but one rich in petroleum. Centuries ago, an evaporating inland sea left thick deposits of sediment and minerals, including oil and the largest deposit of Permian rocks in existence. Petroleum mining and related activities have dominated the basin since 1923, when the Santa Rita No. 1 well opened near Big Lake.

Together the Edwards Plateau and the Permian Basin blaze a path through West Texas that over the centuries has been crossed by Native Americans, Spanish explorers, soldiers of various nations, gold seekers, cattlemen, and petroleum entrepreneurs. About 1450 or so, the place was nearly barren of humans, but coyotes, deer, bear, antelope, and bison abounded. In fact, the bison drew a new wave of Indian hunters, and by the 1500s Jumanos and others had established villages in the region. The Spanish wanderer Álvar Núñez Cabeza de Vaca in 1534 stayed at one of the Jumano villages. Almost a century later, between 1629 and 1632, Franciscans Juan de Salas and Diego López conducted Christian services at a thriving Jumano community.

Eventually, Spanish traders from Santa Fe became frequent visitors among Jumanos, especially villages on the Concho and upper Colorado rivers. Some Spaniards collected shells, for which the Concho River was named, and harvested them for fresh water pearls. Trading in the area came to an abrupt halt when in 1680 the Pueblo Revolt in Santa Fe and the upper Rio Grande cut lines of communication.

Yet Spanish activity continued. In 1683, a delegation of seven Native Americans, including Jumanos, appeared before Governor Domingo de Cruzate in El Paso seeking a resumption of trade and the return of missionaries as aid against eastern Apache groups that had begun to move into the region. The governor appointed Juan Dominguez de Mendoza, a former visitor to the Jumanos, to lead an expedition that would explore the resources of the region and reestablish trade. Mendoza traveled to the Pecos River, crossed the stream near the current Horsehead Crossing, and continued east to the Middle Concho River, which he followed to its junction with the North Concho at present-day San Angelo.

From there Mendoza with his party continued east to a river he called the San Clemente, which was probably the Colorado River. He described the river water as "clear and good" and noted that "the country is well supplied with nuts and other food products, such as wild turkeys, sweet potatoes, buffalo, and many other kinds of animals. The river is supplied with many fish: catfish, boquinete, and matalote; and with shells; and with a variety of very agreeable songbirds." While camped on the Colorado near the present site of Ballinger, Mendoza wrote, "The bottom lands of the river are luxuriant with plants bearing nuts, grapes, mulberries, and many groves of plums; with much game, wild hens, and a variety of animals, such as bear, deer, and antelopes . . . [and] the number of buffalo is so great that only the divine Majesty, as owner of all, is able to count them."[1]

On May 1, 1684, the Mendoza expedition began its return. Conversion of Jumanos to Christianity had been slow and Lipan Apaches, who were challenging Jumanos for hunting land, had attacked Mendoza's camps. Although Mendoza was not ready to quit, Spanish attention turned away from the Jumanos. Apache problems in West Texas was one reason, but a more important factor was that government concern now centered on foreign incursions, led by Frenchman Robert Cavelier, Sieur de La Salle, along the Spanish Gulf Coast.

Apaches in West Texas were not forgotten. In response to repeated Indian raids, Don Juan Antonio Bustillo y Ceballos, the governor of Texas, in 1732 led a punitive expedition against Apaches, attacking a village of 400 tents in what is now Menard County. He reported 200 Apaches dead and 30 women and children captured along with 700 horses and cattle and 100 loads of pelts.

Then Spaniards found silver and copper. In 1756 Don Bernardo de Miranda discovered a rich vein of silver in a cave on a tributary of the Llano River and brought back three pounds of silver ore. Although the Spanish did little mining in the area, this discovery led prospectors on an endless search for the lost San Saba mines, said to have been exploited by the Indians as a source of silver. Treasure hunters continue to search for the San Saba mines.

Such expeditions led to a period of greater stability and the founding in 1757 of a mission for Apaches along the San Saba River. The houses, church, and stockade of the Mission Santa Cruz de San Sabá, near present-day Menard, were built of wooden posts and poles with thatched roofs in the method known by the Spanish as *jacal*. The Spaniards also built a presidio to fortify the area—unfortunately, this installation was four miles upstream, on the other side of the river.

Perhaps 3,000 Apaches camped near the mission in June 1757. They refused to enter the compound, however, saying they would return after a bison hunt. Upon returning, they still refused a priest's entreaties to enter the stockade facility. The refusal, combined with news of impending attacks by northern tribes, discouraged the missionaries, and by the end of the year some had left.

Then, in March 1758, the expected attack occurred. A force of 2,000 Comanches, accompanied by warriors from Tonkawa, Tejas, Wichita, and Caddo tribes surrounded the mission. The warriors forced their way into the mission courtyard and stole food, clothing, and horses and killed two of the mission priests who tried to appease them. A small group of mission folk took refuge in the church as the Comanches celebrated and set fire to the stockade. The refugees later managed to make their way to the presidio. Comanches and their allies followed. At the post, because some garrison soldiers were absent on patrols, 30 men stood off the Indians. Only the return of the patrols the next day saved the presidio from being burned to the ground. Afterward, as the Spanish government attempted to determine its strategy for securing mining operations and trade routes across West Texas, the Presidio San Luis de las Amarillas de San Sabá, as that site came to be known, was strengthened. Yet by 1772 it had been abandoned, its ruins used only occasionally as shelter for Indian fighters.

With no Spanish presence in the region, West Texas increasingly came under the control of Comanches, the fearless horsemen of the plains. And as political jurisdiction in West Texas passed in 1821 from Spain to Mexico, to the Republic of Texas in 1836, and finally to the United States in 1845, Comanche power and influence increased. In 1849, following the end of the war with Mexico, American citizens began crossing the Edwards Plateau and the Permian Basin. Some wanted to trade with Indians. Others sought routes to California gold fields.

In response, the United States Army surveyed various trails and proposed that a line of military posts be established through Comanche country. The forts would provide safety and enforce peace through a strong military presence. Fort Mason, among the first of the outposts, was established in 1851 near Comanche and Centennial creeks in the northern part of what was then Gillespie County. In 1852, troops manned Camp Joseph E. Johnston, a temporary site on the North Concho River. At the same time, the army chose a site on the San Saba River, about twenty miles southwest of the abandoned Spanish presidio, to establish Fort McKavett. In October, the sandstone walls of Fort Chadbourne went up, on Oak Creek, a tributary of the Colorado River. Army surgeon Ebenezer Swift recalled traveling from Fort Mason to his new station at Camp Johnston. "Fort Mason," he wrote, "is some distance in advance of the settlements, and we are of course in advance of it, in a wild country, inhabited by Indians, prairie dogs and rattle snakes."[2]

As permanent buildings at the outposts rose, the "wild country" became a bit less feral. Stage lines appeared, and with troopers of the Eighth Infantry and Second Cavalry patrolling the region, travelers felt more secure. In 1855, soldiers established Fort Lancaster on Live Oak Creek, a tributary of the Pecos River. It provided protection for a new southern mail road, and from 1858 to 1861, the short-lived Butterfield Overland Mail route crossed the region on its way to Horsehead Crossing on the Pecos River before continuing to California.

In addition, of course, some pioneers determined to settle on the Edwards Plateau. A number of towns appeared near the army outposts. A few families, beginning with that of William S. Gamel in 1846, settled near what became the site of Fort Mason, even before the post was established. The towns of Mason, San Saba, and Lampasas were established in 1855. Llano appeared in 1856. In 1858, settlers established Menard, first known as Menardville, on the San Saba River near the ruins of the old Spanish presidio. Just west of the Pecos, the army in 1859 constructed Fort Stockton at Comanche Springs, a site on the Comanche War Trail. The post was intended to protect expanding mail and freight lines.

Such rapid growth in the region all but ceased in 1861, when the Texas secession convention voted to pull Texas out of the United States. Federal soldiers withdrew from military posts along the edge of Comanche territory. Noah Smithwick, traveling west to escape Confederate territories, wrote that "[at] Fort Chadbourne we encountered the first visible effects of impending war in the absence of the American flag from the fort where it had fanned the breeze for so long."[3]

During the Civil War, Texas state troops replaced some of the U.S. soldiers. A company of Texas Rangers under command of Captain Robert Halley, for example, manned Fort Chadbourne in an attempt to protect settlers in the area. Ranger companies manned other outposts and patrolled areas between the forts in an effort to block Kiowa and Comanche raids. Confederate Army contingents also entered the fray.

Sometimes there was disaster. In December 1864, Captain Henry Fossett of the Confederate forces assembled a battalion at Fort Chadbourne to attack nearly 600 Kickapoos known to be moving through the region. The Kickapoos were migrating—peacefully—from Indian Territory to Mexico, but Fossett's command and a militia group under Silas Totten encountered the Indians in early January along Dove Creek. The Kickapoos routed the Confederates, who were outnumbered and had no clear plan of action. The Indians then resumed their trek into Mexico. In this much-criticized fight, Fossett and Totten lost 22 men dead and 19 wounded, the largest loss by Confederate troops on the Texas frontier.

Despite such efforts or perhaps because of them, civilian settlement in southwestern Texas did not increase during the Civil War. Lieutenant Sidney Green Davison observed, "The country is very poor, but pretty. . . . There are no settlers in this country except two or three Dutch cow drivers—no women."[4] After the war, Federal forces reoccupied Texas, but initially did not man the western forts. Their efforts concentrated on administering Reconstruction and providing a show of force against the French government of Maximilian in Mexico. Nonetheless, Fort Mason was reoccupied in December 1866 and then repaired and improved through the use of civilian artisans and military labor. By this time, too, Texans had begun to herd cattle across the Edwards Plateau. Indeed, soon after the Dove Creek fight, Richard F. Tankersley, one of the first American settlers on the Concho River, brought cattle into the area, foreshadowing the new wave of settlement.

In the spring of 1867, General Phillip Sheridan proposed reestablishment of additional outposts. He wanted to protect the growing number of cattlemen and settlers in the region. Partly in response, Company G of the Fourth Cavalry, under Captain Michael J. Kelly, arrived in May 1867 to reopen Fort Chadbourne. By June, 331 soldiers were at the fort. Fort Chadbourne's return to active life was brief. The army needed a site with a more reliable source of water, grass, and wood. Besides, buildings at the post were too small and in some cases irreparable, with bad roofs and broken walls. Fort Chadbourne continued in use as a subpost for a few years, but it was abandoned in 1873.

Meanwhile, in June 1867, Lieutenant Peter M. Boehm arrived at the Middle Concho River and established a temporary camp as a possible site for the new post. Three months later a board of officers, including Major John P. Hatch, arrived to survey the North and Middle Concho rivers; they chose to locate the new fort on a plateau at the junction of the rivers. They liked the spot because of "the large quantity and quality of grass—the almost inexhaustible supply of limestone and rock and land for building and the large and never ending supply of good running water."⁵

Construction began on the new post, designated Fort Concho, in January 1868. By the end of the year, the quartermaster's storehouse, the commissary, and one wing of the hospital building had been completed. Construction crews used native limestone quarried from the area south of the post. They made mortar with lime extracted from the stone and with crushed sandstone from along the Concho River. Most wood used for framing they hauled from the Gulf Coast. While local sawmills produced some lumber, most of it was pecan wood, which proved difficult to use because of its hardness and the tendency of green wood to shrink and twist after it had been nailed in place.

During the same period, the Ninth Cavalry reoccupied Fort Stockton and Fort Lancaster, and troops of the Fourth Cavalry occupied Fort McKavett. But construction problems at the outposts were complicated, in that building materials and other supplies had to be freighted by oxen from Indianola on the Gulf Coast through San Antonio to West Texas over rough and often muddy roads. To improve supply lines, soldiers built wagon roads to connect the forts.

Soldiers also engaged in numerous scouting expeditions, for in the early 1870s Comanches continued to hold control of the region's vast grasslands. Most such scouts returned to camp without seeing a single Indian. In March 1872 Sergeant William Wilson assembled a small patrol that followed the trail of some horses recently stolen near Fort Concho. His men soon tracked down the suspected party, whom they believed to be hostile Indians. After a skirmish, the troopers reported two of the enemy killed, three wounded, and one captured out of fourteen engaged. They also recaptured nineteen of the stolen horses, and five mules. Upon questioning the prisoner, Wilson discovered that the party he had attacked was in fact *comancheros,* Hispanics and mixed-blood traders, who had bargained for stolen goods with the Indians.

Sergeant Wilson turned his prisoner over to the post commander, Major Hatch. Hatch soon realized that the captive, Polonio Ortiz, could serve as a scout and guide on campaigns against Comanches. For the rest of the early 1870s Ortiz would serve Colonel Ranald Mackenzie and the Fourth Cavalry on several important expeditions, most of them toward the northwest and across the Llano Estacado.

In 1875, Fort Concho and Fort Stockton became home to the Tenth Cavalry under Colonel Benjamin Grierson. The Tenth enlisted African American troopers, many of whom were former slaves from Virginia, Kentucky, Maryland, and Tennessee. To the army, the Tenth was known as Grierson's Brunets. Their Indian adversaries referred to them with respect as Buffalo Soldiers, perhaps because their hair resembled the dense fur on the mane and forequarters of the sacred bison. The black soldiers helped in the army's efforts to convince Comanches, Kiowas, and their allies to settle on reservations in Indian Territory.

Some western Apaches, who had also accepted reservation life, left their government reserves. Short of food on the reservations and unhappy with confinement, they determined to return to their old hunting grounds. Upon leaving reservations they sometimes raided nearby ranches or settlements for cattle or horses. By January 1878, the situation had become serious enough that the army created the District of the Pecos to control what it considered the Apache problem and to promote settlement in western Texas.

Colonel Grierson became commander of the new district, with headquarters at Fort Concho. His Tenth Cavalry engaged in several operations beyond the Pecos River, helping to return Apache warriors and their families to reservations. As one result, after 1880 few Native American tribes lived on or hunted the Edwards Plateau and Permian Basin. By then ranchers had moved in, bringing cattle and sheep to the rich grazing lands. In 1877, for example, the old Fort Chadbourne grounds became ranch land when Thomas L. Odom founded the OD Ranch and established his headquarters at the abandoned post. In 1881, the town surrounding the post at Fort Stockton officially changed its name to Fort Stockton, and it quickly developed into the center of an extensive sheep and cattle ranching industry. J. B. McCutchen drove a herd of cattle into Coke County in 1889, and other settlers followed, founding the town of Bronte.

As the army built telegraph lines and developed sources of water in the late 1870s and early 1880s, other towns sprang up. Junction, named for its location at the confluence of the North and South Llano Rivers, appeared in 1876. Paint Rock got its start in July 1879 and eventually survived two fires and a flood on the Concho River. Frederick Ede, who moved to Concho County in 1881 and donated 40 acres for a town site in 1882, founded Eden.

Around Fort Concho settlements had grown up at Ben Ficklin, Lone Wolf, and Veck's store. Veck's store frequently was described as a place where "frontier characters came to buy tobacco, ammunition and arms—but principally to get whiskey and to gamble where there was no law to restrain them."[6] As early as February 1870, Post Surgeon William Notson reported an attempt by Bartholomew J. DeWitt, a government contractor, to establish a town just across the North Concho River from the post. The new village, known as Saint Angela for DeWitt's wife, appeared to be almost completely made up of former post sutlers opening stores and saloons to attract the soldiers' business.

Such establishments also attracted many less desirable citizens. In April 1871, three weeks after his arrival at Fort Concho, Post Chaplain Norman Badger ventured across the North Concho to conduct the first worship services in the small collection of saloons and shanties. Doctor Notson noted in his monthly report that it was "probably the first time that the name of the Deity was ever publicly used in reverence in that place." Notson also claimed that by the end of 1871 more than 100 murders had been committed "within a radius of ten miles from the Adjutant's office," one of them when "a man called another a louse." Even in 1878, after the town had begun to prosper, conditions remained so violent that Dr. Samuel Smith stated, "It is never considered safe to pass through there at night and no officer ever thinks of leaving the garrison after dark."[7]

Buffalo Soldiers from Fort Concho spent much of their off-duty time in the town, which would later become San Angelo, and sometimes they became victims of gamblers, ruffians, and other miscreants. Friction was a result. Incidents that occurred in January and February 1881 reflect the animosity. The fatal shooting of a Tenth Cavalryman led to a confrontation in which troopers and sheriff's officers confronted one another. Later, 40 soldiers fired some 200 shots into a local hotel. Five of the cavalrymen were arrested. The murder suspect, Tom McCarthy, was not punished.

The strained relations improved over the next few years. In August 1882, when a flood destroyed the county seat at Ben Ficklin and badly damaged areas of San Angelo, Fort Concho soldiers provided rations, shelter, and medical care for the survivors. And despite the growing pains of its early years, San Angelo prospered. It soon became the center of Edwards Plateau cattle and sheep raising operations. James L. Millspaugh, a land promoter

*Freighters hauling wool, San Angelo country, early 1900s. (Courtesy Southwest Collection, Texas Tech University)*

who had helped lay out the San Angelo town site, opened an ice factory in 1884. He also operated the first water works and in 1888 brought the Santa Fe railroad to San Angelo.

By 1888, railroads had crossed many sections of the Edwards Plateau and Permian Basin. They carried cattle and sheep to market and brought new towns to life. The Texas and Pacific Railway in 1881 established Midway Station halfway between Dallas and El Paso. The first resident, Herman Garrett, arrived with a herd of sheep in 1882. When the town could not acquire a post office under the name Midway because of other sites with the same name, residents changed the name to Midland. In June 1886, when the Gulf, Colorado, and Santa Fe Railway built through the site of Ballinger, 6,000 people arrived for the sale of town lots. A similar land promotion turned Odessa, a water stop named for the railroad workers' home in Russia, into a thriving community.

Railroads and new settlers aside, drought sometimes plagued the region. Sterling County rancher Harry Tweedle observed, "Only the just and righteous seemed to get all the rainfall. It was up to the unjust and unrighteous to get some buckets and haul water to their land."[8] Serious droughts affecting most of the Edwards Plateau in two periods, 1909–12 and 1924–25, devastated many farms, ranches, and other businesses.

Drought did not hamper the petroleum business. Prospecting for oil and gas had begun in the Permian Basin about 1900, but high costs at the time kept exploration at a minimum. The first commercial oilfield was completed in 1921 in Mitchell County with a discovery well in the Westbrook field at a depth of 2,498 feet. Prospectors discovered the huge Yates oilfield in October 1926 in southeastern Pecos County. The first Yates well produced 450 barrels a day, but by the spring of 1927 there were five wells producing an average of 9,099 barrels a day. In January 1985 the Yates field produced its 1 billionth barrel of oil, proving to be one of most prolific discoveries in the world.

As a result of such success, many oil and gas companies moved production to the Permian Basin. After the first producing oil well in Ector County came in on the W. E. Connell ranch in December 1926, the cow town of Odessa became a major distribution and processing point. In neighboring Midland extended droughts and a depressed agricultural economy had caused many residents to leave before 1926, but with its prime location at the center of oil production, the town boomed again. By 1929 thirty-six oil companies had offices there.

Most of the oil was found in sandstone at less than 4,500 feet until 1928, when a large flow of oil and gas in Reagan County was discovered at 8,525 feet. The sudden increase in production brought thousands of oilfield workers and support industries to the Permian Basin. Bill Briggs, a credit man for oil companies, remembered, "It was a rather wild and hectic life." Unprepared for the boom, ranching towns were stretched beyond their limits. Many people moving into Midland and Odessa lived in tents or trailers. Helena Grant, a schoolteacher in Odessa, recalled that in 1925 they "were just beginning to smell oil in Ector County. People began to move in with their small children. Of course, my room, being the first grade, filled up first. The school kept filling up and filling up and filling up. They moved me down to the courthouse [and] one year I enrolled 145. Not all at one time, but they came and went."[9] Martha Lyle of Odessa remembered the crowded living conditions. "The trailers," she said, "were pretty close together in the courts. There was never any privacy, no yard. . . . We did have some nice neighbors when we lived in a trailer. . . . Everybody was in and out of everybody's trailer all day long."[10]

Many towns in the region benefited from the oil boom of the 1920s. The opening of the Yates field gave an economic boost to Fort Stockton. San Angelo businesses benefited from increased population demands, and numerous oilfield supply companies and steel manufacturers set up operations in the growing city. San Angelo College, later Angelo State University, opened in 1928.

The economic depression of the 1930s stifled the oil boom, causing a major cutback in oil production. By 1932, about one-third of the oilfield workers had become unemployed, bringing the first oil boom to a halt. A second boom came during World War II, when the newly mechanized army, navy, and air force insured a continued need for oil. The war also heralded the return of the U.S. military to the Edwards Plateau and Permian Basin. The wide-open air spaces proved ideal for flight training and led to the establishment of the Midland Army Air Force Base and the San Angelo Army Air Field Bombardier School, which later became Goodfellow Air Force Base.

In 1944 the Horseshoe Atoll and Sprayberry-Dean oilfields, sandstone fields on the northern end of the Edwards Plateau, were discovered, estimated to contain more than 10 billion barrels of oil. Development of the fields led to a drilling frenzy, attracting workers and additional companies. By 1950, 215 oil companies had located in Midland, making the city the financial and administrative center of the Permian Basin.

The rise in oil production sustained the region during the 1950s, when serious drought devastated many cattle and sheep ranchers. This interval proved to be the most severe dry spell reported on the Edwards Plateau. From 1954 through 1956 the eastern part of the region recorded a cumulative rainfall deficit of more than twenty inches. Nonetheless, the oil industry did not sustain its 1950s high rate of production. Rather, during the succeeding decades it rose and fell, experiencing a constant, and now familiar, cycle of boom and bust. Because of increased competition from foreign oil producers, an economic slump occurred during the 1960s. By the 1980s, production had substantially increased again, and the need for oilfield workers found families living in trailers, tents, or even their automobiles. In 2014, still another oil boom occurred, this one relating to new recovery methods.

Today oil production and distribution as well as sheep and cattle raising continue to be major industries on the Edwards Plateau and Permian Basin. Crop agriculture is limited largely to pecans and grain sorghums. Much of the grassland is considered an endangered ecosystem, caused by overgrazing, erosion, drought, and modern development. Deer hunting has become an important source of income for many smaller communities. In recent years, exotic animals have been introduced to the area, providing an additional resource for hunters. Midland (pop. 106,561), Odessa (98,801), and San Angelo (91,880) are the region's major urban centers.

Many notable people have called the once empty grasslands home. Screen actor Tommy Lee Jones hails from San Saba, and Woody Harrelson is from Midland. Elmer Kelton, named Best Western Writer of All Time by the Western Writers of America, lived and worked in San Angelo. Over his long career (from his first book in 1957 until his last in 2009), Kelton won seven Spur Awards and a Golden Saddleman Award from the Western Writers and a record four Western Heritage Awards from the Cowboy Hall of Fame. The forty-third president of the United States, George W. Bush, spent much of his youth in Midland and returned there to work and to marry Midland native Laura Welch.

Clearly, the Edwards Plateau and Permian Basin country has enjoyed a long past. The region has been home to humans since long before recorded history, sustaining Native peoples for millennia and, over recent centuries, newcomers from many lands. Hunters, missionaries, traders, miners, soldiers, farmers, and many others have lived there, but in the twentieth century, its rich grazing lands promoted its distinctive cattle and sheep industries, and later substantial deposits of oil and gas led to the growth of its major cities and modern lifestyles and businesses. Today, in 2014, the region plays a vital role in the society, culture, and economy of greater West Texas.

## NOTES

1. Cited in Herbert Eugene Bolton, ed. *Spanish Exploration in the Southwest, 1542–1706* (New York: Charles Scribner's Sons, 1916), 336, 338.

2. Cited in M. L. Crimmins, "Experiences of an Army Surgeon at Fort Chadbourne," *West Texas Historical Association Year Book* 15 (1939), 35–36.

3. Noah Smithwick, *The Evolution of a State: Or, Recollections of Old Texas Days* (Austin: University of Texas Press, 1983), 252.

4. In Stanley S. McGowen, "Life and Death on the Texas Frontier: Letters of Sidney Green Davidson and Mary Kuykendall Davidson," *West Texas Historical Association Year Book* 74 (1998), 114–15.

5. Capt. George G. Hunt to Lt. Alexander H. M. Taylor, September 28, 1867, Records of the Headquarters, Fort Concho, Texas, RG 393, National Archives.

6. Cited in Barbara E. Fisher, "Forrestine Cooper Hooker's Notes and Memoirs on Army Life in the West, 1871–1876," master's thesis, University of Arizona, 1963, 113–14.

7. Cited in John Neilson, "'I Long to Return to Fort Concho': Acting Assistant Surgeon Samuel Smith's Letters from the Texas Military Frontier, 1878–1879," *Military History of the West* 24 (Fall 1994), 146.

8. Cited in Harold M. Gober, "The Sheep Industry in Sterling County," *West Texas Historical Association Year Book* 27 (1951), 35.

9. Quotes in Roger and Diana Olien, *Life in the Oilfields* (Austin: Texas Monthly Press, 1986), 241, 168.

10. Olien and Olien, *Life in the Oilfields*, 76–77, 152.

# FOR FURTHER READING

Bolton, Herbert Eugene, ed. *Spanish Exploration in the Southwest, 1542–1706.* New York: Charles Scribner's Sons, 1916.

Hindes, V. Kay, Mark R. Wolf, Grant D. Hall, and Kathleen Kirk Gilmore. *The Rediscovery of Santa Cruz de San Sabá, a Mission for the Apache in Spanish Texas.* Austin: Texas Historical Foundation, 1995.

Jordan, Terry. *Texas: A Geography.* Boulder, Colo.: Westview Press, 1984.

Matthews, James T. *Fort Concho: A History and a Guide.* Austin: Texas State Historical Association, 2005.

Olien, Roger, and Diana Olien. *Life in the Oilfields.* Austin: Texas Monthly Press, 1986.

Wallace, Ernest, ed. *Ranald S. Mackenzie's Official Correspondence Relating to Texas 1871–1873 and 1873–1879.* Lubbock: West Texas Museum Association, 1967.

# CHAPTER 5

# The Trans-Pecos–Big Bend Country

*Miguel A. Levario*

The Trans-Pecos–Big Bend region is basin and range country, bounded on the south by its long border with Mexico along the Rio Grande and characterized by desert ranch land and large state and national parks. Levario reviews the history of this large section of West Texas, including its Indian and Hispanic background; traces the central role of its major city, El Paso; explores its border troubles, past and present; and describes its growing importance in the state's tourism industry.

An early Spanish explorer, Álvar Nuñez Cabeza de Vaca, once described the Trans-Pecos–Big Bend region as a "deserted spot, uninhabited . . . [it] contains steep places, dry places, few watering holes, and great distances . . . for this reason it cannot be inhabited by rational Christians."[1] This early observation is a reflection of the contradictory and complex nature of the far western Texas landscape. The Trans-Pecos is home to impressive mountain ranges, vast deserts, canyons, forests, and a grand river that served as the region's lifeline. These diverse environments sustain a wide variety of wildlife. They also have been home to diverse and eclectic groups of people who have wrestled with and sometimes tamed the vast, isolated, and unforgiving land that exhibits breathtaking topography and once was thought to be too harsh and isolated for human habitation.

The Trans-Pecos–Big Bend subregion of West Texas comprises the region's large southwestern zone. South across the Rio Grande is the state of Chihuahua, Mexico. To the north of the subregion lies New Mexico. The zone's eastern edge geographically is the Pecos River, but geologically its terrain extends into the western Permian Basin. The Big Bend area may be roughly defined as the portion of Trans-Pecos lying within the great bend in the Rio Grande as its flow turns from southeastward to northeastward before ultimately curving toward the Gulf of Mexico.

Only two major rivers, the Pecos and the Rio Grande, water this vast area. The Rio Grande begins in the mountains of southern Colorado and flows south, diagonally crossing the state of New Mexico, and turns southeast at El Paso toward the Gulf of Mexico. The Pecos, which also runs through New Mexico, empties into the Rio Grande below Langtry. A third river, the Rio Conchos in Mexico, meets the Rio Grande along the southern South Texas border at a site near Presidio that early Spanish explorers named La Junta de los Rios, a place important in Big Bend history.

Other geological hallmarks of the Trans-Pecos–Big Bend landscape include its majestic mountain ranges. At the western tip of El Paso are the Franklin Mountains, which extend from the heart of the city northward into southern New Mexico. Northeast of El Paso along the Texas–New Mexico state line are the Guadalupe Mountains, which include Guadalupe Mountains National Park. Although most of that mountain range is located in New Mexico, the highest and southernmost portion, which includes the national park, lies in northwestern Culberson County, Texas. At the extreme south of the Trans-Pecos lie the Davis and Chisos mountains plus Big Bend National Park, Big Bend Ranch State Park, and Black Gap Wildlife Management Area.

Native peoples inhabited the rough and arid Trans-Pecos for thousands of years. By the early 1600s the predominant tribes of the region were the Sumas and Mansos. Both groups were closely related to the Janos and Jumanos, also present along the Rio Grande. The Sumas and Mansos made little use of clothing and regularly painted themselves. They lived in *jacales*, permanent dwellings made of poles, grass, and mud. Their communities generally consisted of a political hierarchy led by a head chief. Over time the Mansos intermarried and formed political alliances with other tribes, including Apaches.

The first Europeans to cross the Trans-Pecos area were survivors of the shipwrecked Pánfilo Nárvaez Expedition of 1527–28. The group washed ashore near present-day Galveston, off the Texas coast. Among the survivors was Álvaro Nuñez Cabeza de Vaca, treasurer of the expedition and one of the most resourceful men to emerge from the shipwreck. For eight years he endured a dynamic array of events that included a near fatal illness, enslavement, and service as a medicine man. In 1534 he found himself in a village near La Junta de los Rios, accompanied by an entourage of Indian scouts and aides who had guided him along established trails.

To Cabeza de Vaca, native peoples along the Rio Grande "had the best physiques of any we saw. They were the liveliest and most skillful, and the ones who understood and answered our questions best."[2] People in communities along the river grew a variety of vegetables that included squash, beans, and corn. They resided in flat-roofed jacales, a style of construction that Spanish settlers later modified by introducing sun-dried adobe bricks. Adobe, because it was well suited for a wide range of climate changes and was comprised of readily available materials, had been used elsewhere in the Americas for thousands of years, but the Old World brick technology revolutionized building architecture along the Rio Grande.

Cabeza de Vaca's travels through Texas exposed him to the area's presumed riches, which at times yielded precious metals. Indians showed Spanish travelers rare stones and turquoise. The travelers in turn believed the existence of such valuable commodities was proof of the mythical Seven Cities of Cíbola, rich cities that, according to legend, had been established by seven Catholic bishops who in the eighth century had fled the Muslim conquest of Spain, setting sail across the Atlantic. The myths and related reports of riches prompted officials in Mexico City in 1539 to commission Francisco Vásquez de Coronado to search the northern country. After Coronado failed to find the fabled Cíbola, the Viceroyalty of New Spain largely ignored the northern deserts, known as the Tierra Depoblada (The Uninhabited Land) for several decades.

By the end of the sixteenth century renewed interest in the north encouraged the crown to appoint Don Juan de Oñate as both the leader of an expedition of conquest and governor of the northern provinces. On April 20, 1598, the Oñate expedition reached the lands along the Río Grande. Ten days later, with pomp and ceremony, he took formal possession of the territory in the name of King Philip II of Spain, and christened the domain the Kingdom of New Mexico. The formal act occurred some nineteen miles southeast of present El Paso. Oñate established his political headquarters in northern New Mexico, and the El Paso area became a midpoint between the new colony and much of the rest of the viceroyalty.

Because spreading Catholicism was a primary objective of many such early colonizing expeditions from Europe, missionaries formed an active part of most of the first Spanish settlements. In 1659, missionaries established Nuestra Señora de Guadalupe, a modest church made of adobe, in present-day Ciudad Juárez in Chihuahua. They built a more permanent structure in 1668, which served as the spiritual center for European Catholics and Christianized Indians in the Rio Grande area. The mission also served an important role when several Spanish settlers and missionary Indians, including Tiguas, fled from upper New Mexico during the region's Pueblo Revolt in 1680, an event that caused some 2,000 Spaniards to hurry south.

Thus El Paso, already a small village in 1680, in part owes its beginnings to the Pueblo Revolt. Its strategic location between Ciudad Chihuahua (founded 1709) and Santa Fe to the north (once that city was reestablished) allowed El Paso to emerge as a flourishing commercial and military center in the eighteenth century. Merchant interests grew, and before long El Paso served upper New Mexico as a supplier, way station, and trade center.

In 1726 Colonel Pedro de Rivera de Villalón reported a large population in the El Paso area—on both sides of the river. He reported that the land yielded fine vineyards and high-quality fruit, largely because of irrigation ditches that carried water from the Río Grande to area farms. Settlements near El Paso in 1750 reached more than 3,000 in habitants, and in 1754 Franciscan friar Father Manuel de San Juan Nepomuceno y Trigo reported that the "great Río [Grande] is a beautiful image of the celebrated Nile."[3] In 1760 the bishop of Durango reported nearly 5,000 people living in the El Paso region. The area's commerce and population continued to grow, and at the close the eighteenth century the far Trans-Pecos projected an image of success.

By 1806, population of the greater El Paso area had ballooned to nearly 7,000, and with its growth the region evolved into more than a commercial center and trading way station. Schools and churches existed on the south bank of the Rio Grande. Mail service between Santa Fe and Ciudad Chihuahua commenced in 1805. The main economic staples—agriculture, ranching, and commerce—flourished.

In 1821 Mexico gained independence from Spain. New, liberal land laws followed, but few people took advantage of what essentially was free land. As a result, the Mexican government appropriated funds for the construction of forts. Along the Rio Grande several presidios were constructed, most manned by convicts. Because Apache and Comanche raids had become frequent, life near the presidios from La Junta de los Rios to the Big Bend proved too difficult for many Mexican settlers.

Near what became modern El Paso, on the other hand, land grants related to the new laws encouraged additional settlement. One of the most profitable grants endowed some 215 acres of mud flats on the north bank of the Rio Grande (in present-day downtown El Paso) to a landed aristocrat, Juan María Ponce de León. He received the grant in September 1827 and immediately developed the tract. He dug *acequias* (ditches) that carried water to the fields; planted corn, grapes, and wheat; and built several adobe roadhouses for protection. He prospered.

In the spring of 1836, during the Texas rebellion, El Paso and much of the Big Bend witnessed little trouble. In December, however, the new Republic of Texas declared the Rio Grande from its source to the Gulf of Mexico to be the western and southern boundary of Texas. Yet the struggling little government failed to establish dominion over the El Paso area or over most of eastern New Mexico. Repeated attempts by Texas officials to exercise such authority failed. The issue was not resolved until the end of the war between the United States and Mexico and the Compromise of 1850 two years later.

Afterward, Major Robert S. Neighbors, Superintendent of Indian Affairs in Texas, organized the new counties of Presidio and El Paso. Presidio County was regarded as unsafe on account of continued Indian resistance and little was done there, but the Neighbors Commission successfully organized El Paso County. In February 1850, elections were held, and by March, El Paso County was fully established, with elected officials in place. Presidio County remained unorganized and was attached to El Paso for judicial purposes until 1875.

Still, the large region needed protection not only for its new residents but also for commerce and trade. In an effort to provide safety, the U.S. government established a military garrison in the area. It began in February 1848 when Major Benjamin Beall and a detachment of the First Dragoons arrived. Brevet Major Jefferson Van Horne was the first commanding officer, and his garrison consisted of 257 men of the Third United States Infantry. In September 1849 General Order No. 58 created the post of El Paso, near the village of the same name, to protect such local merchants and pioneers as James Magoffin from bandits and resistant Indians. In 1851 the army withdrew from the area except for a small detachment on guard at Magoffin's property. Because of increased Indian raids, the U.S. War Department in 1853 reestablished the post of El Paso in Franklin, a village in the vicinity of the original locale. The following year the name was changed to Fort Bliss in honor of William Wallace Smith Bliss, who had served in the war with Mexico and had died in 1853.

In a similar measure to protect settlers, the government in 1854 established Fort Davis. Located near the Davis Mountains in modern Jeff Davis County, the post initially served as a stage stand to help transport mail, but it quickly emerged as a key army post protecting the southern trading route from San Antonio to El Paso. After the Civil War it became the major military installation in the upper Big Bend country.

The Trans-Pecos region played a limited but complex role during the Civil War. The Texas–Mexico borderland was a major artery for the cotton and munitions trade, but much of the political and military struggles occurred elsewhere. El Paso pioneers offered their allegiance and sympathy to the Confederacy, whose presence in El Paso was short-lived. Confederate forces occupied Fort Bliss in 1861, but Union forces overtook the fort the following year.

Fort Davis had a similar fate. General David E. Twiggs, commander of the Eighth U.S. Military District, evacuated the fort, and Colonel John

R. Baylor with his Confederate forces replaced him in 1861. The fort was occupied for almost a year but abandoned after a failed campaign by Confederate forces to capture New Mexico. For five years, Fort Davis stood empty, but in 1867 federal troops reoccupied it.

In the mid-1880s Fort Davis reached the height of its importance. At that point the post held 600 men, and more than sixty adobe and stone structures spotted the grounds. Between 1867 and 1885, the garrison was composed of white officers and black enlisted men of the Ninth and Tenth U.S. Cavalry and the Twenty-fourth and Twenty-fifth U.S. Infantry regiments. Before closing as an active garrison in 1891, Fort Davis played a major role in the latter stages of the western U.S.–Indian wars.

Although the region experienced little bloodshed during the Civil War, the Trans-Pecos–Big Bend country experienced plenty of trouble in the San Elizario Salt Wars of 1877. That conflict involved a dispute over free access to salt licks located in El Paso County. American and Mexican citizens from both sides of the Rio Grande had drawn from the salt licks for many generations, but in 1872 local officials privatized the area and denied free access. Many Mexican residents continued to frequent the salt licks and eventually decided to challenge the privatization of the land. Louis Cardis, an Italian stagecoach manager and local political boss, and Judge Charles Howard, who had bought the disputed land and declared it off limits to local residents, became embroiled in a bloody feud.

An angry mob, allegedly organized by Cardis and upset with the move to privatize the land, kidnapped Howard and held him for ransom for three days in San Elizario. Howard won his freedom by promising to give up his claim to the salt licks and by agreeing to leave El Paso. But on October 10, 1877, Howard found Cardis in an El Paso store and fatally shot him.

Many of Cardis's supporters, most of whom were Mexicans, demanded Howard's arrest. Tensions escalated. A contingent of Texas Rangers arrived to support the local sheriff and protect Howard, but a group of Mexican militiamen forced the sheriff and the Rangers to surrender both Howard and their guns. Soon a firing squad executed Charles Howard and a few of his cohorts.

Texas Rangers retaliated. Accompanied by some civilians they attacked the village of San Elizario and killed several residents. African American army units, or Buffalo Soldiers, from Fort Davis ultimately suppressed the uprising and restored order. In 1878 El Paso area residents were once again allowed access to the salt licks, upon payment of a nominal fee.

Law enforcement in far West Texas in the late nineteenth century differed from other areas of the state in part because residents resisted outside influence and authority. Much of the defiance was attributed to the great geographic distance between the Trans-Pecos and Austin, the seat of state authority. Such isolation encouraged local officials to seek their own justice or retribution. Problems included rebellion, defiance, and general disorder.

Each of these problems was evident in 1896, when a local resident hosted a prizefight near Langtry but across the international border and beyond the jurisdiction of Texas police. The incident began when a boxing promoter named Dan Stuart offered heavyweights Bob Fitzsimmons and Peter Maher $10,000 to fight in Dallas. Governor Charles Culberson quickly backed an anti-prizefighting law that forced Stuart to seek an alternative location. When news outlets reported that the fight would take place near El Paso, Governor Culberson sent a company of Texas Rangers to the city to enforce the state's new legislation.

Stuart then got help from Judge Roy Bean of Langtry, a showman and charlatan who referred to himself as "the Law west of the Pecos." While Bean erected a fight ring on a sandbar in the Rio Grande on the Mexico side of the river, boxing fans were told on February 20 that a special train would leave El Paso that night to take them to the secret location for the boxing match. A large collection of law enforcement officers, including the Texas Rangers, had also assembled in Langtry, but they held no jurisdiction in Mexico.

The prizefight occurred. Fitzsimmons won the match with a right-hand punch to Maher's jaw only a minute and a half into the first round, disappointing people in attendance, who had wanted a longer match. Judge Bean, who had hoped to sell refreshments during what was supposed to be a long fight, had plenty of beer left over.

The much ballyhooed prizefight was made possible by railways stretching across the southwestern Texas landscape. In 1870 the Texas legislature had granted the Galveston, Harrisburg, and San Antonio Railway (GH&SA) rights to lay tracks across the state. The first train pulled into San Antonio

*Southern Pacific Railway bridge across Pecos River west of Del Rio, 1909. (Courtesy Southwest Collection, Texas Tech University)*

in 1877, and soon thereafter traffic along the Chihuahua Trail through La Junta de los Rios and the Big Bend to San Antonio increased, justifying a rail line through Southwest Texas.

At roughly the same time, railroad baron Collis P. Huntington of Southern Pacific Railroad was developing a line eastward from California. He negotiated a deal with GH&SA and agreed to join the two lines at a location between El Paso and San Antonio. The Southern Pacific Railroad reached El Paso on May 19, 1881 and in 1883 met up with the GH&SA.

El Paso and the surrounding area flourished, but the railroad further isolated the lower Big Bend. Transporting goods by train was cheaper and faster than by wagons or pack mules, and as a result the old Chihuahua Trail became obsolete for long hauls. Not all was lost, however, for Marfa, established in 1883 as a water stop and freight headquarters for the GH&SA, served as a Big Bend trade center. Indeed, the little stop quickly evolved as a modern town with a bank, post office, two saloons, and, in 1885 a hotel.

Meanwhile, in 1882, a few railroad workers and their families founded a tent community near a spring-fed creek just twenty-six miles east of Marfa. After brokering a deal with the railroad, residents of Murphyville, as their community was called, folded their tents and soon developed a small western town that laid claim to a dozen houses, a few saloons, a hotel, and several other establishments. In 1888 it changed its name to Alpine.

At the same time, El Paso began to look like a modern, industrialized city, complete with banks, newspapers, churches, a fully functioning city government, and hotels. The first public school opened in March 1883, the same year that El Paso became the county seat. The first school for African American children was built, and Olivas V. Aoy organized a school for children of Mexican origin. El Paso boasted a population of more than 10,000 residents in 1890.

Because of railroads, industry made its way into the region. The Kansas City Smelting and Refining Company constructed a large smelter in El Paso in 1887. In 1899 the company merged with several others and formed the American Smelting and Refining Company (ASARCO), which served as a major smelter for northern Mexico and the southwestern region of the United States. Cotton became a major cash crop when workers completed the Elephant Butte Dam in 1916 in southern New Mexico. The steady stream of water turned the unforgiving desert into an oasis for thirsty crops.

Other major industries flocked to West Texas. They included the Standard Oil Company of Texas, and by the late 1920s the Phelps Dodge Company had located major refineries in El Paso. The city's geographic location as a gateway to its southern neighbor and its proximity to northern Mexico's rich mining areas contributed significantly to El Paso's industrial transformation.

Farther east, modernization gradually took hold of the lower Big Bend. A greater military presence ushered in a new era for the region. Cavalry troops arrived, and the army established Camp Albert, later named Camp Marfa and then renamed Fort D. A. Russell, igniting a population boom. By 1930 Marfa had grown to nearly 4,000 residents. Meanwhile, in 1921 Alpine welcomed the establishment of Sul Ross Normal College (now Sul Ross State University). This school, along with large-scale ranching in the area, made Alpine a center of commercial and cultural activity.

In El Paso other events were troubling. Among them was the role the American city played in the Mexican Revolution of 1910–20. Many of the revolutionary leaders organized their initiatives in El Paso, and across the river in Ciudad Juárez some fighting occurred. American and Mexican residents in the twin cities and along the international boundary did not escape some of the violence of the revolution. Ranch raids and other activity caused great distress among property owners on both sides of the border.

On December 25, 1917, a group of Mexican bandits raided the L. C. Brite Ranch, located near Valentine. Ranch foreman Van Neill and his family were at the ranch and engaged in a ferocious gun battle with the bandits. They succeeded in killing one bandit and seriously wounding several more. Some of the bandits, who wanted items in the ranch's general store, filled their bags with various goods and left.

When word reached him in Marfa, ranch owner Lucas Brite immediately organized a posse of law enforcement officials, soldiers, and civilians to pursue the bandits. Van Neill and others immediately pointed the finger at Chico Cano, a bandit familiar to many in the region, as among those in the raiding party. Texas Rangers set their sights on one of Cano's hideouts, a small Texas village along the border called Porvenir.

On January 27, 1918, the Rangers approached Camp Evetts (Diez y Ocho Camp), a military post near Porvenir, and requested army assistance. Because they believed Cano and his gang would be in Porvenir around midnight, the Rangers expected trouble and wanted help. The Army's Eighth Cavalry, stationed at Camp Evetts, had already investigated the Brite Ranch and concluded that the Porvenir residents were innocent of wrongdoing.

Nonetheless, the Texas Rangers, some cavalrymen, and several local ranchers headed for Porvenir. Upon arrival the Rangers forced themselves into homes, removed men from their beds, and pushed them to an isolated area not far away. While Rangers and ranchers ransacked Porvenir, the cavalrymen at the makeshift camp stood watch over the inhabitants, who were disoriented and huddling around a fire. While searching the Porvenir homes, the Rangers rounded up fifteen men and boys and corralled them at a spot down the road. Then they shot the captives. The event was shocking. Porvenir and the surrounding area of the Big Bend were abandoned. The Texas Rangers were condemned and those involved in the bloody affair were discharged from the force, but they were not brought to trial for the extralegal executions.

The Trans-Pecos–Big Bend region experienced a short-lived economic and social boom during the Prohibition years of the 1920s. With the Eighteenth Amendment and the Volstead Act the manufacture, transportation, and sale of alcoholic beverages was banned. Residents and others passing through El Paso and the Big Bend region soon discovered that substantial profits could be made in smuggling liquor from Mexico, especially at such border towns as Ciudad Juárez and Ojinaga, where saloons and related entertainment activities prospered.

Prohibition proved extremely difficult to enforce. American consumers went to great lengths to obtain beer, wine, and distilled liquors, and many people were willing to pay exorbitant prices for it. One hundred cases of bourbon, for example, purchased in Juárez at the wholesale price of $25 might sell upon delivery in Saint Louis, Kansas City, Denver, or Dallas for $6,000. Tourist dollars also poured into the border cities as many Americans flocked to the saloons, gambling tables, dance halls, and racetracks located across the Rio Grande.

The prosperity of the 1920s abruptly ended when the stock market crashed in October 1929. Tourist dollars dried up, and the entertainment industry in Ciudad Juárez was virtually abandoned. The harsh realities of the ensuing Great Depression were felt in the region, although their extent was seemingly less intense in El Paso. Many amenities, such as gas and food, saw little change in price. Entertainment in El Paso was relatively affordable, and after revision of the Volstead Act in 1933 (it was repealed late in the same year), a quarter could purchase three bottles of beer. The first annual Sun Bowl football game was played in 1935. A radio station, KTSM, began service in 1938, and a second radio station, KROD, came on the air in 1940.

There is little doubt that World War II revived El Paso and the rest of the Trans-Pecos. El Paso and Marfa became major contributors to the war effort. Fort Bliss led the way. The facility expanded from its original 1,200 acres to 436,000 acres by the time the United States entered World War II. A new chapter began for one large unit, the First Cavalry Division. When it received orders for assignment in the Pacific Theater in 1943, its soldiers turned in their horses and horse equipment, marking the end of an era for the "Glorious First." By 1944 Fort Bliss had been transformed into the nation's primary anti-aircraft artillery installation.

The war's impact was also felt in Marfa. The federal government stationed its Chemical Warfare Brigade in town and constructed a prisoner of war camp nearby. The Marfa Army Air Field was established just a few miles east of town for advanced flight training. By the war's end in 1945, Marfa boasted a population of 5,000. Any promise of continuing population and economic growth for the busy town ended when both military installations closed the following year. At the end of the twentieth century, Marfa counted just over 2,100 residents.

The postwar years marked a period of significant growth for El Paso. The city's downtown skyline experienced marked change in 1955 with the completion of the El Paso Natural Gas Company's eighteen-story headquarters. Additional buildings, as well as major transportation projects, proliferated throughout the decade. The Cordova Bridge, later renamed Bridge of the Americas; the Interstate 10 east–west corridor; and the Transmountain Road, a roadway cut through the Franklin Mountains at one mile above sea level, were all completed during the decade.

A new public library (1954), a referendum approving new hospital facilities (1959), and a new complex for the El Paso Museum of Art (1959) represented further evidence of El Paso's growth. In addition, in 1949 the College of Mines and Metallurgy changed its name to Texas Western College to reflect its expanded enrollment and curriculum offerings. By 1963 the college had completed the construction of a 30,000-seat football stadium nestled within a small mountain located on the campus. It hosts the annual Sun Bowl, which (behind the Rose Bowl in southern California) is college football's second oldest operating bowl game.

Political changes kept pace. In 1923 the Texas legislature had passed a law prohibiting black Texans from voting in Democratic primaries. To test the law, physician Lawrence Nixon and his wife, with the sponsorship of the El Paso chapter of the NAACP, took their poll tax receipts to a Democratic primary polling place. Refused ballots, the Nixons and their El Paso attorney, Fred C. Knollenberg, sued and twice carried the case to the U.S. Supreme Court. Nonetheless, the Nixons were not allowed to vote until the decision in *Smith v. Allwright* (1944) ended the Texas white primary.

El Paso's further experience in civil rights issues preceded that of many of its Texas counterparts. In 1955, for example, Thelma White, a black woman, was admitted to Texas Western College. She broke the state's rigid color barrier by making Texas Western the first formerly all-white Texas public college or university to open its doors to black students. The city council followed suit by passing ordinances providing for open accommodations and open access in the purchasing and renting of housing. In 1957 Raymond Telles won the city's mayoral race, the first Mexican American to be elected to that office in a major U.S. city. Another major milestone occurred in sports. Texas Western College, renamed the University of Texas at El Paso in 1967, won the 1966 national men's basketball championship with the first all-black starting lineup in NCAA history. Coach Don Haskins and his players defeated Adolph Rupp's all-white team from the University of Kentucky.

Clearly, the Trans-Pecos–Big Bend country has a history as expansive and colorful as its landscape. Its endless horizon, majestic mountains, and howling deserts are the signature of a landscape that attracts millions of visitors to the area's state and national parks. Big Bend National Park, which was established in 1944, saw over 450,000 visitors in 1976, the nation's bicentennial year; visitation remains high (more than 290,000 in 2011). Today, in 2014 the region's people continue a long tradition of fortitude and ingenuity as they deal with the area's isolation and solitude. Sustained by the independent spirit of its native peoples, the grand explorations of its Spanish adventurers, the pioneering spirit of its Anglo settlers, and the revolutions of its Mexican and Texan peoples, the Trans-Pecos–Big Bend region, including El Paso, remains an indomitable part of the soul of West Texas.

# NOTES

1. Quoted in Glenn Justice, *Little Known History of the Texas Big Bend: Documented Chronicles From Cabeza de Vaca to the Era of Pancho Villa* (Odessa: Rimrock Press, 2001), 1.

2. Quoted in Jefferson Morganthaler, *The River Has Never Divided Us: A Border History of La Junta de los Rios* (Austin: University of Texas Press, 2004), 22.

3. Quoted in W. H. Timmons, *El Paso: A Borderlands History* (Austin: University of Texas Press, 1990), 39–40.

# FOR FURTHER READING

Casas, Juan Manuel. *Federico Villalba's Texas: A Mexican Pioneer's Life in the Big Bend*. Houston: Iron Mountain Press, 2008.

Cool, Paul. *Salt Warriors: Insurgency on the Rio Grande*. College Station: Texas A&M University Press, 2008.

García, Mario. *Desert Immigrants: The Mexicans of El Paso, 1880–1920*. New Haven: Yale University Press, 1981.

Justice, Glenn. *Little Known History of the Texas Big Bend: Documented Chronicles From Cabeza de Vaca to the Era of Pancho Villa*. Odessa: Rimrock Press, 2001.

Morgenthaler, Jefferson. *The River Has Never Divided Us: A Border History of La Junta de los Rios*. Austin: University of Texas Press, 2004.

Ragsdale, Kenneth Baxter. *Quicksilver: Terlingua and the Chisos Mining Company*. College Station: Texas A&M University Press, 2008.

Romo, David Dorado. *Ringside Seat to a Revolution: An Underground Cultural History of El Paso and Juárez, 1893–1923*. El Paso: Cinco Puntos Press, 2005.

Timmons, W. H. *El Paso: A Borderlands History*. Austin: University of Texas Press, 1990.

Tyler, Ron C. *The Big Bend: A History of the Last Texas Frontier*. College Station: Texas A&M University Press, 1996.

Wooster, Robert. *Frontier Crossroads: Fort Davis and the West*. College Station: Texas A&M University Press, 2005.

# Part II

# THE PEOPLE

Many diverse populations live across the wide territory of West Texas. Many diverse peoples have likewise occupied most parts of the region in the past, some for a very long time—Indian peoples for millennia, and early Hispanic colonists and their descendants since at least the sixteenth century. Authors of the four chapters of part II explore the past and modern experiences of these and other contributors to the region's history and evolving traditions who have too often been underrepresented in historical and sociocultural studies of the region.

As the authors demonstrate, some of these groups have histories in West Texas as surprising as they are important. Centuries before Spaniards and other European Americans came to dominate West Texas, various groups of American Indians individually rose and fell in influence. Much reduced in population and political influence today owing to the conflicts of recent centuries (Indians in 2014 comprised approximately 1.0 percent of the region's general population), they are increasingly recognized for their strong, lasting influence on the land and its cultural traditions. Hispanic peoples, who were the first Europeans to settle in West Texas and who exercised supreme political power over it until quite late in its history, have placed an indelible stamp on the region's character. Yet their place in its affairs today has become ambivalent as a result of several generations of Anglo political dominance and, in more recent decades, because of increased socioeconomic pressures from Hispanic nations to the south. African Americans, beginning with a few who arrived with the earliest Hispanic explorers, have been a lasting presence in the region, especially after the rise and fall of the slave economy in the East brought various responses in West Texas and surrounding territories. Yet their history among the people of the region was often ignored and, later, neglected, until public interest and serious scholarship began to redress the balance, especially from the later twentieth century onward. And women, who have naturally been a substantial part of the region's changing populations since the very beginning, continue even now to seek equal footing and recognition in the history and current affairs of West Texas.

The four chapters gathered here represent not only new material, but up-to-date ideas and fresh interpretations.

# CHAPTER 6

# Native Americans in West Texas

*Thomas A. Britten*

Native Americans have inhabited West Texas since shortly after the first humans arrived on the North American continent. Britten demonstrates how these prehistoric societies and cultures changed, merged, declined, or adapted to shifting environmental currents. His emphasis here, however, is on Indian groups of the early historic era and their social and material cultures, as well as their interactions with the first Spanish and Anglo-American explorers and settlers of the region.

At the dawn of the twenty-first century, American Indians constituted one of the smallest minority groups in Texas—larger only than Native Hawaiians and Pacific Islanders. Two centuries before, dozens of socially and culturally diverse Indian tribes comprised the dominant majority of the population of what is now the American Southwest, successfully repelling the efforts of Spanish, French, and, for a time, Euro-American settlers to eject them and establish dominion over the land.

The Indians of West Texas, in particular, posed a challenge to would-be conquerors and were among the last indigenous peoples to succumb to the combined might of the U.S. Army and the demographic onslaught of countless farmers, ranchers, settlers, miners, and merchants who moved west during the latter half of the nineteenth century. From the 1840s through the 1870s, Native peoples resisted efforts to force them onto reservations or to expel them from Texas altogether. But by the late 1870s, Indian wars in Texas were over. So too was the epic history of Indian dominance that reached back some twelve millennia.

We may never know with certainty the specific origins of the first humans to occupy West Texas, but scholars from a variety of disciplines agree that there were people occupying the region some 10,000 to 12,000 years ago. These early peoples, often called Paleo-Indians, resided in small, nomadic bands and subsisted on such large game animals as mammoths, bears, and bison. The precise weapons and techniques they used and the game animals they depended upon varied from place to place, but the first West Texans must have been fearless people, employing primitive stone and wooden weapons against huge and formidable animals. In some respects, the nomadic hunting economy that the Paleo-Indians introduced into West Texas persisted (albeit with significant modification) into the historic period. Nomadic bands of Comanches and Eastern Apaches, for example, relied upon bison hunting as their primary subsistence activity well into the nineteenth century.

West Texas Indians of the Archaic period (8,500 years ago to about 2,000 years ago) differed from their Paleo-Indian ancestors in a number of significant ways. First, they became more culturally diverse as immigrant peoples pushed into North America, bringing new ideas and technologies with them. Archaic peoples were typically hunters and gatherers who moved seasonally to take advantage of specific subsistence opportunities, but their range was somewhat more restricted than in Paleo-Indian times, and over their extended time in the region they became increasingly territorial. Some scholars also point to the Archaic hunters' expanded and sophisticated tool kit, which included stone dart points, scrapers, knives, axes, choppers, picks, and drills. By around 600 C.E., bow and arrow technology appeared in West Texas, transforming hunting and war-making alike. Mortars and pestles also appeared during the Archaic period, indicating the growing reliance of some Indian communities on seeds and plant foods.

Although there is no consensus regarding just where and when West Texas Indians first attempted to grow corn, some scholars speculate that Indian peoples may have attempted agriculture in the western Trans-Pecos area between 3,500 and 3,000 years ago. As time passed, the "three sisters" (corns, beans, and squash), arriving from lands farther south, spread northward and eastward across Texas, permitting some Indian groups to adopt sedentary or semisedentary lifestyles. By the time Spaniards appeared in the region in the sixteenth century, virtually all native peoples practiced at least desultory agriculture as well as hunting.

The various Indian communities that existed in West Texas during the millennium preceding European contact continued to adapt to the world around them. In the Trans-Pecos subregion, Indian peoples settled along the Rio Grande and its tributaries and adopted a sedentary lifestyle dependent upon agriculture. One important group, the Jumanos, were farmers and traders who congregated around what later became known as La Junta de los Rios, where they tended their irrigated fields of beans, squash, corn, and watermelons. Additional Jumano farming communities scattered along the middle Rio Grande as far west as present-day El Paso.

At some point in their history, Jumano groups conducting seasonal hunts on the southern plains decided to remain there, shifting their encampments in response to migrating bison herds. Over time, this tribal division became somewhat permanent, although the corn-growing "River Jumanos" and the bison-hunting "Cibola Jumanos" remained in contact with each other, exchanging meat and hides for corn. Both groups also traded with the Pueblos in New Mexico and became intermediaries of sorts connecting the Pueblos with various indigenous groups in eastern Texas.

In the Texas Panhandle, meanwhile, the Lake Creek people (200–900 C.E.) resided in several camps or villages situated on or near the Canadian River. They maintained an economy based on hunting bison, deer, and pronghorn antelope as well as rabbits and other small game, and they did some gathering of nuts and seeds. They also engaged in trade with Woodland Indian groups to the east and with Southwestern Indian desert dwellers to the west.

From the thirteenth century through the early sixteenth century, Antelope Creek people settled in numerous semipermanent villages and temporary hunting camps throughout the northern Texas Panhandle. Archeological evidence indicates that Antelope Creek inhabitants were skilled in working with bone, shell, pottery, and stone and that they were involved in an extensive trade network both with the Pueblos to the west and with Plains Caddoan speakers to the northeast. From the Puebloans the Antelope Creek people secured luxury goods such as obsidian, turquoise, and painted pottery. In exchange, the Antelope Creek traders provided elbow pipes, bone tools, and various perishable items, such as bison hides and meat.

When Spanish expeditions ventured into Texas between the sixteenth and eighteenth centuries, the Europeans encountered hundreds of Indian communities of varying sizes, economies, and cultures. In the Trans-Pecos area, more than sixty tribes or bands resided along the Rio Grande from near modern day Del Rio west to El Paso. They were principally farmers and traders, possessing a market area stretching 800 miles from northeast Texas to northwest Chihuahua. Some only wintered on the Rio Grande, spending their spring on the southern plains hunting bison. Near the important trading settlement at La Junta de los Rios lived Abriaches, Cabris, Mesquites, and the aforementioned Jumanos. Upriver closer to El Paso were Tanpochoas and Caguates, and along the Río Conchos in northern Chihuahua lived several tribal groups that visited West Texas to trade.

On the Texas High Plains, Spaniards encountered a large number of nomadic and seminomadic bison-hunting tribes. In May 1541 Spanish conquistador Francisco Vásquez de Coronado set out from Pecos Pueblo, east of present day Santa Fe, New Mexico, on an expedition in search of Gran Quivera, the legendary Indian settlement on the northern edge of New Spain. Ten days after crossing the Pecos, Coronado came upon a vast plain covered with an immense herd of bison calves, cows, and bulls. Some of his men noticed marks in the ground and suspected that these had been made by warriors dragging their lances. Curious, the party followed the tracks to a *ranchería* (village) of some fifty nomadic bison hunters who, Coronado reported, lived "like Arabs" in hide tents and employed well-trained dogs to carry loads of bison meat, hides, and other items. It was the dogs dragging tent poles, the Spaniards quickly discerned, that had caused the scratches they had seen in the ground. Coronado later referred to these nomads as the Querechos, and he described them in glowing terms—as being gentle, faithful in their friendship, and skilled in the use of sign language. Five to six days' march west from the Querecho encampment lived a second group of bison hunters who were enemies of the Querechos, painted their bodies and faces, and lived in "pueblos of rancherías." Coronado referred to these people as Teyas.

Some fifty years later, in the mid-1590s, the Humana-Leyva expedition explored West Texas. After several days of travel, the Spaniards encountered great herds of bison near the Canadian River and the deserted rancherías of nomadic bison hunters whom they called Vaqueros. The Vaqueros hunted bison on foot, constructed blinds near watering places, and then waited for the animals to come to drink so that they could shoot them with bows and arrows. Dogs, sometimes carrying sixty or more pounds of supplies each, served as beasts of burden as the Indians had not yet acquired horses.

Although the identity of the Teyas remains a matter of considerable debate, there is general agreement among scholars that Spanish reports of the Querechos and Vaqueros were actually referencing the very same group of people. They were nomadic bison hunters who resided on the grasslands of the northern Llano Estacado between the Canadian River on the north and the tributaries of the Red River in the south. They had a close trade relationship with the Pueblos and participated in annual or seasonal trade fairs. At times, especially during the winter months, they established encampments in the foothills just east of their Pueblo associates. Some scholars believe that the Querechos and Vaqueros may have been proto-Apaches, a population who by the seventeenth century dominated much of the bison trade on the Llano Estacado.

At some point during the late seventeenth and early eighteenth centuries, the Apaches began leaving the Texas Panhandle. A factor influencing their migrations was the pressure of powerful Indian newcomers. Tribes such as the Shoshonean-speaking Comanches moved eastward onto the Great Plains through passes in the Front Range. Harried by Cheyenne, Kiowa, and Pawnee warriors armed with French guns, the Comanches turned south, challenging both the Apaches and the Wichitas for access to hunting grounds and control of the bison-hide trade.

Desirous of gaining a foothold on the southern plains and eager to position themselves closer to trade outlets and bison herds, Comanches visited the Pueblos in 1705. During the ensuing decades, Comanche strength steadily increased across West Texas, and by the close of the eighteenth century the Comanches had transformed themselves into a mounted, well-equipped, and powerful people.

In addition to Lipan Apaches and Comanches, other native groups that inhabited West Texas at various times during the eighteenth and/or nineteenth centuries included Kiowas, Kiowa Apaches, Jumanos, and Tiguas. One might also add such frequent visitors as the Mescalero Apaches, who ventured from their mountain sanctuaries in southeastern New Mexico into the Big Bend region to hunt bison; Tonkawas from central Texas who, like the Mescaleros, sought hunting opportunities in West Texas; and Coahuiltecans, a hunting and gathering people who resided along the lower Rio Grande valley in widely dispersed settlements.

Cultures and lifestyles of West Texas Indians varied considerably. They were influenced by the confluence of geography, climate, available flora and fauna, proximity to Native and European markets, and the unique history and mythology of each tribe. The cultures and lifestyles were not static but exhibited remarkable adaptability as a particular group's circumstances changed over time. The Lipan Apaches, for example, were predominately nomadic bison hunters when they lived on the southern plains of Texas during the seventeenth and early eighteenth centuries. When the Comanches forced their relocation in the 1720s to south-central Texas, they adopted a semisedentary, hunter-gatherer economy and relied increasingly on native plants such as sotol (desert spoon) and agave.

Nonetheless, the cultures and lifestyles of many West Texas tribes shared several traits. All Indians of the region were hunters. Migratory peoples such as the Comanches, Lipan Apaches, Kiowas, Kiowa Apaches, and at least some Jumanos based their subsistence almost entirely upon bison, although women supplemented this diet with an immense variety of wild fruits, nuts, and plants. Following their acquisition of horses at some point in the early eighteenth century, hunters became exceptionally proficient at locating herds and conducting hunts.

Many West Texas Indians believed that huge herds of bison and other game animals originated in a "country" under the ground or inside mountains, and that every spring they swarmed up out of great cave-like openings in the earth that were situated somewhere on the Llano Estacado. Upon their arrival near a herd, the women and children set up camp while the men set out for the hunt. As they drew near the animals, the lead hunter directed the hunting party to break up into smaller units, each with its own leader. These smaller groups surrounded the herd and, at a prearranged signal, advanced simultaneously from all sides, dispatching the animals with bows and arrows, spears, or muskets. The hunters usually dressed larger game animals such as bison or deer at the place where they had made the kill. After removing—and usually consuming—the entrails, the men skinned the animals and cut up the meat into large pieces that they wrapped in hides and transported back to the main camp.

The women of these hunting bands understood that their workload would increase significantly once the hunt ended. Preparing and preserving the meat, tanning the hides, and transforming bones and entrails into tools, utensils, bags, containers, and other specialty items while simultaneously caring for children, hauling water, and tending to the fire must have overwhelmed them at times. To cure and preserve the meat, women cut it into thin strips, and cooked it slowly until it dried. They also stored it in *parflèches* (skin bags), in straw, or in slab-lined pits dug into the ground. Another common method of storing dried meat was by pulverizing it with a mallet and mixing in melted fat, bone marrow, and dried paste from crushed wild fruits. Some recipes called for the addition of pecans, walnuts, or honey. The resultant pemmican, when stored properly in airtight bags, could last for years and was a nutritious, high-energy food that Indians took on long trips, stored for emergencies, or ate during the bleak winter months.

Some West Texas tribes diversified their subsistence efforts, and at least a few were farmers. The Jumanos residing at La Junta de los Rios were excellent farmers and impressed visitors with their bountiful fields of corn, beans, squash, and melons. The Tiguas, a Puebloan people who lived in several settlements near the early Spanish village of El Paso, were also farmers who raised corn, beans, squash, and cotton in large, communally owned fields. The Lipan Apaches and Tonkawas also experimented with farming, but their preference for hunting, frequent conflicts with Comanches, and disinclination to remain in one place for long undermined such pursuits. Coahuiltecans, who resided along scorching, arid stretches of the Rio Grande valley, eked out a living hunting small game animals and gathering wild plant foods, including mesquite beans, prickly pear, acorns, pecans, and a variety of roots and tubers.

The types of homes or domiciles that sheltered West Texas Indians were dependent in many ways upon subsistence patterns. Migratory peoples lived in tepees constructed of bison hides strung over several stout poles. Large tepees could house a family of ten or more, while smaller ones accommodated only three or four individuals. Women could assemble or disassemble a tepee in minutes—an important skill for a people constantly on the move. A second type of dwelling, the wickiup, was common among Lipan and Mescalero Apaches and consisted of several slender poles bent into arches and assembled into a dome-like structure. Cracks and crevices between the poles could be plastered over with mud to keep out the wind, or filled in with grass, bark, or branches. Otherwise, hides thrown over the top and sides provided cover. The sedentary Jumanos and Tiguas, on the other hand, resided in much more substantial Pueblo-style dwellings comprised of hardened clay and timber. The impoverished Coahuiltecans lived in simple huts of sticks and hides.

Indian people of West Texas spoke a wide variety of languages. Comanches spoke a Uto-Aztecan language similar to that of the Shoshones. Lipan, Mescalero, and Kiowa Apaches spoke Southern Athapaskan, while the Kiowas spoke a Tanoan dialect. Linguists disagree about the Jumano language, with some arguing Tanoan and others Uto-Aztecan. The Coahuiltecans spoke what the Spaniards called Coahuilteco, and the Tiguas spoke Tiwa, a branch of Kiowa-Tanoan. To communicate cross-tribally, Texas Indians may have resorted to sign language. The closely associated but linguistically distinct Kiowa Apaches and the Kiowas, for example, are known to have communicated with each other in this way.

West Texas Indians also displayed characteristic diversity in regard to reckoning kinship. The various Apachean peoples and the Tonkawas observed matrilineal kinship patterns, meaning that children determined their lineage through their mother's family and newlyweds took up residence with the wife's parents. Comanches and Coahuiltecans, on the other hand, observed patrilineal kinship patterns and traced their heritage through the father's family. The Kiowas employed a bilateral kinship reckoning system, meaning they traced their ancestry through both male and female links. Kinship patterns played a critical role in virtually every aspect of Indian societies, and the strength and durability of tribal subdivisions or bands often reflected the stability of kinship relations.

When European trade goods became available, the desirability of gaining access to them spawned a frenzy of Indian raiding and captive taking—usually women and children—to exchange for manufactured items such as gunpowder and firearms. Comanches and Lipan Apaches preyed on each other throughout the eighteenth century, and the staggering loss of Apache women contributed to unprecedented social upheaval and the near extinction of the matrilineal Lipans. Comanches, on the other hand, grew in number, as they were better equipped to assimilate captive women, due in part to their patrilineal kinship traditions.

Compared to the powerful Iroquois League of New York, the Cherokee Nation of Georgia, or the Caddo Confederacy of East Texas, the tribal organization of most West Texas Indians—with the exception of the Tiguas and Jumanos—appears at first glance relatively unsophisticated. Lacking any formal tribal or religious hierarchies, Comanches, Apaches, Coahuiltecans, Kiowas, and Kiowa Apaches resided in widely scattered, autonomous bands comprised of extended families bound together by kinship ties. Men of influence exercised leadership at the band level, and the adult males usually selected chiefs informally. Leaders formulated opinions and decisions based on consensus and by understanding the various needs and desires of their people. Decisions were not mandates but rather expressions of the general will, and individuals who disagreed could always pack up their belongings and join a new band more to their liking. Once it became clear that a leader no longer enjoyed the support and approval of his people, he simply stepped aside for whomever the consensus selected, assuming the role of a respected elder.

Other important aspects of West Texas Indian sociocultural existence shared basic similarities as well. Men spent a good deal of their time hunting, making weapons, conducting raids, and managing horse herds, while women prepared food, cared for children, gathered edible plants for food and medicine, hauled wood and water, and tended to the upkeep of tepees or wickiups. Mothers doted on their children, and adopted (at least from a European perspective) a rather permissive attitude regarding punishment.

Parents often arranged marriages for their children outside their kin group, but the marriage ceremony was a simple affair, and elopement was common—as was divorce. Some tribes observed taboos regarding interaction between in-laws, and couples understood that marriage incurred obligations to the extended family, such as providing food or seeking permission to remarry after the death of a spouse.

Religion was both animistic and polytheistic but mostly an individual affair, the supplicant seeking visions and divine protection or intervention through prayer, fasting, or other rituals. Kiowas, and perhaps the Comanches, participated in large communal religious activities, such as the Sun Dance. Death rituals were of particular importance to West Texas Indians, and burial took place within a day or so after death. Elders interred the body, dressed in finest clothing, along with other material objects (weapons, tools, amulets) that had held special significance to the deceased. Some tribes harbored acute fears of ghosts and went to great lengths to avoid contact with the spirits of the recently deceased. They repeatedly moved their encampments, they no longer mentioned the name of the deceased, and they burned sage to ward off what they feared might be angry or vindictive spirits that possessed the power to cause harm to the living.

Indian people participated actively in the profound changes that swept across West Texas during the eighteenth century. As they moved into the area in the early 1700s, Comanches dislocated the Lipan Apaches, who in turn headed southward into south central Texas. Spanish soldiers, missionaries, and ranchers, meanwhile, endeavored to expand their reach northward across what they considered to be Spanish Texas. Trapped in the middle of these ever-shifting borders were Jumanos and Coahuiltecans, who faced the unenviable choice of subjugation and assimilation by either Spaniards or Apaches. By the mid-eighteenth century, both of these Indian peoples had vanished from the historical record.

In 1785 the Comanches, under the leadership of a remarkable chief named Ecueracapa (sometimes called Cota de Mala or Camisa de Fierro), made peace with the Spaniards and turned their collective energies toward exterminating their mutual enemy, the Lipan Apaches. Over the course of the next decade, the increasingly fragmented and scattered Lipans looked to bandleaders Zapato Sas, Chiquito, and Canoso for direction, but the intertribal war continued into the 1790s.

The collapse of the Spanish empire in the 1820s and the new Republic of Mexico's detachment from Indian affairs along its northern frontier accelerated Indian raiding and attacks on the isolated settlements in West Texas. Native peoples remained aloof from the Texas Revolution of 1836, although Lipan Apache oral tradition suggests that tribal members witnessed the Mexican army's siege and attack on the Alamo. By most accounts, Lipans got along well with officials in the new Republic of Texas. Lipan Chief Cuelgas de Castro (or Castro), who spoke Spanish and English in addition to his native Apachean dialect, nurtured close ties with Sam Houston and in 1837 signed a treaty of friendship with the Republic of Texas.

*Comanche winter encampment near the Llano Estacado, ca. 1872. Indians sought canyons and river valleys for cold weather quarters. (Courtesy Southwest Collection, Texas Tech University)*

The powerful Comanches, on the other hand, viewed Texans with suspi-
cion and as adversaries for control of West Texas. Given the long history of
Lipan–Comanche animosity, it came as no surprise when Lipans served as
scouts and auxiliaries for Texan troops in campaigns against the Comanches. In February 1839, for instance, Lipans under Castro's leadership
fought alongside Captain John H. Moore in the latter's attack on Comanche Chief Muguara's encampment near Spring Creek in Archer County.

The rapidly expanding non-Indian population of Texas, along with the
region's annexation by the United States in 1845, heightened Comanche
insecurity. In a well-intentioned but poorly conceived effort to keep
Comanches and Texas settlers from annihilating each other, government
officials established a 23,000-acre reservation in 1854 on the Clear Fork of
the Brazos River for Comanche bands willing to settle there. Most Comanches, however, preferred to continue their nomadic and autonomous existence in West Texas. Unable to keep Comanches on the reservation and to
keep white settlers out, government officials in 1859 moved the reservation
Comanches to the Indian Territory, in what would become Oklahoma.
Comanches remaining in Texas continued to raid exposed settlements in
a last-ditch effort to preserve their freedom and forestall the onslaught of
Anglo pioneers moving into West Texas.

During the 1870s the sporadic violence that had marked the contest for
control of West Texas escalated into full-scale war. The Treaty of Medicine
Lodge Creek (1867) had established a reservation for Comanches, Kiowas,
and Kiowa Apaches in southwestern Indian Territory, but the agreement
did not greatly improve conditions in Texas, as most Comanches and
Kiowas would not stay on the lands assigned them and continued to conduct raids into Texas. Evidence of the Comanches' growing desperation
was their decision in 1874 to embrace the Sun Dance and the leadership
of Isa-tai (White Eagle), who promised victory over whites. In June 1874
a collection of Quahada Comanches under the leadership of Isa-tai and
Quanah, Kiowa warriors led by Lone Wolf and Satanta, and some Cheyennes attacked an encampment of Anglo bison hunters at Adobe Walls
in Hutchinson County. The fight not only failed to dislodge the hunters
but also provided a rationale for a concerted military campaign against the
Indians to force them back onto their reservation in Indian Territory.

The resulting Red River War was a decisive episode in the Indian wars of West Texas. Although the number of casualties was modest, the various Comanche, Kiowa, Cheyenne, and Arapahoe bands that participated suffered the destruction or confiscation of their winter supplies and horse herds. Unable to continue resistance in the face of these staggering losses, Indian participants began a long march back to their reservations in Indian Territory.

The U.S. military followed up on its victory in the Red River War with a methodical search-and-destroy campaign across West Texas. In 1874 American soldiers in Texas logged an estimated 19,000 miles enacting this campaign, and a year later they rode an additional 40,000 miles in an effort to subdue remaining Indian holdouts. The tactics employed in this war of attrition included the year-round, constant search and pursuit of Indians, staking out their watering places, invading favorite hunting and camping sites, and destroying (or seizing) the Indians' horses, weapons, equipment, and stores of food. On April 14, 1881, a small party of seven Lipans committed what may have been the last Indian raid on Texas soil when they attacked and killed a fourteen-year-old boy named Allen Reiss (or Allen Lease) and Mrs. John McLauren, who were working in a garden along the Frio River. In 1882, twelve military expeditions set out from various Texas posts and covered 3,662 miles, but without finding the slightest trace of Indian raiders.

At the beginning of the twentieth century, census officials counted fewer than 500 American Indians residing in Texas. Comanches, who just a century earlier may have numbered 20,000 or more, now resided alongside the Kiowas, Kiowa Apaches, and Tonkawas on reservations in Oklahoma. The few remaining Lipan Apaches, whose forefathers had challenged Spaniards and Comanches for dominance of West Texas, were scattered across northern Mexico or living with their Mescalero kinsmen on the Mescalero reservation in New Mexico.

The Tigua story is a bit different. Tiguas struggled to maintain a unique tribal and cultural identity in the face of the rapidly growing community centered around El Paso. Their persistence paid off when in April 1968 President Lyndon B. Johnson signed legislation extending federal recognition to the Tiguas. With state and federal government assistance, Tiguas opened a restaurant, a visitor center, a museum, and, in 1993, the Speaking Rock Casino. At its height, the casino employed some 800 people. It closed in 2003

The only other federally recognized tribe in West Texas is the Kickapoo Traditional Tribe of Texas. An Algonkian-speaking people originally from the central Great Lakes region, the Kickapoo Nation splintered in the early nineteenth century and a division migrated south through Texas to northern Mexico. Under the sponsorship of the Mexican government, Kickapoos raided settlements in South Texas and served as a first line of defense against marauding Lipans and Comanches. In return for their service, Mexican authorities granted them lands around Nacimiento in northern Coahuila. The Mexican Kickapoos retained their traditional way of life, raising corn and hunting into the 1940s, when, in the face of drought and the fencing of surrounding ranches, they moved across the Rio Grande into Texas seeking employment as farm laborers.

Living in encampments near the International Bridge connecting Piedras Negras, Coahuila, and Eagle Pass, Texas, the Kickapoos found seasonal employment as migrant workers, at times traveling across the country to harvest fruits and vegetables. They did not legally hold title to land in Texas until 1985, when federal authorities granted them permission to purchase tracts near El Indio, Texas, and they became eligible for federal aid. Like the Tiguas, the Kickapoos ventured into casino gambling in the 1990s and in 2004 established the Lucky Eagle Casino in Eagle Pass. Although gaming proceeds have provided jobs and enabled Kickapoos to construct ancillary businesses, casino operations have also contributed to serious tribal divisions over control of the proceeds.

The various Indian peoples of West Texas played a pivotal role in American history. Their attachment to the land and to the preservation of their way of life thwarted the northern advance of the Spanish empire and checked the expansion of Euro-American settlement west. Their active participation in the complex trade network connecting the Pueblos in New Mexico to East Texas and beyond, conversely, attracted the attention of merchants and settlers who sought to displace them. Federal and state military campaigns hastened the removal of Comanches, Kiowas, and Kiowa Apaches from West Texas and led to the establishment of forts and other military installations in the region, while trans-border raiding across the Rio Grande remained a critical diplomatic issue facing Mexican and U.S. policy makers into the twentieth century.

The Indian population of West Texas reached a nadir in the early 1900s, with only a few hundred still present, but has since recovered, to more than 10,000 in the early decades of the twenty-first century, concentrated mainly in the region's urban areas (4,600 in El Paso, 1,500 in Amarillo, 1,000 in Eagle Pass, 650 in Lubbock). Indian cultural expression, at one time the target of assimilationist reformers, is now celebrated each year at powwows, reenactments, and parades and in schools and many regional and national museums. Modern-day West Texans of all racial and ethnic backgrounds are proud, resourceful, and resilient. In such ways they owe much to the Native Americans who first inhabited the giant side of Texas and who have continued ever since to leave an indelible mark on its history.

## FOR FURTHER READING

Anderson, Gary C. *The Conquest of Texas: Ethnic Cleansing in the Promised Land, 1820–1875*. Norman: University of Oklahoma Press, 2005.

Britten, Thomas A. *The Lipan Apaches: People of Wind and Lightning*. Albuquerque: University of New Mexico Press, 2009.

Carlson, Paul H. *The Plains Indians*. College Station: Texas A&M University Press, 1998.

———. *Deep Time and the Texas High Plains*. Lubbock: Texas Tech University Press, 2005.

Foster, William C. *Historic Native Peoples of Texas*. Austin: University of Texas Press, 2008.

Hamalainen, Pekka. *The Comanche Empire*. New Haven: Yale University Press, 2008.

Hickerson, Nancy P. *The Jumanos: Hunters and Traders of the South Plains*. Austin: University of Texas Press, 1994.

LaVere, David. *The Texas Indians*. College Station: Texas A&M University Press, 2004.

Mayhall, Mildred P. *Indian Wars of Texas*. Waco: Texian Press, 1965.

Newcomb, William W. *The Indians of Texas: Prehistory to Present*. Austin: University of Texas Press, 1961.

Pertula, Timothy K., ed. *The Prehistory of Texas*. College Station: Texas A&M University Press, 2004.

Smith, F. Todd. *From Dominance to Disappearance: The Indians of Texas and the Near Southwest, 1786–1859*. Lincoln: University of Nebraska Press, 2005.

Wade, Maria F. *The Native Americans of the Texas Edwards Plateau, 1583–1799*. Austin: University of Texas Press, 2003.

# CHAPTER 7

# Tejanos in West Texas

*Arnoldo De León*

Hispanic people, mainly Mexican Americans, have steadily increased their role and population numbers across West Texas since the arrival of the first Spanish explorers on the North American continent in the sixteenth century. They came as town builders and ranchers, as dons and priests and pastores, as migrant workers and permanent settlers. In the twentieth century, especially, their numbers have increased in the region, and Tejanos—Texans of Mexican descent—have assumed prominent positions of all kinds in the affairs of West Texas. De León focuses on some central, themes, ideas, and issues relating to their presence and contributions.

During the mid-nineteenth century, people of Hispanic, usually Spanish-Mexican, descent constituted some 70 percent of the total white population living in West Texas. Until the last decades of that century, people of Hispanic origin outnumbered Anglos (non-Hispanic white settlers and residents) in what today are referred to as the Edwards Plateau and Trans-Pecos areas of the region. In modern-day Oldham, Hartley, and Deaf Smith counties in the Texas Panhandle, *pastores* (sheepherders) from New Mexico similarly held a demographic advantage over Anglos as late as 1880.

Some prominent Hispanic names of the present day can be identified with West Texas before 1900: Casimero Romero, Pablo Alderette, and Paula Losoya Taylor. Romero led sheep ranchers from New Mexico into the Panhandle around 1876 and established the town that came to be known as Tascosa. Alderette arrived in the San Angelo area with his family around 1869 or 1870 and served as a Tom Green County commissioner in 1875. History credits Losoya Taylor with co-founding Del Rio.

For the most part, however, ordinary Tejanos, of Mexican origin or descent, worked as ranch and farm hands, as day laborers, as freighters, and as unskilled workers in an assortment of occupations in the predominantly agrarian society of West Texas. Though post–Civil War Anglo immigration to the region began to dwarf the Mexican American presence there, people of Mexican descent remained a visible element in 1900. As present-day statistics show, in recent years they have again come to outnumber Anglos in many counties stretching from the Rio Grande to the Texas Panhandle.

Tejanos, the name used today for Texans of Mexican descent, originally applied to people who inhabited the geographic area of Texas. In colonial times, when Texas was a northern territory of Mexico and most residents other than Indians spoke Spanish, "Tejanos" simply meant "Texans," people who lived in Texas. During the years of Texas independence the same geographical sense prevailed, and residents of the new republic were sometimes referred to as Tejanos. The shift in meaning, such that "Tejano" also denoted Hispanic language and culture as distinct from "Anglo" counterparts, seems to have gradually occurred over the mid- to late nineteenth century as the Anglo population rose and English became a more prevalent language.

Even so, West Texas was, and remains today, a land of geographic diversity, and Tejanos and Mexican immigrants, along with other ethnic incomers to the area in the early twentieth century, gravitated toward areas offering hospitable prospects for cattle, sheep, and goat raising. This pattern of settlement took them to Trans-Pecos ranch counties like Terrell, Pecos, and Reeves, but also to Edwards Plateau livestock counties like Sutton and Val Verde. Others sought work in developing enterprises, such as the quicksilver (mercury) operations in the Big Bend. The Chisos

Mining Company in Terlingua, for example, attracted workers from both sides of the border, so many that one contemporary in the early 1900s remarked that 1,000 to 1,500 Mexicans lived in tents and stone huts near the mine.

During the period after World War I all of West Texas experienced new improvements in range management, in farming practices, and in oil drilling. The number of towns multiplied. Mexican American communities that had arisen before 1900 kept pace with the times despite dire conditions: poverty, racial discrimination, condescending attitudes toward Mexican culture and intelligence, and even violence. In towns like Marfa, Presidio, San Angelo, Fort Stockton, and Ozona, *barrios* (labeled "Little Mexicos" by Anglos) sprouted around railroad depots or livestock yards, sites where unskilled jobs might be readily accessible to Mexican workers. These barrios afforded opportunities for community building, and Tejanos organized mutual aid societies to help members in need or to sponsor cultural activities; they founded churches of every denomination, celebrated *fiestas patrias* (patriotic Mexican holidays) under the tutelage of local *comités patrióticos*, and enjoyed sports events—almost every community had its own *equipo*, or baseball team.

New arrivals from Mexico or other parts of the state (many came from South Texas) augmented the existing Hispanic population in the region. But not all of them pursued their destiny in ranch settlements, as so many earlier Mexican workers had done. Instead they sought new beginnings in counties such as Schleicher, Runnels, Concho, and McCullough, which were turning more and more to farm cultivation.

They also further pursued possibilities for livelihood in sections of West Texas then undergoing oil exploration and discovery: Reagan and Ector counties in the Edwards Plateau, and Pecos County in the Trans-Pecos region; in the Panhandle; and in such Rolling Plains counties as Scurry, Fisher, Jones, Howard, and Taylor. This new thrust drew Tejanos into the fledgling oil towns of Big Lake and Snyder and into embryonic barrios growing in Odessa, Midland, Abilene, Lubbock, and Amarillo.

By 1930 people of Mexican origin or descent represented a rather insignificant proportion of the inhabitants settled throughout the wide expanse that is West Texas. According to calculations derived from population figures provided by federal census of 1930, Americans of Mexican descent made up 7.6 percent of a total West Texas population of 843,922.

The Great Depression and World War II led a greater number of Mexican workers northward from their homes in South Texas and in Mexico, as well as from southern West Texas counties, where many already resided. Although the Depression extended its reach into West Texas, it hardly caused the devastation there that it did in other parts of the country, and the region survived, due to the quick rebound of ranching, government help to farmers, and a surge in the oil industry.

But the 1930s and 1940s did not bring better days to the Tejanos of West Texas or to Hispanic workers and families moving into the region. Whether in ranching, farming, oil fields, or towns, most faced trying times. Traditionally ranchers had paid Mexican and Tejano cowboys less than they paid Anglo cowhands for doing the same work. Anglo sheep and goat men negotiated through *capitanes*, or crew chiefs (themselves forced to survive on meager payments) for getting their sheep sheared, a system encouraging wage unfairness that hit the common *tasinque* (sheep shearer) hardest. In the San Angelo area in 1934, Mexican American sheep shearers went on strike protesting employment practices and low pay. The strike ended in failure.

Migrant farm workers dealt with their own tribulations. By the early 1930s Mexican workers were responding to calls for cotton pickers throughout the region, and the demand came strongest from farm counties in Northwest Texas. Setting out from South Texas, the migrant laborers followed a trail that kept them on the road from about March to December. They crossed through the Coastal Bend counties on their way to Central Texas farms, then through Tom Green, Runnels, McCullough, and Concho County cotton fields, and up to Lubbock, Hale, Lamb, and Bailey counties.

On the Big Swing, as people called this cycle, Mexican American migrants encountered difficult conditions. They traveled at their own expense, either in an old car or on the bed of a large truck—they paid a *troquero*, a truck driver, to transport them over the hundreds of miles along their route. Circumstances forced them to find shelter on their own, to determine what stores sold goods to Mexicans (some towns discouraged Mexicans from even stopping within their city limits), and to trust that work would await them once reaching their destination. Once arrived, they were plagued by a range of further problems, among these lack of proper sanitary facilities, lack of adequate protection from the weather (winters are cold in Northwest Texas), troqueros who might cheat them of their earnings, ill-treatment by farm owners, and, of course, low wages for back-breaking labor.

The recovery of the oil industry during the 1930s augured well for Permian Basin counties, Panhandle counties, and some southeastern counties in Northwest Texas, and many Tejano workers sought jobs in and around the oil fields. For the most part, racial and ethnic attitudes of the era precluded their taking the more desirable positions and better-paying tasks. They faced relegation to the dirtiest chores, including grubbing the land, cleaning oilfield debris, and helping transport oilfield supplies and heavy equipment. In small oil towns close to the oilfields, they survived by taking any type of employment: pick and shovel work, house cleaning, construction, dish washing, or perhaps seasonal jobs in neighboring farms and ranches.

Town life offered these workers no advantages over rural living. Housing in urban areas reflected the ambient poverty level in which most lived; dwellings were built with whatever earnings they could muster, generally on affordable property at the outskirts of a municipality. In any case, most Anglos in West Texas followed segregationist policies and prohibited "Mexicans" (meaning anyone Hispanic) from setting up homesteads in the white areas of settlements and municipalities. Public facilities such as restrooms parks were often off limits to "Mexicans," as were schools. Educators seldom made provisions for schooling Tejano adolescents, and in any case, there existed unwritten rules that Mexican children could not attend school past the elementary grades.

Still, the clearest expression of Hispanic culture throughout West Texas was discernible in the towns—at least that is where present-day scholarship, albeit thin, has so far focused. Within the boundaries of the barrios, as in remote ranch and farm homes, life marched on as normally as people could possibly make it. Entrepreneurs set up business establishments, among them *tienditas* (small "mom and pop" general stores), restaurants offering Mexican-style food, Spanish-language theaters, and dance halls. Spanish-speaking priests and ministers tended to the spiritual needs of believers. Within the Hispanic community, people carried on old folkloric traditions, families observed conventional courtesies when interacting with one another and with friends, and the young abided by established rules of courtship. Leisure included the observation of important religious and secular anniversaries, both Mexican and American (Fourth of July), or participation in recreational clubs that sponsored cultural activities, picnic outings, and dances. *Lo mexicano,* "the Mexican way," thus persisted during the Depression years throughout West Texas: in the Big Bend, in border towns such as Del Rio, in urban centers like San Angelo, and in Trans-Pecos towns such as Fort Stockton and faraway Van Horn.

Despite their persistent socioeconomic problems, collectively and individually, Hispanics made efforts at community improvement. Mexican American leaders took it upon themselves to address local issues, as in the case of the League of United Latin American Citizens (LULAC), active in towns like San Angelo and Fort Stockton by the 1930s. By the war years, at least a few students had broken past societal barriers in West Texas to graduate from high school. Many young Hispanic men met the qualifications for military service and either enlisted or responded to draft calls, fighting gallantly both in Europe and in the Pacific.

The Mexican and Mexican American influx into West Texas intensified after World War II, at least as indicated in population figures. In 1950, about 95,000 people of Mexican origin or descent lived in West Texas (8.6 percent of the total population) and this amount increased to more than 306,000 (20 percent of the total population) in 1980.

Although between 1950 and 1980 the oil industry experienced fluctuations and farmers and ranchers faced their own woes, West Texans of Mexican descent still found options for material advancement in many sections of the region. Ranch counties attracted some workers, and cattle feeding enterprises and meat packing plants established in Northwest Texas during the 1960s drew hundreds directly from Mexico and from poverty-stricken areas throughout the state. But the greater lure to West Texas were the counties that continued to offer work in farming and oil production. Farms, now irrigated by electrically powered pumps, had a greater need for field hands, and oil counties along the northern rim of the Edwards Plateau and Trans-Pecos now offered new job possibilities to Hispanic workers,

*LULAC rally, ca. 1960. (Courtesy Southwest Collection, Texas Tech University)*

who until past midcentury had not been permitted direct employment in oil drilling operations. And by the 1960s Tejanos and other Hispanic workers also saw better opportunities in the cities of West Texas, some of which emerged as centers of finance, hubs for the ranching and farming industries, focal points for conducting financial transactions, or simply as oil towns. Thus by the 1960s and 1970s the general demographic trend was movement from rural areas into large cities such San Angelo, Midland, Odessa, Del Rio, Lubbock, and Amarillo and also into several county seats of less populous counties.

Individually or as a group, Mexican Americans in West Texas attempted to find solutions to festering problems. Throughout the region, they still felt a need to tread lightly when entering public places; the route from Marfa, through Fort Stockton and then to Junction during the late 1940s (and presumably later) had a notorious reputation for "not serving Mexicans" at restaurants. During World War II even Mexican Americans in uniform experienced rejection at eateries, barber shops, and gas stations.

Barrio leaders during the 1950s and 1960s bravely addressed such matters as ethnic prejudice, police harassment, and de facto segregation in West Texas schools, among them the systems in Pecos, Midland, Ozona, Sonora, Alpine, and Snyder. In these endeavors they found encouragement and support from LULAC and the American G.I. Forum (AGIF), the two leading groups at that time that looked into Mexican American concerns in Texas. In the hostile environment of that era, representatives from LULAC and AGIF went before city councils to request that attention be given to Mexican American neighborhoods needing city lighting, paved roads, and garbage collection. In rural areas, these advocates inquired into cases of Anglo abuse of Hispanic farm and ranch hands. To help uplift Hispanic communities, LULAC councils and AGIF chapters set up citizenship classes, encouraged people to pay their poll taxes and to vote, held dances to raise funds for school scholarships, sponsored athletic activities, and encouraged Mexican Americans to contribute to worthy causes, among them Red Cross drives. When Henry B. González of San Antonio launched his drive for governor in 1958, he counted on LULAC and the AGIF to help in his West Texas campaign. (He was defeated but went on to a long career in the U.S. House of Representatives, 1961–99.)

A more intense political drive intended to remove long-standing obstacles to Mexican American advancement occurred during the 1960s and 1970s. This was the Chicano Movement, a sometimes militant campaign led by young people coming of age during the tumultuous Vietnam era and by middle-class members of the World War II generation who had become increasingly dissatisfied with circumstances that stifled Mexican American ambitions. Chicanos joined such militant groups as the Mexican American Youth Organization (MAYO) and Raza Unida Party (RUP), or they joined older, mainstream organizations such as LULAC, AGIF, and the Mexican American Legal Defense and Education Fund (MALDEF). Assisted by liberal allies from such entities as Texas Rural Legal Aid (TRLA), they launched frontal attacks on racism and ethnic prejudice, on the political structure, on the capitalist system, and on social injustices generally.

While area universities such as Texas Tech, Angelo State, and Sul Ross State often received a lot of attention as a result of Chicano students' militant activism, many West Texas communities became politicized and active at the micro level. In 1972 and 1974, when RUP put up candidates for statewide offices, many Mexican Americans in West Texas supported the party's platform, which called for a better funding system for schools, for single-member election districts, for the elimination of the Texas Ranger force, and for women's equality. Here and there RUP won some offices, among them in Marathon in Brewster County. The momentum of the 1970s allowed for the election of Froy Salinas of Lubbock as state representative in 1978.

Chicano activists also dealt with the plight of the migrant farm laborer. In the late 1970s and continuing into the 1980s, the Texas Farm Workers Union (TFWU) arrived in Northwest Texas counties of Bailey, Castro, Deaf Smith, Hale, and Lamb to challenge the dire conditions—long hours, very low pay, and little social support—that had long afflicted Mexican Americans in the vegetable and cotton fields. TFWU organizers held marches, union rallies, and boycotts in efforts to win concessions from growers. TRLA, TFWU's main ally, filed suits of various sorts, and court victories gradually prepared towns (such as Hereford) where migrants increasingly yearned for the day when Tejanos would gain office in municipal, county, and school district governance.

During the latter decades of the twentieth century and into the first years of the twenty-first, Mexican Americans solidified their presence in West Texas. Having comprised about 20.0 percent of the total population in 1980, by the year 2000 Tejanos accounted for fully 30.8 percent of the total population in the region. This occurred as West Texans wrestled with uncertainty. The oil industry, while still a mainstay in many counties, contended with its usual ebbs and flows, and farmers and ranchers annually struggled with bad weather and with a dwindling supply of the great reserves of water essential for irrigated lands. These and other factors led to a marked decline in the Anglo population and a rapid rise in the number of Tejanos who chose West Texas as their permanent home.

Continuing population increase was not the only demographic development to occur among Tejanos. Americans of Mexican descent also continued their earlier movement away from the more remote ranch counties toward the oil counties of the Edwards Plateau and Trans-Pecos and the oil and farm counties of northwestern Texas. Though they remained a discernible presence everywhere in West Texas, the trend that had begun at midcentury, in the postwar years, was toward the urban areas, such that Lubbock, Amarillo, and Big Spring in northwestern Texas became magnet cities for many. On the Edwards Plateau, the cities of Del Rio, Midland, Odessa, and San Angelo together housed about 50.0 percent of the entire Hispanic population living from the Hill Country in the region's east to Hudspeth County in Far West Texas.

In sum, Mexican Americans stayed in or migrated into West Texas for a variety of reasons. As other West Texans did, Tejanos found that the region offers a pleasant environment for raising families and enjoying life in general. As opposed to big city problems such as pollution, congestion, highway traffic, crime, and drug dealing, rural areas for many residents offered generous space and a greater sense of safety and security. Also, Tejanos were following a general trend in American society whereby minority groups found rural areas more to their liking.

Economic and social inducements also explain the Tejano preference for life in West Texas. Recent arrivals from Mexico, as well as native-born Tejanos, have taken jobs in the region's numerous farms and ranches, and in its oil fields, in the feedlots of Northwest Texas, in restaurants, hotels, and construction sites in cities, and in every business seeking unskilled manual labor. Enterprising Mexican Americans, even in disadvantaged circumstances, have often established business enterprises catering to Hispanic tastes or meeting Hispanic needs for professional services. Attorneys' offices displaying signs reading "Se habla español" proliferated, for instance, in towns and cities where Tejanos came to live and work. In the wake of the social reforms won in the 1960s and 1970s, Hispanic professionals—previously an almost nonexistent class—have found openings in the educational field as teachers and college professors, in hospitals as doctors and nurses, and in local and federal government service. Others who once worked the fields have prospered sufficiently to buy farm land.

Hispanics have also found politics, once closed to them, attractive. The work of groups such as LULAC and the AGIF, the impact of the Chicano Movement, the initiatives taken in West Texas by the San Antonio–based Southwest Voter and Education Project (SWVRP), and TRLA's court victories in the early 1980s forced cities, counties, and school districts to hold single-member district elections. This opportunity, coupled with the increase in the Hispanic population (and thus in voting numbers), allowed Tejanos to win political appointments or elections to government posts. By the end of the twentieth century they had become increasingly visible in West Texas county commissioners' courts, in school boards, in the constabulary (including sheriffs), and on the judge's bench.

Over the now nearly five centuries since the founding of the first Hispanic settlement, Tejanos have sunk deep roots in just about every county in West Texas, gaining a demographic majority in 2014 in Sutton, Reagan, Presidio, Pecos, Deaf Smith, and Castro counties. Demographers have predicted further population gains in other counties and have reasoned that even counties far removed from the Rio Grande border could well follow trends now well established in South Texas, with its prominent Spanish-language advertisements, bilingual transactions, commemorations of the holidays such as Cinco de Mayo, and much more that marks the incontestable presence of a Hispanic West Texas. Easy to overlook in the landscape of West Texas until recent decades, Tejanos have gained a secure foothold in the mainstream of the region's affairs and have seen their culture come to be celebrated as another component of the American way of life.

## FOR FURTHER READING

De León, Arnoldo. "Mexican Americans in the Edwards Plateau and Trans-Pecos Region, 1900–2000." *Southwestern Historical Quarterly* 112 (October 2008), 148–70.
———. *San Angeleños: Mexican Americans in San Angelo, Texas.* San Angelo: Fort Concho Museum Press, 1985.
———. "Tejanos in Northwest Texas: Rural Folks or Urbanites?" *West Texas Historical Association Year Book* 86 (2010), 8–32.
Flores, María Eva, CDP. "The Good Life the Hard Way: The Mexican American Community of Fort Stockton, Texas, 1930–1945." Ph.D. dissertation, Arizona State University, 2000.
Gómez, Arthur. *A Most Singular Country: A History of Occupation in the Big Bend.* Santa Fe: National Park Service; Salt Lake City: Charles Redd Center for Western Studies, Brigham Young University, 1990.

Martínez, Camilo Amado, Jr. "*Vamos Pal West:* Let's Go West." *West Texas Historical Association Yearbook* 70 (1994), 40–56.

Olien, Roger M., and Diana Davids Olien. *Oil Booms: Social Change in Five Texas Towns.* Lincoln: University of Nebraska Press, 1982.

Rangel, Jorge C., and Carlos M. Alcalá. "Project Report: De Jure Segregation of Chicanos in Texas Schools." *Harvard Civil Rights–Civil Liberties Law Review* 7 (March 1972), 307–91.

Romero, Yolanda. "Hispanics in the Texas South Plains." In *The Future of the Southern Plains*, edited by Sherry L. Smith, 199–218. Norman: University of Oklahoma Press, 2003.

Taylor, Anna J. "Hispanic Settlement of the Texas Panhandle–Plains, 1876–1884." *Panhandle–Plains Historical Review* 70 (1997), 36–58.

Torres Smith, Anita. "Shearing: *La Traquila* in the First Half of the Twentieth Century." *Journal of Big Bend Studies* 6 (1994), 99–117.

Wright, Paul. "A Tumultuous Decade: Changes in the Mexican-Origin Population of the Big Bend, 1910–1920." *Journal of Big Bend Studies* 10 (1998), 163–87.

CHAPTER 8

# African Americans in West Texas

*James M. Smallwood*

Although they have seldom represented more than ten percent of the region's population, African Americans have been in West Texas since the time of the first Europeans in North America. They have played key roles in the area's economic, social, cultural, and political life, but their important stories have too often been obscured. Here, using several specific examples, Smallwood provides a thoughtful overview of Black Americans, their activities, and their experiences in West Texas.

Black slaves from Africa accompanied Spanish explorers to Texas before the region possessed such a name. The first was Esteban (Estevan or Stephen), a Moor from Azamor in Morocco. Although not an African American by birth, he became the first recorded black man to set foot on Texas soil. He was a survivor of a shipwreck near Galveston Island in 1527 and a slave of Captain Andrés Dorantes de Carranza. Local Indians captured Esteban, Dorantes, and a shipmate, Álvar Nuñez Cabeza de Vaca, only to see them escape in 1534. Trying to find Mexico City, the three wayfarers explored southward to the Rio Grande, turned northwest, crossed land that would include present-day Presidio in West Texas, and reached an area near today's El Paso before turning south again and winding up in Culiacán, a place of safety, after they had

traveled approximately 2,000 miles on foot. Cabeza de Vaca became famous for his published account of their travels. Esteban died on American
soil in 1539, while accompanying an expedition among the Zunis.

African slaves accompanied Francisco Vásquez de Coronado when in
1541 he made his famous reconnaissance while looking for the mythic
Seven Cities of Cibola, supposedly a land of great wealth. From a base near
present-day Albuquerque, New Mexico, the expedition took an eastward
course across the Llano Estacado of western Texas. After resting in Blanco
Canyon, Coronado sent most expedition members home and, with a small
force, trekked to what is now southern Kansas, where he saw no cities of
gold but found a poor village of Wichita Indians. As members of subsequent Spanish expeditions, some blacks eventually settled in West Texas, as
did a number of Spaniards, of course. Some early Spanish explorers noted
that former black slaves were already living with a few Indian tribes that
the Spaniards encountered on their expeditions across parts of West Texas.

Although some blacks were in West Texas at an early date, development
of a significant presence and population took many decades. In 1792, for
example, only 448 blacks lived in Texas, some clustering around El Paso and
a few others living with various Indian tribes of West Texas. The number
expanded rapidly. By 1800 approximately 1,000 black people called Texas
home, and the numbers continued to rise as the decades passed. Some of
these were new arrivals who settled in West Texas.

Much later, when white settlers from the eastern United States and Canada (usually termed Anglos, though of varied European origins) began to
occupy West Texas, some of the new settlers brought slaves with them. In
Young County, for example, Anglos began arriving in the 1850s, and in the
county's early history slaves numbered one of every three settlers. Coming
in wagon trains with their owners, African Americans became teamsters,
cooks, laborers on farms and ranchers, woodcutters, and domestics, or
engaged in such other useful pursuits as road building, an important occupation in the area because roads crisscrossed Young County and opened
remote areas. Yet in West Texas considered broadly, slavery remained an
insignificant development. Young County's large number of slaves appears
to have been an exception, for El Paso County numbered only eight slaves
in 1860.

Activities of black soldiers (infantry and cavalry) from the 1860s to the turn of the century impacted the history of West Texas. The Plains Indians called them Buffalo Soldiers because the soldiers' hair reminded the Indians of the buffalo's coat, perhaps especially the distinctive curly, rough mane that covers the animal's shoulders. It was a term of respect, for the Indians believed that bison were sacred animals who furnished them most of their needs, including their homes (tepees), clothing, blankets, and other goods, such as water bags and domestic implements, such as knives and needles, fashioned from bison bones and horn. The long history of Buffalo Soldiers actually began during the American Civil War.

Approximately 186,000 African Americans fought for the Union during the Civil War, and in the summer of 1866, when Congress reorganized the peacetime army, its solons recognized the valor of the men by authorizing two black cavalry units: the Ninth and Tenth U.S. Cavalry regiments and six regiments of infantry that in 1869 were reduced to two, the Twenty-fourth and Twenty-fifth United States Infantry regiments. From mobilization in 1866 until 1900 Buffalo Soldiers served in a variety of posts and in a variety of tasks in West Texas, the broader Southwest, and the even larger Great Plains. Often broken into various detachments, black soldiers fought Indians; they performed sundry garrison chores; they built roads; they escorted all manner of civilian parties, including mail carriers; and undertook various difficult tasks relating to both military and civilian life. As soldiers, they were tough, aggressive, and efficient when they took the field against Comanches, Kiowas, Apaches, Cheyennes, and Arapahoes, in addition to Sioux on the Northern Plains. Their commanders, all white, were a widely experienced cadre whose names read like a who's who in American military history: the legendary Civil War hero General Benjamin H. Grierson, immortalized in the movie *The Horse Soldiers* (1959); William R. Shafter, Edward Hatch, Abner Doubleday, Ranald S. Mackenzie, and Joseph A. Mower.

The Buffalo Soldiers were an elite group, and many of them were rewarded for their valor. Thirteen of their enlisted men won the Medal of Honor during the Indian wars. Six of their white officers won the same distinction. Five additional black soldiers won the same prize during the Spanish–American War in 1898.

The most famous Buffalo Soldier was Henry O. Flipper (1856–1940). His military career, unfortunately, was marred by white discrimination, insults, and questions regarding his character. Born a Georgia slave, after manumission he sought an education, a path that eventually took him to West Point, where in 1877 he became one of the school's first black graduates. His field was engineering. As a lieutenant in the Tenth Cavalry, he served at various posts in Texas and at Fort Sill in Indian Territory (later Oklahoma). Using his skills as an engineer, he supervised the drainage of malarial ponds; he directed the construction of a road from Gainesville, Texas, to Fort Sill; and he supervised the construction of a telegraph line from a Texas military post to Fort Supply, Indian Territory. He also served with units that fought Indians in West Texas, personally engaging in two battles near Eagle Springs, Texas. He was appointed quartermaster of Fort Davis and took control of the fort's supplies and physical plant—whereupon his woes began.

Colonel William R. Shafter became commanding officer of Fort Davis in 1881. Shafter determined to get rid of Flipper and immediately relieved him as quartermaster. Shafter also planned to relieve him as commissary officer as soon as a replacement showed up. Warned by area civilians in 1882 that Shafter planned to purge him, Flipper waited for the inevitable. Soon, disaster struck. Apparently, due to theft by others, Flipper had lost commissary money and had tried to hide the fact until he could replace it, but Shafter learned of the incident. Ultimately dismissed from the army following a court-martial, Flipper returned to private life, remained in the Southwest, and made his livelihood in various ways including surveying and other work that called for a competent engineer. For a time he worked for Albert B. Fall, a prominent political leader from New Mexico. He worked into the 1930s and died in 1940.

Black Seminoles also contributed to the nation's military forces and to the development of West Texas. Their history was complex, originating in seventeenth-century Florida, where they first emerged as a separate ethnic group made up of a racial mix including Indians and blacks. Sometimes called Maroons, they numbered some 5,000 by 1822 and lived among the Seminoles in Florida. Because Spain controlled Florida and offered asylum to runaway slaves, a development that began when the American colonies still belonged to the British, the number of Maroons steadily increased. Even after Spain transferred Florida to Britain in1763, the region remained a haven for escaped American slaves, with most settling among the Seminoles, where they lived in separate villages. In the era of forced removals in the 1830s, they were dispersed to Indian lands that became part of present-day Oklahoma and Texas. From those areas, most Maroons migrated to Northern Mexico to live under a more tolerant government than those they had found in the American states and in Indian Territory.

In 1870, during the U.S.–Indian wars on the Great Plains, the United States Army recruited a number of Black Seminoles, including John Kibbetts, a black Seminole warrior, to serve as scouts and Indian fighters. They originally numbered but twelve and worked out of Fort Duncan in West Texas. As time passed, the number rose to several dozen. Later, additional former slaves, or freedmen, joined the group, ultimately bringng it to about 300. Many of them served under Colonel Ranald S. Mackenzie and Lieutenant John L. Bullis. Most notably, many fought in the Red River War (1874–75) in West Texas, including the epic Battle of Palo Duro Canyon (1874), the results of which drove the young Comanche Chief Quanah and his band back to their reservation in Indian Territory. After Indian conflicts ceased in the region, later in the nineteenth century, Black Seminoles, even though denied the land they had been promised by the U.S. Army, helped settle West Texas, many working for Anglo ranchers, farmers, and townspeople.

Like the Black Seminoles, black cowboys also contributed to West Texas life and work. Most notably they helped to expand the emerging range cattle industry. Formed in South Texas shortly after the Civil War, that industry by the 1880s had expanded all the way to Montana and other points north and west. According to the classic study *The Negro Cowboys* (1983) by Philip Durham and Everett L. Jones, black cowboys made up at least 25 percent of all those who worked the range in West Texas. Black cowboys were indeed an important component of range labor. Later a few survived as rodeo performers as well as landowners and cattle raisers.

One of the earliest African Americans in West Texas to achieve note was Britton "Britt" Johnson, called Black Fox by his Kiowa adversaries. Born in 1840, Britt was a Tennessee slave who belonged to Moses Johnson. After moving to Texas with his master, he spent his young years in the old Peters Colony (near present-day Fort Worth) working on Moses's ranch. Apparently treated well by his owner, Britt learned to read, to write, and to perform minor mathematical functions. After Moses bought a ranch in Young County's Elm Creek Valley, Britt became his foreman, a job that allowed him much freedom along with the accompanying new responsibilities.

Britt was frequently gone from the ranch, performing such tasks as hauling freight or moving horses or cattle; yet apparently he never thought of running away. Perhaps because he was faithful to his owner, he was also allowed to raise his own horses and cattle. As well, when Britt came of age, Moses gave him permission to marry another slave. With his wife, Mary, Britt raised three children: one son and two daughters.

In 1864, while Britt was away from the ranch on business, Kiowas and Comanches—several hundred strong, led by Comanche Chief Little Buffalo—raided some ranches in Young County, including Moses's place. During this attack, now known as the Elm Creek Raid, the Indians killed several settlers and stole hundreds of cattle and horses. They captured seven people, including all members of Britt's family. Because he had to find and rescue his wife and children, Britt asked Moses to give him his freedom papers so that he might travel without fear of arrest as a runaway slave. Moses complied.

Once freed, Britt searched for his family for almost a year without results. Finally, in 1865, Comanche Chief Asa-Havey, to curry favor with the American government, accepted a ransom for Mary and her daughters; Kiowas had killed Britt's son, Jim, shortly after his capture. With his surviving family, Britt settled in Parker County and became a successful teamster. He expanded his business by acquiring new wagons and by hiring employees and became modestly prosperous. But he was cut down in his prime in 1871, when a Kiowa war party attacked his train of three wagons. The Indians killed Britt and his two helpers, afterward mutilating their bodies. Although he died young, Britt demonstrated to his contemporaries that black men could master any work and build successful businesses, no small achievements for men born to slavery.

If Britt was an pioneering black cowboy in West Texas, "Nig" London was a latter-day counterpart. Born in 1910 on a small family ranch,

London hailed from Throckmorton County. As a youth, he performed chores around the ranch. In 1923, when he was just thirteen years old, he participated in his first cattle drive, helping to move a herd of 1,800 head from Shackelford County to his home county. By that age, he also excelled as a horse breaker and trainer and worked throughout Throckmorton County and adjacent counties, charging $5.00 per head.

London also lived long enough to see great changes come to cow country. One important change came from the transportation revolution, when mechanized vehicles became readily available and affordable in the 1940s. Use of pickup trucks and hauling trailers replaced cattle drives, for example. London also saw the transition in range water management whereby shallow livestock tanks created by mules pulling fresno scrapers were exchanged for bigger, deeper pools created by bulldozers, another sign that the old days of the cattle industry were passing by. Raising cattle had slowly become an agribusiness.

Not many black cowboys in West Texas became as successful as Britt Johnson or Nig London, but a few became foremen or managers. Many became wranglers, cooks, or "security officers" to handle problems caused by others on the trail. Several achieved distinction for one skill or another. Bose Ikard worked for Charles Goodnight as a top hand as well as becoming his major detective when Goodnight lost cattle to rustlers who, when caught, were not dealt with kindly.

Another such "officer" was James Kelly, born in Williamson County in the 1830s to former slaves who had been freed by the prominent Olive family. He in turn worked for the Olive clan, becoming a trail boss on long cattle drives and serving as an enforcer when necessary. Kelly's first drive was notable, as he helped herd several thousand head of cattle up the Sedalia Trail to Sedalia, Missouri, after an eastern railroad reached there in 1866. Thereafter for several years, Kelly headed other drives to both Kansas and Nebraska, once trails were laid out to those areas. Such work made the Olive family rich. In one notable drive, Kelly and Prentice "Print" Olive drove a large herd to Abilene, Kansas, and returned home with $50,000, a small fortune by nineteenth-century standards. In his work for the Olive family, Kelly led parties looking for rustlers, and he shot several such robbers. As the era of the open range was fading, he sometimes terrorized farmers and was not afraid to cut barbed

*Daniel Webster "80 John" Wallace, 1880s, a cowboy who became a highly respected cattleman and rancher in Mitchell County. (Courtesy Southwest Collection, Texas Tech University)*

wire fences. As white cowboy E. C. "Teddy Blue" Abbott said: "It takes a hard man to work for them [the Olive family], and believe me, they had several of those all the time." Despite his life of hard work and occasional violence, Kelly lived into his seventies, dying in 1912.

Daniel W. "80 John" Wallace (1869–1939), born in Victoria County, was a black cowboy who ultimately became rich by the standards of his time. Working for cattlemen Gus O'Keefe and Winfield Scott, Wallace took part in the "long drives" to Kansas when he was but a teenager. Savvy with his money, he eventually saved enough to buy land. Over time, he became the owner of almost two sections of land near Loraine, in Mitchell County, on which he ran about 500 to 600 head of cattle. Another black cowboy who achieved fame was William "Bill" Pickett (1870–1932), a native of Travis County, who became a "Wild West" rodeo performer and invented what became known as the rodeo event bulldogging.

African Americans continued to work on ranches into the twentieth century, and Mollie Stevenson, a fourth-generation owner of the Taylor-Stevenson Ranch near Houston, acknowledged their contribution to the Texas economy by founding the American Cowboy Museum in 1987, which highlights the work of black, Indian, and Hispanic cowboys. Also significantly, in the 1940s, rodeos featuring black cowboys became the rage and remain popular among cowboy fans. Formed in 1947, the Negro Cowboy Association supervised several rodeo programs.

Looking back, it becomes clear that in the nineteenth century, many African Americans became cowboys or soldiered in West Texas. They moved into such careers because in them they experienced less overt discrimination than in other occupations. Generally, in the United States, African Americans were treated poorly. Often segregated, discriminated against economically and socially, and denied full rights as American citizens, black Americans lived through it all. But the West, including West Texas, was a land that represented opportunity, becoming a safety valve, as it were. In part, status was gained in the West simply by being good at one's work; skill sometimes outweighed whites' beliefs in racial supremacy.

As the United States entered the twentieth century, blacks in West Texas felt the same allure of urban areas as their white counterparts. During the World War I era and afterward, blacks moved to cities and towns seeking good jobs, a better standard of living, a more exciting cultural life, and perhaps also an escape from the loneliness they had experienced in life in rural areas. Because of segregation, however, blacks who moved to the cities, including those in West Texas, could not aspire to quality jobs with relatively good pay. They became day laborers; they worked in businesses located in areas where blacks were numerous; and they worked as porters, cooks, busboys, and the like. African American women often became seamstresses, cooks, and domestic servants of various kinds. Many black women took in clothes for washing and ironing. Others managed households and child care for white families.

As time passed, some blacks turned to professional occupations and mainly served various African American communities. Members of this group became physicians, barbers, dentists, lawyers, ministers, and store owners, for example. in more recent times, African American professionals, both men and women, have come to participate in the larger Anglo-dominated world of West Texas.

The 1920s represented a prosperous decade, but some African Americans enjoyed only limited participation in that prosperity. Nonetheless, during the decade such major West Texas towns as El Paso, Amarillo, Lubbock, Midland, Odessa, San Angelo, and Wichita Falls saw their black population rise.

The Great Depression (1929–40) adversely affected most blacks, as it did most ethnic groups, even whites. Conditions seemed worse for black Americans. Always "the last hired and the first fired," they saw whites taking jobs previously reserved for blacks, further creating higher unemployment among African Americans. Nationwide, at the height of the Depression, 56 percent of blacks were unemployed. Statistics for West Texas mirror the national figures.

President Franklin D. Roosevelt and his New Deal efforts (enacted 1933–36) alleviated some of the severe economic and financial problems. Roosevelt and the "New Dealers" mandated that blacks be allowed to fill jobs created by the various New Deal work programs in proportion to their population in the areas where they lived or served. Some New Dealers seemed to favor blacks, the model being the young Texan Lyndon B. Johnson, one of Roosevelt's favored group of up and coming young politicos. As the Texas director for the National Youth Administration, Johnson hired more blacks than any other director in the nation. Then, sent to Washington as a congressman, he remained a solid New Dealer, supporting all of Roosevelt's initiatives. He also established his own initiatives anytime he could help Hispanics and African Americans.

The enormous spending associated with World War II pulled the nation, including West Texas, out of the Great Depression. When President Roosevelt began a war preparedness campaign in 1940, New Dealers decided to take advantage of the nation's manpower, meaning that wartime government contracts would be spread nationwide rather than depending fully on the eastern industrial centers. War contracts came to such West Texas cities as Lubbock, Amarillo, El Paso, San Angelo, and Midland. Smaller towns also received war contracts, and many West Texas communities became home to military air bases.

The World War II era and its aftermath also saw developments in the budding Civil Rights Movement. On behalf of blacks nationwide, labor leader A. Phillip Randolph began a crusade for fair employment in defense industries that spent federal tax money. Bowing to what could become nationwide racial marches and actual physical clashes, President Roosevelt issued Executive Order 8802, which banned racial discrimination in the defense industry. Suddenly, black West Texans in major cities and towns found new work opportunities at higher wages. Thousands emerged from poverty, as did their white counterparts in defense works.

Meanwhile, the United States courts made rulings that spurred the movement onward. In 1944 the Supreme Court in *Smith v. Allwright* abolished the Democratic Party's white primary; the case involved a potential black voter who had been denied a vote in the Democratic primary because he was black. In 1949 in *Sweatt v. Painter*, the court commanded integration of the University of Texas School of Law. Other rulings followed. In effect, these contributed to the liberation not only of civil rights for Texas blacks, but of African Americans nationwide. For education, the most important ruling, perhaps, was *Brown v. Board of Education of Topeka* in 1954. The ruling reversed the 1896 *Plessy v. Ferguson* decision that had established a "separate but equal" doctrine. Now the Supreme Court demanded that public schools integrate. In West Texas, people reacted to the new ruling in different ways. In San Angelo, for example, white leaders obeyed the court and integrated schools voluntarily. They experienced very little trouble. In Odessa, Anglo leaders resisted and fought the ruling politically for as long as they could. School integration was not complete in West Texas until the 1970s. After becoming the nation's president, Lyndon B. Johnson continued his civil rights efforts. In 1964 he pushed the Civil Rights Act through Congress, later adding the Voting Rights Act (1965), and the Open Housing Law (1968). In toto, a revolution occurred between 1945 and 1968. Now, in West Texas as in the rest of the nation, black Americans would have full rights as U.S. citizens. As years passed, their living standards rose accordingly.

The world of sports illustrates gains that black Americans have made. Black people now fully participate in college and professional games. Black West Texans attending college have many sports outlets. Schools such as Texas Tech University, West Texas A&M University, Angelo State University, and the University of Texas at El Paso offer a full range of competitive sports, including men's football, basketball, baseball, and other sports while also supporting women's basketball, volleyball, and counterparts to men's programs. Most important to black youngsters are the sports scholarship programs, for without a sports subsidy, many of them probably could not attend college. In that sense, sporting activities are a leveler available to African Americans, and they offer a way up and out of poverty, especially for students who earn a degree.

Area junior or community colleges also offer sports programs, all open to black youngsters. Midland College and nearby Odessa College, for example, are members of the Western Junior College Athletic Conference, as are Howard College in Big Spring and South Plains College in Levelland. All of them field men's basketball and baseball teams and women's basketball teams and participate in other sports as well. Midland College has won twenty national championships since 1975.

Although most West Texas cities are too small to host major professional sports, several provide homes to minor league baseball, soccer, and indoor football. Midland has a baseball team in the Texas League and a professional soccer team. Amarillo and San Angelo have indoor football and a minor league baseball team. Again, for young blacks who stake their future on professional sports careers, the college programs and minor league sports provide a chance for participants to be seasoned and, perhaps, to grow into players who have major professional football, baseball, and basketball careers.

Today, in 2014, population demographics of select cities and towns in West Texas reveal that blacks are still very much a minority. Yet modern black Americans prosper in a land that the early nineteenth-century American explorer Stephen Long labeled the Great American Desert. Indeed, blacks are present in increasing numbers. In Abilene in 2000, for example, blacks represented 8 percent of the population of 115,930. Lubbock's population of 199,564 in 2000 comprised 8.7 percent African Americans.

Its sister city Amarillo contained 173,627 people, 6 percent of whom were black. Midland's 94,996 population in 2000 comprised 8.4 percent blacks. Its sister city Odessa counted 6.9 percent of its 90,943 people as black.

Through the past five centuries there have been black Americans in West Texas. They have lived in its towns and cities and in its rural areas. They have participated in the region's economic, political, social, and cultural life. They have made various and enormous contributions to the quality of life in West Texas. They have been doctors, educators, day laborers, lawyers, domestic employees, business owners, ranchers, farmers, judges, and politicians, among other career activities. Some, as noted earlier, became soldiers and cowboys. In 2014 they represent less than 10 percent of the area's population, but through those five centuries of their steady presence, black Americans have contributed significantly to the giant side of Texas.

## FOR FURTHER READING

Arrington, Carolyn. *Black Explorer in Spanish Texas: Estevanico*. Austin: Eakin Press, 1986.

Barr, Alwyn. *Black Texans: A History of African Americans in Texas*. 2d ed. Norman: University of Oklahoma Press, 1996.

Durham, Philip, and Everett L. Jones. *Adventures of the Negro Cowboy*. New York: Bantam Books, 1969.

———. *The Negro Cowboys*. 1965. Lincoln: University of Nebraska Press, 1983.

Fowler, Arlen L. *The Black Infantry in the West, 1869–1891*. Westport, Conn., 1971; Norman: University of Oklahoma Press, 1996.

Glasrud, Bruce A., and James M. Smallwood, eds. *The African American Experience in Texas: An Anthology*. Lubbock: Texas Tech University Press, 2007.

Glasrud, Bruce A., and Laurie Champion. *Exploring the Afro-Texas Experience: A Bibliography of Secondary Sources about Black Texans*. Alpine: Center for Big Bend Studies, 2000.

Glasrud, Bruce A., and Paul H. Carlson, eds. (with Tai D. Kreidler). *Slavery to Integration: Black Americans in West Texas*. Abilene: State House Press, 2007.

Harris, Theodore D., ed. *Negro Frontiersman: The Western Memoirs of Henry O. Flipper*. El Paso: Texas Western Press, 1963.

Leckie, William H. *The Buffalo Soldiers: A Narrative of the Negro Cavalry in the West*. Norman: University of Oklahoma Press, 1967.

Massey, Sara R., ed. *Black Cowboys of Texas*. College Station: Texas A&M Press, 2000.

Mulroy, Kevin. *Freedom on the Border: The Seminole Maroons in Florida, the Indian Territory, Coahuila, and Texas.* Lubbock: Texas Tech University Press, 1993.

Porter, Kenneth Wiggins. *The Negro on the American Frontier.* New York: Arno Press, 1971.

Smallwood, James M. *The Struggle for Equality: Blacks in Texas.* Boston: American Press, 1983.

Stewart, Paul W., and Wallace Yvonne Ponce. *Black Cowboys.* Broomfield, Colo.: Phillips, 1986.

CHAPTER 9

# West Texas Women

*Tiffany M. Fink*

The role of women in West Texas, an important, but until recently often neglected aspect of the region's history, has increasingly attracted the attention of historians and other writers. Women have been ranchers, landowners and dealers in real estate, writers and journalists, entrepreneurs, teachers and scholars, lawyers, and, in fact, like men, have succeeded in work of all kinds. This chapter highlights several overarching themes relative to West Texas women and offers specific examples to illustrate the discussion.

Jane Gilmore Rushing, one of the region's most gifted literary figures, reminds us that the land of West Texas "encompasses more than climate and landscape; it's a breed of people, a style of life, a way of freeing and extending the mind."[1] Women, of course, are an important part of that breed of people and that style of life. In West Texas women have been visionaries, entrepreneurs, organizers, heads of households, and leaders in many other ways. From the time of the first American Indians in the region, when they often were responsible for the family's daily decision making, to the present day, when they have headed city and state governments, busy hospitals, and large independent school districts, women have been important figures in West Texas and, by extension, in the greater American West.

The earliest female West Texans migrated in and out of the region as important members of Native American groups of the Southern Plains. Comanche, Kiowa Apache, and Tonkawa women were part of a society and culture that provided them with large amounts of responsibility, independence, respect, and, in some cases, authority. Captain Randolph Barnes Marcy of the Fifth United States Infantry observed on one of his trips across West Texas in the 1850s that women and children accompanied Comanche men at a camp near present-day Throckmorton. The presence of the women and children in such camps was seen as evidence that Comanches possessed peaceful intentions. Gender equality was usual among Plains Indian tribes, and women normally possessed significant influence. The culture afforded opportunities for women far beyond the stereotypical hide preparation, porcupine-quill embroidery, and erection and disassembly of tepee homes during times of travel. The first Native American women of West Texas enjoyed opportunities for equality and responsibility perhaps greater than their counterparts among the first Anglo settlers who arrived in West Texas in the nineteenth century.

Perhaps the most famous Comanche woman associated with West Texas was Naduah, also named Cynthia Ann Parker. Taken from her Anglo home at age nine by Comanches in 1836, she grew up among the Indians, married a warrior, and learned to contribute to Comanche society through tanning hides, preparing buffalo meat, and assembling a tepee. She married Peta Nocona and gave birth to two sons, Pecos and Quanah, and a daughter, Prairie Flower. Naduah adapted to her new society and culture and built a family life with Nocona. In 1860 federal troops and Texas Rangers took her from the Indian life she had lived for a quarter of a century.

Forcibly removed from her Comanche friends and family, she again became Cynthia Ann Parker, but her return to life among Anglo friends and family remained tragic. She never saw her husband or her sons again, and her efforts to reenter Anglo society failed. After the death in 1864 of her young daughter, Prairie Flower, who had come with her into white society, Cynthia Ann mourned violently, lacerating her breasts. On several occasions she tried to escape back to her Comanche relatives. It is believed that grief for her lost family undermined her health and may have caused her death in 1870.

Sallie Reynolds Matthews (1861–1938), another notable West Texas figure, recorded the complexities of frontier existence, such as those in Parker's life, during the long struggle between Anglo settlers and Native Americans. *Interwoven: A Pioneer Chronicle* (1936), her account of pioneer life in West Texas during the latter nineteenth century, formed the basis of the original script for the Fort Griffin Fandangle, an annual celebration in Albany. The book contains stories of Native Americans coming for various reasons to Fort Griffin, near the Matthews family's home. Matthews was distressed at the inhumane treatment of Native Americans by settlers intruding from the East: "What could we expect," she asked, "of a people that were gradually driven from their home and country, their hunting grounds being taken without remuneration?"[2]

As settlers of various origins increasingly interacted in West Texas in the nineteenth century, land ownership became a key women's issue. Spanish law in Texas allowed women a greater measure of land management and ownership than did laws of Anglo origin, which generally governed settlements farther east. Partly as a result, West Texas women experienced a more prominent role as equal partners with their husbands or with others in the community than women in the East. And, later, as in the experience of Mollie Jarrott Abernathy in early twentieth-century Lubbock, the Spanish legal precedent of women as landowners would remain a significant influence in modern affairs.

Many histories of women in West Texas during the Spanish colonial period are limited to tales of female residents at missions or to describing Plains Indian women as traveling with family units. A different story, one only beginning to receive attention, was the role of women in relation to property rights. Hispanic family law upheld important rights for women in terms of asset division in the matrimonial relationship. Women experienced a strong measure of independence and self-sufficiency under the Spanish system in West Texas. These heavy Hispanic influences set important precedents for women of all origins in later generations.

Pioneer women settling nearly anywhere in West Texas reaped other benefits, some of them as a direct result of harsh conditions. Men—whether husbands, fathers, uncles, or brothers—depended upon women, often as equal partners in the pioneer quest. Although farm life represented a familiar, characteristic backdrop for women's experiences in West Texas, life on cattle ranches offered some extraordinary experiences. *Texas Women on the Cattle Trails,* Sara Massey's collection of essays by several contributors that appeared in 2006, provides much information on this subject. Of the sixteen women whose lives are detailed in the book, ten hailed from or lived in West Texas, including Bettie Matthews Reynolds, Molly Dyer Goodnight, and Anna McAdams Slaughter. Their histories in particular illustrate how West Texas women enjoyed multifaceted experiences in the American past.

On the early cattle trails that stretched across West Texas, women distinguished themselves in notable ways. Bettie Matthews Reynolds (1851–1935), born Lucinda Elizabeth Matthews, was one of the first women to follow the famed Goodnight-Loving Trail from Fort Belknap in Young County into southern New Mexico, making the trek with her husband, George Reynolds, in 1868. At that time the journey may have been the longest trip of that kind undertaken by any woman. During most of the journey, she drove a military ambulance wagon obtained by her husband as an extra vehicle. As she directed a team of as many as six horses, she rode in the covered passenger partition of the wagon, which looked much like the Butterfield stagecoaches of the mid-nineteenth century. The task required great physical strength and skill as well as tremendous knowledge of horses, all of which she possessed.

Like other West Texas women, Mary Ann "Molly" Dyer Goodnight (1839–1926) and Anna McAdams Slaughter (1856–1948) assisted their husbands in critical activities along western cattle trails and in establishing what would become sprawling and lucrative ranches. In 1876, Charles and Molly Goodnight moved their home from southern Colorado to Palo Duro Canyon, which cuts deep into the Texas High Plains. Over the twelve-day journey, Molly took charge of the herd while her husband, Charles, went ahead to scout for water.

Once settled in the Panhandle of Texas, Molly Goodnight led a rather isolated life. In fact, she often remarked about the important companionship afforded her by the presence of three chickens she kept as pets. Later, as more settlers moved to the plains, Goodnight visited cattle camps and tiny communities, a black satchel of home remedies in hand, ready to aid persons in need of medical attention; no doctors lived in the region. Seeing these needs,

*Ranch women visit their roundup crew during a lunch break, Lynn County, ca. 1895. (Courtesy Southwest Collection, Texas Tech University)*

Molly and Charles encouraged a physician to open a practice in Clarendon, in Donley County. As the modern age unfolded in her part of West Texas, Molly also worked to establish educational opportunities, to protect the last of the Southern Plains bison herds, and to tend to the business of large-scale cattle ranching—all areas of pioneer life that benefitted greatly from her influence and expertise.

Anna McAdams Slaughter, who had connections with both her father's and her husband's ranching families, found double opportunities for expanding women's roles in frontier life. At any given time on either of the family ranches, she undertook almost any job in a capable manner. "While leaders like [Susan B.] Anthony were demanding their rights," says historian James Smallwood, "Anna and other cow women simply *took* their freedom, much to the relief of their men, who always needed help."[3]

Mollie Jarrott Abernathy (1866–1960) understood the hard conditions and requisite adjustments for a West Texas settler. She has been described as a woman with a sophisticated, educated background who successfully entered a male-dominated culture. The sudden murder of Abernathy's first husband, Jim Jarrott, occurred in 1902, shortly after the family's relocation to an area outside the newly established community of Lubbock. Although encouraged by friends to forsake her efforts and return to more familiar terrain in the East, Mollie persisted in building a new life in Texas. Favoring a strong education for her three children, she sent them to a Catholic school near Big Spring, where they would be safe from the difficult conditions of frontier life. Then she focused her energies on building the cattle ranch she and her late husband had dreamed of. Though she missed her children and felt quite alone with little companionship beyond the hired ranch hands, Mollie built a thriving business.

Within a few years, she met and married Monroe Abernathy of Lubbock. Continuing the precedent of female land ownership established in the Spanish period, she received from Monroe some prime real estate in the center of the fledging town and reaped handsome profits from it. In her long life on the South Plains of West Texas she lived to experience the dawn of the modern age, participating in the promotion of Progressive Era ideas through Lubbock politics. At the center of these ideas were the concepts of liberty and social justice.

Challenging the status quo and effecting social and political change remained dominant themes in the lives of West Texas women. As they broke down barriers and forged new avenues, new opportunities emerged in the realms of education, journalism, medicine, economics, politics, and the military. Women's organizations in West Texas emerged as important centers for social interaction and activities.

Women's clubs had become increasingly popular as the frontier era waned. In 1897 the Texas Federation of Women's Clubs reported twenty-one registered literary clubs. By 1901, the total had increased to 132, and by the eve of World War II, 1,200 clubs existed on the official list. Statewide, the clubs totaled membership of more than 60,000 women. Literary clubs developed early on as a key component of these organizations and remain a valuable source today for understanding the culture of women in the region. For many women, literary clubs provided opportunities, unavailable elsewhere, for intellectual growth and expression that fulfilled social and intellectual needs. Though many such clubs existed in West Texas, two deserve mention here: the Manuscript Club of Wichita Falls and the Panhandle Pen Women of Amarillo.

The Manuscript Club, founded in 1922, provided a creative outlet and supportive environment for women, especially for those who grappled with feelings of isolation and alienation. The organization afforded women a sense of liberation, even if social and political constraints remained intact. Although some of the members claimed status as native West Texans, most had migrated to the region. Fania Kruger, for example, a club member, had moved to Wichita Falls after consenting to an arranged marriage, which had resulted in her relocation. A Russian Jewish immigrant, she eventually wrote poems reflecting themes that related to her personal background. Her work attracted international attention during and after World War II.

Betty Holland Wiesepape, author of *Lone Star Chapters: The Story of Texas Literary Clubs*, observed in retrospect that "Women's literary clubs may have been the primary creative outlet for some of the region's most intelligent citizens."[4] Certainly, Laura Hamner (1871–1978) and Phebe Warner (1866–1936) fit that assertion. Pioneers of a different brand than Sallie Reynolds Matthews or Molly Goodnight on the range frontier, Hamner and Warner, with four other women, established the Panhandle Pen Women of Amarillo in April 1919 and forged careers in Texas journalism and social activism. Their footprints on the modern development of the Texas Panhandle remain evident today.

Activities of members of the Panhandle Pen Women indicate that their lives were marked by a great deal of freedom and independence. Hamner fit this pattern, having been in the early twentieth century most likely the lone woman in a large group of men who went by train from Texas to the Oklahoma Panhandle ("No Man's Land," as it was sometimes called, a place favored by outlaws on the run) to claim land in that sometimes wild and untamed place. She remained in Oklahoma for some years, residing alone in a log cabin to meet homestead requirements. A writer as well as a homesteader, Hamner, who was already in her mid-fifties when she co-founded the Panhandle Pen Women in Amarillo, eventually authored nine books of poetry and nonfiction. She received literary honors from the Texas Senate, the Texas Institute of Letters, and the Texas Press Association.

Warner, like Hamner, worked diligently in West Texas, receiving recognition for her work promoting social causes, including the designation of Palo Duro Canyon as both a state and a national park. A pioneer doctor's wife, she had assisted, prior to joining in the formation of the Panhandle Pen Women, in the formation of several agrarian women's clubs, thus allowing the same creative outlet to rural women that existed for their urban counterparts. She also promoted adult education classes throughout the Panhandle.

Like Hamner and Warner, Virginia Boyd Connally, a medical doctor with a specialization in diseases of the eyes, ears, nose, and throat, pioneered the new frontiers that began to open for women in the twentieth century. A 1933 graduate of Simmons College (now Hardin-Simmons University), she enrolled in the Louisiana State University School of Medicine, completing her Doctor of Medicine degree in 1938. On September 22, 1940, the *Abilene Reporter-News* announced that the city's first female doctor was practicing medicine from her office near downtown. According to journalist Loretta Fulton, the Taylor-Jones County Medical Society elected Connally its president in 1948, and in 1960 she accepted appointment as the first female chief of staff for Hendrick Medical Center in Abilene. In addition to practicing medicine for forty-two years, Connally balanced roles as mother, wife, and active community servant. In addition, she traveled to support Baptist missionary efforts around the globe. Today, in 2012, celebrating her centennial year, Dr. Connally remains an active servant-leader in the Abilene community and continues to encourage women to pursue education and contribute positively to the world about them.

The twentieth century also saw a rise in independence and public service among minority women. Herlinda Wong Chew (ca. 1894–1939), daughter of an Aztec mother and a Chinese father, lived in Mexico and United States. She arrived in West Texas when violence near Ciudad Juárez during the Mexican Revolution after 1910 forced her family to abandon their Mexican residence for El Paso. Later she would relate stories of "crossing the Rio Grande while dodging bullets and carrying . . . small children."[5] Permission to remain in the United States lasted only briefly. Under the threat of a forced return to Juárez, Chew began researching immigration law. She borrowed law books and studied the provisions for official, permanent relocation to the United States. Hanging her hopes and the future of her family on a solitary provision allowing Chinese immigrants to enter the United States legally as merchants, she and her family opened a business in El Paso in 1921, the New China

Grocery. She continued to research and study and soon became known as a trusted expert on immigration law.

Herlinda and her husband, Antonio, traveled several times to China. Becoming aware of discrimination directed at Mexican women married to Chinese men, Chew began helping such women and their children return to Mexico. She also worked in her Texas community to improve the economic viability of shop owners, helping them to compete with the chain stores. Chew's life experience and contributions to public service brought another new dimension to the portrait of West Texas women as pioneering figures in every field of endeavor they entered.

In social activism and pivotal community leadership, African American women of West Texas have also been outstanding. The achievements of important leaders such as Mae Simmons of Lubbock, Allie Ward of Abilene, and Bernice Love Wiggins, who was born in Austin and resided for a time in El Paso, are closely connected to the communities of which they were part. Simmons is remembered as an excellent teacher and beloved leader, and Ward was a pioneer in education. Wiggins is honored even today as one of the twentieth century's most accomplished Texans.

Mae Simmons (1911–1981) taught in the Lubbock public school system from the 1930s through the 1970s. In the 1920s, with the rise of the cotton industry in West Texas, the first African American migrant farm workers arrived to seek employment. In 1920, records indicate, the total population of black citizens in Lubbock County numbered sixty-three. Within the span of a decade, however, more than 1,100 African Americans called Lubbock home. As the population grew during the era of strict racial segregation in public life, the demand for educators willing to serve in segregated schools likewise increased.

In 1939, Simmons relocated with her husband to Lubbock. Soon she began work as a substitute teacher in the newly established Dunbar School, an African American institution. Upon completion of her bachelor's degree and with strong encouragement from the founder and leader of Dunbar School, Edward C. Scruggs, Simmons joined the faculty as a full-time fourth-grade teacher.

Simmons had multiple opportunities to teach elsewhere, such as in the Houston area, where she had completed her bachelor's degree. Something about West Texas, however, pulled her back to Lubbock. Eventually she served as principal of the Ella Iles Elementary School, and she remained as well an active community servant in Lubbock.

Allie Ward (1899–1981), of Abilene, also an educator, was born in Weatherford and received her bachelor's degree from Prairie View A&M University. In 1921, she accepted a teaching position in a small, two-room, segregated school on Abilene's north side. She later taught at two other schools in Abilene, including the Carter G. Woodson School. A visible and active member of her adopted community, Ward taught thirty-six years in the Abilene Independent School District. Her passion as an educator focused on elementary school children, and many Abilenians, including Jewell Pritchett (in a published memoir), remembered Ward as "one of the very best" teachers in the city.[6]

Upon her retirement in 1957 Ward opened a day care facility in her home, mainly for working-class families. At the time, she may have had the only child care program in Abilene. Her new efforts allowed mothers flexibility and freedom to work, improving their families' economic situations. When members of Abilene's First Baptist Church wanted to start a child care program as a mission effort to help low-income families, church members contacted the city's foremost expert, Ward, for guidance. When asked about her long years of service to the children and families of the city, she commented that she wished "to have known how to appropriate God's gift to me at an earlier age."[7]

Whereas Mae Simmons and Allie Ward deeply influenced their communities through education, Bernice Love Wiggins (1897–1936) of El Paso celebrated her city through her skills as a writer and as a voice for African Americans. Esteemed across the nation as among the most celebrated of black woman poets in her time, she used her skills at crafting verse in many ways. During World War I she used poetry to question the federal government's greater zeal in calling African American men into service than their white counterparts. In a famous poem, "Ethiopia Speaks," she grappled with the related moral and ethical question concerning the circumstances under which African American mothers sent their sons to war. But the majority of her poems emphasized daily life. In many ways, her work paralleled that role played by literary clubs for Anglo women.

Wiggins also addressed the horrors of lynching and on that point joined her voice with other writers, including Countee Cullen, Langston Hughes, and Zora Neale Hurston. She must be placed among the great writers of the Harlem Renaissance. In 1925 she published *Tuneful Tales,* a collection of more than one hundred poems, a powerful literary work that brought to light important issues about the life of black Americans, whose freedom remained at stake during the her era, the twentieth century.

Many other women writers have captured the beauties of West Texas, its rugged environment, and the charm of its people. Like Wiggins, authors such as Dorothy Scarborough (1878–1935), Loula Grace Erdman (1898–1976), and Jane Gilmore Rushing (1925–1997) left a strong literary imprint on the region. Today, nearly a century after it first appeared, Scarborough's novel *The Wind* (1925) continues to ignite discussion in conversations about the West Texas environment. The book was published anonymously to boost publicity, but Scarborough's powerful descriptions of the wind, the heat, and the vast space of the Rolling Plains, near Sweetwater, prompted readers to speculate that the author was male. Elements of climate play roles in the story as villainous creations, attempting to wear down a woman's resolve to settle in such a harsh land.

Scarborough's book drew immediate response from Judge R. C. Crane, then-president of the West Texas Historical Association, who challenged her austere depiction of the region, using major Texas newspapers as his forum. In defense of her work Scarborough responded, "Has the West Texas wind got on your nerves, Mr. Crane, and the sand blinded you to the difference between a novel and a historical treatise?"[8] Exchanges between the two culminated in Crane's taking Scarborough on a tour of West Texas for the purpose of demonstrating to the author her errors. Their conversation during the trip ended ironically and abruptly upon the arrival of a West Texas "norther," precisely the kind of wind that she had portrayed in her novel. Metro-Goldwyn-Mayer released a film version of the book in 1928, one of the last silent films issued by the company. Both the book and the film remain classics.

Loula Grace Erdman contributed to the West Texas literary tradition in a long writing career spanning the 1930s until nearly the time of her death in1976, her publications most notable for a lively series of novels for children.

She migrated to the Texas Panhandle in 1950 and taught there in a variety of capacities, ultimately settling into a position at West Texas State University in Canyon. Her works gave voice to the plight of homesteaders in the Panhandle and represented at the time of their writing a departure from popular themes that highlighted cowboys and ranch life. Adding to the appeal of her stories, Erdman interviewed Panhandle residents and incorporated their stories into her fiction. Her novels, which often feature women of different types and backgrounds, offer readers a varied perspective on Panhandle pioneers.

Jane Gilmore Rushing began her literary in her forties, in the 1960s, and published through 1992, some five years before her death. She is recognized for producing novels and short stories that evoke universal themes through a West Texas perspective and has been praised by notable scholars and writers on Texas women's biographies such as Lou Halsell Rodenberger. Rushing captured life and history from a woman's point of view and set most of her fiction on the Rolling Plains during the latter part of the state's frontier era. In her writings she endeavored to paint a truthful picture of people and place, often taking readers through stories of pain and abuse, and relationships outside of the social norms. Although she never left West Texas to promote her works, Doubleday, which published a number of her books, recognized Rushing as a major author. The well know literary critic James Ward Lee included her *Against the Moon* (1968) in his *Classics of Texas Literature* (1987). With Scarborough and Erdman, Rushing stands among the most sensitive literary portraitists of West Texas culture and life.

West Texas women also contributed to American society in ways far removed from literature and intellectual life. World War II marked a watershed for women in West Texas and across the country. Serving the United States during the war, for example, were such all-female military groups as the Women's Army Corps (WAC) and the Women Airforce Service Pilots (WASP). Although until then these kinds of military service had been closed to them, women participated through the WAC and WASP directly in military aspects of the war effort. The West Texas town of Sweetwater is said to have served as "the only all-woman air base in history."[9] More than 25,000 people applied for positions at the newly established Avenger Field, but only 1,074 women passed the requisite examinations. WASP airwomen worked in a variety of support roles related to the United States Army's defense efforts. All totaled, these female pilots logged 60 million miles of flight.

These contributions to military service during the war extended far beyond the boundaries of West Texas and laid the foundation for future generations of women to serve, work, and make a positive difference in the American armed forces and in other professions and institutions previously closed to women. During its existence WASP in particular served in integral ways to protect the entire world, its impact reaching far beyond Sweetwater's Avenger Field and the Southern Plains of Texas.

In addition to military service, West Texas women have increasingly participated in local and state government as elected officials. Two recent and notable examples are Debra McCartt of Amarillo and Susan King of Abilene. McCartt, having served Amarillo on the city commission from 2001 to 2005, made a successful bid for mayor in 2007. Described as a "lively and tireless campaigner who projected a dynamic image of confidence and sophistication,"[10] she upset millionaire Jerry Hodge, who had served as mayor twenty-five years earlier, to become the first female mayor of Amarillo.

King won a hotly contested race for the District 71 seat in the Texas House of Representatives. Today, in 2014, as the first woman to represent the region in that position, she brings to the table a medical background with a strong record of community service. Her work in Austin as a representative has focused on health care, community service, and education. One state law she championed, proposed by a school child in her district, required seat belts on all Texas school buses. This record of attention to health and school issues has placed King at the forefront of efforts to defend and protect future generations of young people.

West Texas women, like other women in the state, have clearly taken leadership roles of all kinds in the past and in the present day. They have taken initiatives in promoting kindergarten programs for children, saving parks and canyons for future Texans, forcing changes on political issues, influencing the state's economy in positive ways, starting their own businesses, and organizing groups for the benefit of women. West Texas women drove wagons, guided herds, built shelters, practiced medicine, raised children, buried husbands, and founded and managed ranches.

They wrote, sang, acted, taught, farmed or ranched, piloted, fought, built, elected, governed, judged, represented, and defended. Many of their names receive slight or even no mention in our regional and state histories, but the few appearing in these pages represent countless others who effected monumental change, the benefits of which people continue to reap on the giant side of Texas.

## NOTES

1. Cited in Sylvia Ann Grider and Lou Halsell Rodenberger, eds., *Texas Women Writers: A Tradition of Their Own* (College Station: Texas A&M University Press, 1997), 161.

2. Sallie Reynolds Matthews, *Interwoven: A Pioneer Chronicle* (College Station: Texas A&M University Press, 1936), 39–41.

3. James M. Smallwood, "Anna McAdams Slaughter," in Sara Massey, ed., *Texas Women on the Cattle Trails* (College Station: Texas A&M University Press, 2006), 175. Both Smallwood and historian Joyce Gibson Roach have noted that women in the early West could complete almost any task. Their skills and contributions were not only accepted by their fathers, husbands, and brothers but also encouraged and appreciated. See also Roach's *The Cowgirls* (Houston: Cordovan, 1977; Denton: University of North Texas Press, 1990) and her edited *This Place of Memory: A Texas Perspective* (Denton: University of North Texas Press, 1992).

4. Betty Holland Wiesepape, *Lone Star Chapters: The Story of Texas Literary Clubs* (College Station: Texas A&M University, 2004), 36.

5. Marilyn Dell Brady, *The Asian Texans* (College Station: Texas A&M University Press, 2004), 22–23.

6. Jewell G. Pritchett, *The Black Community in Abilene* (Abilene, Tex.: Pritchett Publications, 1984), 68–69.

7. Pritchett, *Black Community in Abilene,* 68–79.

8. Cited in Sylvia Ann Grider, "The Showdown between Dorothy Scarborough and Judge R. C. Crane," *West Texas Historical Association Yearbook* 63 (1986), 5–13.

9. Ruthe Winegarten, *Texas Women, A Pictorial History: From Indians to Astronauts* (Austin: Eakin Press, 1986), 130.

10. Paul H. Carlson, *Amarillo: The Story of a Western Town* (Lubbock: Texas Tech University Press, 2006), 223.

# FOR FURTHER READING

Burnett, Georgellen. *We Just Toughed It Out: Women on the Llano Estacado*. El Paso: University of Texas at El Paso, 1990.

Crawford, Ann Fears, and Crystal Sasse Ragsdale. *Women in Texas: Their Lives, Their Experiences, Their Accomplishments*. Austin: State House Press, 1992.

Exley, Jo Ella Powell, ed. *Texas Tears and Texas Sunshine: Voices of Frontier Women*. College Station: Texas A&M University Press, 1985.

Fulton, Loretta. *Virginia Connally, M.D.: Trailblazing Physician, Woman of Faith*. Abilene, Tex.: Loretta Fulton, 2011.

Glasrud, Bruce A., and Merline Pitre, eds. *Black Women in Texas History*. College Station: Texas A&M University Press, 2008.

Grider, Sylvia Ann, and Lou Halsell Rodenberger, eds. *Texas Women Writers: A Tradition of Their Own*. College Station: Texas A&M University Press, 1997.

Massey, Sara, ed. *Texas Women on the Cattle Trails*. College Station: Texas A&M University Press, 2006.

Rodenberger, Lou Halsell, Laura Payne Butler, and Jacqueline Kolosov, eds. *Writing on the Wind: An Anthology of West Texas Women Writers*. Lubbock: Texas Tech University Press, 2005.

Steele, June M. "Phebe Warner: Community Building in the Texas Panhandle." Master's thesis, Texas Tech University, 2000.

———. "Edward Struggs and Mae Simmons: Two African American Educators and the Provisions for Black Schools in Lubbock, Texas, 1930–1970." In Bruce A. Glasrud and Paul H. Carlson, eds., *Slavery to Integration: Black Americans in West Texas*, 119–30. Abilene: State House Press, 2007.

# Part III

# POLITICAL AND ECONOMIC LIFE

C ompared with the area of Texas east of modern Interstate Highway 35, West Texas is sparsely settled. Most of the region's residents live in the larger cities: El Paso, Lubbock, Amarillo, Abilene, Midland, Odessa, San Angelo, and Wichita Falls. Between the cities mostly lie wide stretches of land seemingly dominated by straight roads, mesquite- and juniper-choked rangeland mixed with oil pump jacks and towering wind turbines, cotton fields reaching across thousands of sometimes dusty acres, or, in the far southwest, mountain ranges off in the distance.

These are only some of the features that combine to make West Texas unique. The authors of the four chapters in part III explore unique traits of the region's politics, of its economic activities, and of its closeness to rural life in tandem with a surprising urbanism. In terms of a broad survey, some of the topics are presented here for the first time.

Collectively, the chapters paint a vivid portrait of how West Texas is different from the rest of the state.

# CHAPTER 10

# The Urban Centers of West Texas

*Richard B. Wright*

In many ways West Texas is a rural, agrarian region. Yet urban centers developed over the course of its history, some now quite large and with diverse populations and commerce. This chapter explores major themes evident in the history of these cities, such as growth and development, and describes important issues, such as urban land use trends and the correlation between minorities and urban spaces. Within this framework the author concentrates on the region's major urban centers: Abilene, Amarillo, Lubbock, Midland, Odessa, and San Angelo, all located on the southern Great Plains; and El Paso, the unique "gateway city" at the westernmost point of West Texas, with close ties to the state of New Mexico and to Mexico itself.

At first glance, relating the theme of urbanism to the history of West Texas might seem an unpromising project, as the idea of "cities" does not leap to mind as an initial response to the mental prompt "West Texas." As noted in the introduction to this book, even in 2014 a number of West Texas counties perhaps still qualify as "frontier" areas as originally defined, having population densities of fewer than two people per square mile. In fact, nineteen counties in the region currently fit that criterion, and more counties are sure to join them in the near future as a result of ongoing population loss.

Concomitant to the rural decline, however, has been a gain in the population of the urban centers and smaller cities of West Texas. In fact, about 74 percent of the region's population resides today in a group of seven cities that represent a small part of the country's 363 Metropolitan Statistical Areas (MSAs): El Paso (649,121), Lubbock (229,573), Amarillo (190,695), Abilene (117,063), Odessa (99,940), Midland (111,147), and San Angelo (93,200). At the turn of the twenty-first century, the proportion of the nation's population living in metropolitan areas was 79.8 percent. Thus despite the relatively low total population of West Texas as a region, the distribution of that population was still closely comparable to the general national trend—and with few exceptions the region's seven metro areas continue to grow at a healthy rate.

The historical impression of a primarily rural tenor to West Texas life deserves some modification. Consider, for example, that the U.S. Census Bureau defines as an "urban area" any town with a population of 2,500 or more and a core population density of at least 1,000 people per square mile. In West Texas dozens of cities and towns meet that Census Bureau criterion but are not a part of any MSA. Many such towns, when their populations contain between 10,000 and 50,000 people, have also been categorized since 2003 by the Census Bureau as being Micropolitan Statistical Areas (μSAs). Fourteen of the nation's 576 micropolitan areas are located in West Texas.[1]

Clearly, the region's urban centers and the idea of "urbanism" provide especially relevant perspectives on the history and development of West Texas. David McComb has pointed out in *The Handbook of Texas Online* that "the history of city building is one of the most significant themes in Lone Star history," even if this fact is "often unrecognzed."[2] Texas historiography and literature have always noticed how the state uniquely blends aspects of both the South and the West, yet perhaps the frame of reference most useful in an initial examination of West Texas is its geographical identity as a part of the Great Plains—even though that focus would exclude El Paso and a good part of the Trans-Pecos. What is most revealing about the Great Plains from the perspective of modern urbanism might at first appear counterintuitive: the thriving cities of the plains are at its periphery and not at its core. Surprisingly, only five metropolitan areas are positioned fully *within* the Great Plains of the United States and Canada that have populations of more than 200,000. West Texas cities Lubbock (229,573) and Amarillo (190,695) are two of them; the other three are Wichita (382,368), Saskatoon (222,189), and Regina (193,100).

All around the perimeter of the Great Plains region, though, are even larger metropolitan areas. Denver, Austin, San Antonio, Dallas/Fort Worth, and Kansas City represent just a few of them. These larger locales are defined as "gateway" cities to the Great Plains, traditionally having served as staging locations for the processing and shipment of commodities produced within the immense central area of the plains. Fort Worth, for example, was historically prominent in the livestock industry in the story of West Texas. But in some important ways the deck became stacked against the non-peripheral cities fully contained within the Plains as industrial capitalism began to interlink more and more of the continent through trade, transportation, and communication.

El Paso, of course, was a significant exception, precisely because it was both a gateway city and an international crossroads community rather than just a town at the periphery of the Great Plains. When new railway routes branched out from Fort Worth in the 1880s, linking towns like Abilene and Pecos into the system was not so much a goal as it was a by-product of the desire to complete a line to El Paso, which not only formed a hub on a major trade route into Mexico but also was positioned on the least topographically difficult pathway for rail lines to pass through the Intermountain West to California.

Accessibility to rich mining deposits in the Southwest and Mexico, bountiful natural resources, and access to plenty of cheap Mexican labor also helped El Paso to boom over the course of the nineteenth and early twentieth centuries. It grew from an arrangement of sleepy villages, military encampments, and ranch communities along the left bank of the Rio Grande, opposite the original colonial town named El Paso del Norte, into a city of almost 40,000 by 1910. The arrival of the Mexican Revolution on the city's doorstep at that time contributed much to the further burgeoning of the population to almost 80,000 by 1925. The onset of Prohibition in 1920 enhanced tourism in the area as it did elsewhere along the U.S.–Mexican border. The military has also long been a staple of El Paso's economy, and refining and smelting historically augmented the industrial growth of the area.

The city's development has tilted and steered in a bewildering set of ways. First, it grew through land additions to Anson Mills's original plat for real estate development, mostly to the northwest and east of downtown, and then later in all manner of plat and lot shapes, encouraged by the growth in use of the private automobile. The regular square gridiron blocks of the 1859 plat have been replaced in some areas by long, rectangular blocks, sometimes bisected by back alleys to facilitate utility easements. These rectangular blocks also allowed more flexibility in tailoring lot purchases to the needs of the customer.

Elsewhere in the city lie subdivisions where streets neatly echo a shared set of curves. A common pattern by the 1950s, it was designed to prevent excessive speeds as drivers passed through neighborhoods. The streets in subdivisions near Fort Bliss, for example, might be intricately intertwined, but they follow orderly patterns. Colonias (unplanned housing aggregations) create a checkerboard along the plain between Interstate 10 and the Rio Grande, obscuring to some extent the original appearance and fabric of venerable colonial communities like San Elizario and Ysleta.

El Paso's exceptional character as an urban center, as compared to the other large cities of West Texas, is augmented in that the city in a sense lies beyond West Texas. After all, the geographic center of New Mexico—just north and west of West Texas—actually lies farther east longitudinally than El Paso.

Back toward the center of the state at about the same latitude as El Paso lies the town of Abilene, for almost a century the informal capital of West Texas. The Texas and Pacific Railway promoted and developed Abilene in the early 1880s. Some breaks and discontinuities in the city's physical organization, between the northern and southern halves of the downtown street grid, are a result of the east–west axis originally established by the railway.

Abilene's Parramore Addition, a neighborhood adjacent to downtown, contains noteworthy homes of the early twentieth century. The advent of streetcars about 1908 and the arrival of automobiles in the same era led over the ensuing decades to the platting of other additions to the west and south. The street layouts for subsequent developments, like River Oaks/

Brookhollow, lying even farther from downtown, reflect the suburbanized layouts of curving streets and irregularly shaped lots that we also see in similar areas in El Paso.

From its earliest years, Abilene had a strong reformist spirit. The city was "dry"—it outlawed the use of alcoholic beverages—from 1903 to 1978. It was among the first municipalities in Texas to adopt a home rule charter, and it set up a modified version of the commission form of city government in 1911, a model first adopted in Galveston in 1901. Although no longer in wide use today, this "Texas Idea" of the commission approach to governance was seized upon by Progressive Era reformers nationally.

As in other cities, women in Abilene had a lot to do with the city's reforming spirit. Particularly in the areas of culture and morality, even before they were enfranchised in the years after the First World War, women's strong influence on public affairs contributed to the city's urban identity and quality of life in important ways. The city's Shakespeare Club, founded 1883, is recognized, for example, by the Texas Federation of Women's Clubs as the state's oldest study club.

In general, the relatively high level of cultural achievement found in large West Texas cities must be attributed to members, both male and female, of philanthropically inclined families residing there. All the large urban centers in West Texas have sustained successful professional organizations in the performing arts since at least the mid-twentieth century, and the visual arts are increasingly well represented. Families in Abilene, working with the late Pop artist Clint Hamilton, an Abilene native, have been instrumental in the city's recently having received one of the first "Cultural District" designations granted by the state of Texas. The El Paso Museum of Art has housed a significant regional donation from the venerable Kress Collection of Italian Art since the late 1940s. In Lubbock, the late Helen DeVitt Jones played an instrumental role in the growth of the Museum of Texas Tech University in all its varied facets; a new auditorium and sculpture court bear her name.

The urban centers of West Texas are in part still very young in comparison to their counterparts in some other areas of the United States. As a result they may not have embraced as fully as others such national trends as the City Beautiful Movement of the late nineteenth and early twentieth centuries, or the urban renewal trends that swept the country several decades later. But Abilene, El Paso, and Lubbock, led by their prominent citizens, are examples of cities that have taken seriously their responsibilities as stewards of their citizens' patrimony and their future quality of life.

In the Texas Panhandle, Amarillo's location in relation to the defining escarpments of the Llano Estacado, or Staked Plains, gave it a geographic advantage in the early era of railroad routing and construction, much as El Paso's location had proven essential as a gateway to territories west of Texas. In 1887 the Fort Worth and Denver City Railway (FW&DC) brought a line in Clarendon, in the southeast Panhandle, northwestward into Potter County, thus avoiding a steep climb up either the caprock or Canadian River escarpments of the Llano Estacado. Amarillo, the county seat, soon became the major shipping point and marketing center for cattle in the region. The original town site had moved a bit east by 1890.

As in other West Texas cities, new real estate development soon followed growth at the city center, especially once streetcar service began in 1908. Like those of El Paso and Abilene, Amarillo's street plan, as one moves away from the city center, shifts from a pattern of regular, square blocks in the downtown area and urban center, to longer, rectangular blocks and less regularity of form, both in block size and in orientation to the original grid. Wolflin Place, for example, was platted in the typical gridded pattern about 1923, but the adjoining Wolflin Estates was laid out with a park-like, radial plan in 1927.

San Angelo's original plan, dating from about 1870, began to extend largely along a southeast–northwest axis moving away from the North Concho River as the city began to grow in the late nineteenth and early twentieth centuries. As with Amarillo, subsequent suburban growth sprawled to the southwest with the emergence of the automobile, particularly in an area that sits between parks and lakes that have been developed to the west of town.

Two railroads, arriving in 1888 and 1909, greatly enhanced San Angelo's role as a cattle market in south central West Texas. When woolgrowers also became a significant part of the area's economy, San Angelo soon became one of the country's leading markets for wool and mohair, as well as the country's top market for sheep. The city's population doubled, from 10,050 in 1920 to 25,308 in 1930, because of the opening of the Permian Basin oilfields. A second doubling of population over the course of the 1940s, to 52,095, came with the opening of Goodfellow Air Force Base—still a pillar of the local economy in 2014.

The history of minorities in West Texas cities has perhaps been most deeply researched in San Angelo because of the efforts of Arnoldo De León, who has taught for many years at Angelo State University. His decades of work have provided an invaluable "bottom-up" sociohistorical perspective on the urbanism of the region, despite flaws in available records resulting from neglect of minority public affairs in the city's history until recent decades. Because Anglo (non-Hispanic European American) settlement occurred in West Texas after the state's most radical period of Reconstruction had largely run its course, de facto segregation of black and Hispanic populations was well on the way to becoming institutionalized in the region by the 1880s, when San Angelo was still a young town. Segregation of people naturally implies some form of spatial separation in living arrangements, and soon, as in many American towns and cities of that era, the less desirable areas of San Angelo came to house its marginalized residents.

Despite their increasingly disadvantaged social standing by the 1880s, Mexican Americans born in Texas (or Tejanos) had predominated in the informal little settlement across from Fort Concho that predated San Angelo. With the first 1870 plat, Tejanos were still able to squat on or purchase property, because the newly laid-out town was small and struggling, with plenty of space for all. But when a new landowner took over development of San Angelo in the late 1870s, and especially once the original county seat, Ben Ficklin, was destroyed by a flood in 1882, more Anglos started moving to the new town.

This new demographic, apparently, caused increasing social tensions. As population densities continued to increase in the community, Tejanos and Anglos came into closer contact with one another. By mechanisms not always clear in the historical record, even Mexican Americans long resident in parts of the original settlement began to be relegated to neighborhoods farther away from the original core area of the town, a

trend that increased as land values rose in the older, central districts and
newcomers sought to promote the eastern half of the original settlement
as the center for the new town of San Angela (the current spelling was not
accepted until 1883). De León has suggested that the existing Tejano families in residence were ousted from their homes through several means:
by eviction, if renting; or simply driven off, if squatting and without legal
recourse; or, perhaps, by forced sale or unfair prices offered by Anglo
purchasers who took advantage of them—many Tejanos of that era who
owned their plots may have been unable to grasp the abstract potential of
land's ability to appreciate in value. Fraud and other unscrupulous means
were undoubtedly employed as well to free up real estate in the proposed
new downtown.

With all this resettlement new *barrios* emerged, north across the tracks
and south of the river. In the northern barrio, named Santa Fe, lots had
been sold to Tejanos at discount prices because initial sales had been
slow—the area had been developed around 1890 as an addition to the
newly planned city. The barrio was more than a mile from downtown.
Between Santa Fe and downtown another new enclave emerged, this one
housing African Americans, although little seems to be known about how
that came to be.

The distinct zonal separation of races within San Angelo and other cities of West Texas was not simply an act of imposition from above. As De
León observes, non-Anglos tended to congregate much as Anglos did, and
they did so even before increasing prejudice, the rising price of real estate,
and changing demographics forced them into sequestered neighborhoods.
Newcomers would gravitate to the parts of town where others like them
lived, where customs and cultural practices would be familiar. Anglos, for
their part, were sufficiently pragmatic about the need for a united community to ensure survival in a tough environment that they adopted a
laissez-faire approach to the cultural otherness of the minorities in their
midst. As long as basic public policies (for example, against gambling or
cockfighting) were not being blatantly violated, tolerance was the norm.

Even though racial and ethnic tensions existed in the economic and
political arenas of West Texas, in social and cultural realms differences
were largely respected by all. This dual situation existed in part because

*Downtown Lubbock, 1942, just as the city entered its period of rapid growth, Lubbock became one of the fastest growing cities in the nation in the 1940s and 1950s. (Courtesy Southwest Collection, Texas Tech University)*

racial and ethnic minorities seemed less interested in challenging Anglo majorities in mainstream social and cultural practices, preferring to per-petuate their own customs and social behaviors instead. It is worth noting that desegregation of schools occurred in some areas of West Texas fairly quickly, promptly, and with little fanfare. Such was the case, for example, with Howard College in Big Spring.

Lubbock, Odessa, and Midland are all fully twentieth-century cities, having reached maturity a generation or so after most of the large cities of West Texas. Thus their urban histories are somewhat less varied, but what they may lack in terms of historic accretion and variation is made up for in vitality and versatility. By the end of the 1940s, for example, Lubbock, founded in 1890, was the second-fastest growing city in the United States (after Albuquerque). In fact it has been said (without too much exaggera-tion) that "almost all up-to-date American cities west of the Mississippi are variations on a basic prototype, and that prototype is Lubbock, Texas. . . . on a small scale Lubbock tells us what those new [Sunbelt] cities look like."[3] The expansive feel of a place like downtown Lubbock, with its wide, flat, perfectly straight streets, reflects somewhat more emphatically than most other West Texas cities the car-oriented phenomena so typical of the post–World War II era. This impression of openness is not an illusion: the average 1990 population densities of all metro areas in Texas were almost 10 percent lower than for the nation at large.

On the west side of Lubbock, the campus of Texas Tech University and the former Reese Air Force Base form an axis along 4th Street. This axis may have the potential to form a component of a "multiple nuclei" pattern of urban development. In this pattern each nucleus is somewhat like a unique block in a patchwork quilt of irregular rectilinear zones in apparently random interrelationships, ranged around a dominant motif—the central business district—and exhibiting one or more commercial-industrial nodes of various sizes, each with its own complex of businesses and land-use zones.[4] A university district and a military base, each with its peripheral commercial services, and are both excellent examples.

Urban centers like Lubbock that have undertaken the bulk of their development since World War II often demonstrate a tendency to spawn such multiple centers of activity beyond the downtown city center. The largest Texas cities and metroplexes, including El Paso, reflect a blend of this "multiple nuclei" pattern and an older "sector" form, in which different types of land use radiate outward in all directions—but in irregular, varied, vaguely wedge-like sectors—while maintaining a direct connection with the "hub" of the central business district.[5]

The "sector" model could explain the directional growth of suburbs in some areas rather than others, because of factors like cheap land acquisition and relative ease of expanding public services. The implication here is that in the sector model, there appear to be more radially coherent connections between sectors, and to the central business district. In the multiple-nuclei model, which describes a pattern that developed later in time, there is not always the same sense of organic connectivity between the different nuclei or nodes. Multiple-nuclei nodes of activity may include or create factors that at first seem random, or beyond the rationalism of city planning—such as real estate speculation and venture capital investments, which are generally given a freer rein, in regulatory terms, in Texas than elsewhere.

Lubbock, sitting alone in the midst of the plains, has also been described, with admiring irony, as a "city that never should have been."[6] Yet the Permian Basin cities of Midland and Odessa represent even more improbable enterprises. Their metro area populations combined may have almost exactly matched the total for Lubbock alone in 2009, such that each obviously makes a lesser impression than Lubbock in terms of spatial expanse. But in terms of high-rise aggregation the story is different.

One of the most common remarks made about Midland is how impressive the skyline is for a city that until recently had never topped 100,000 inhabitants. The famous twelve-story Petroleum Building of 1928–29 was completed less than a decade after Midland's population stood at less than 1,800. Street paving had only recently begun in the area. Yet by the late 1950s, Midland had eight skyscrapers and more than 2 million square feet of office space—with a population of only about 60,000. The city, which was basically a town of shacks in the early 1880s, took aim at San Angelo from its earliest days, arguing that it should be the seat for the original Tom Green County because it was closer to the county center and on a rail line.

Instead, Midland soon became the seat of its own county (also named Midland). And, in the late 1920s, when the main oil activity in West Texas shifted farther to the west, Midland supplanted San Angelo as the regional management center for the sequence of Permian Basin oil booms that would make the region as internationally famous as its corresponding busts would make it notorious.

The increasingly technocratic thinking that marked the oil business in the twentieth century also affected Midland's public image. Modern technology, together with many of its residents' lack of roots in the Permian Basin region, seems to have enhanced a civic mentality oriented to the present and the future, clear-eyed and unsentimental. This attitude may have proved especially receptive to the rigorously functional aspects of modernist design—although more for high-image corporate headquarters, perhaps, than for the comforts of home.

If Midland has become a corporate and managerial headquarters with correspondingly tonier, capacious ranch-house suburbs, Odessa is its blue-collar complement, a major regional center for services and supply. This situation came about in part because during the twentieth-century boom in the petroleum industry Ector County (Odessa is the county seat) undertook an aggressive program to build roads to the oilfields. The city enjoys a preponderance of suburban housing developments with curving streets and irregular lots. Many of Odessa's houses were built fairly quickly and cheaply to accommodate the tremendous influx of workers during the midcentury boom phases. The city today, in the early twenty-first century, retains its flavor of heavy industrial and engineering services but now (like most twenty-first-century cities) courts greater diversification.

What allowed these West Texas cities to succeed, and not others in the region, especially since cities have generally not prospered in the interior of the Great Plains? Three cases here are special: El Paso, not a plains city, has tremendous locational advantages and access to important resources and labor. Midland and Odessa, though plains cities, sit near enormous reserves of petroleum in an otherwise out-of-the-way location on terrain unpromising for agriculture. As for the other four cities, though in varying degrees interior to the West Texas Plains or near the edge of the Edwards Plateau, they all originated as county seats. They gained early access to railroads, even younger Lubbock, which sits on the eastern doorstep of Texas's "Last Frontier" (Bailey, Lamb, Cochran, and Hockley counties). Three of the cities were also regional leaders in farming or stock raising: Lubbock in cotton (thanks to the development of the Ogallala Aquifer); Amarillo in cattle; and San Angelo in sheep, wool, mohair, and cattle. Petroleum played an important sustaining role at crucial times in all four, although, interestingly, it never dominated their local economies for any extended length of time.

These successful city foundations and the urban quality of life they produced begat other economic benefits and further growth. They all became important as transportation and service centers for their areas, and they all enjoyed the arrival of light industries. Most important, perhaps, each courted and obtained institutional bonds with the military and with higher education, especially so in the case of Abilene and Lubbock, as well as in smaller towns like Plainview and Canyon.

Growth rates suggest that the future is bright for West Texas metro areas. The ability to adapt will be crucial as the current century unfolds, but the history of these relatively young cities so far suggests that their ability to adapt is unquestionable.

## NOTES

1. Del Rio, Andrews, and Dumas are among the few growing micropolitans in the region. Although the positive impact of modernization on the *growth* of metropolitan areas is a time-honored theme in American historiography, its concomitant, as one historian has noted, has been very little studied so far: the correspondingly negative impact of modernization over time on the growth rates of small cities, towns, and rural areas generally. See Richard O. Davies, *Main Street Blues: The Decline of Small-Town America* (Columbus: Ohio State University Press, 1998), x.

2. David G. McComb, "Urbanization," http://www.tshaonline.org/handbook/online/articles/hyunw (accessed August 1, 2013).

3. J. B. Jackson, "The Vernacular City," *Center: A Journal for Architecture in America* 1 (1985), 27–43 (quotation, 27).

4. Terry G. Jordan, with John L. Bean, Jr., and William M. Holmes, *Texas: A Geography* (Boulder: Westview Press, 1984), 240.

5. Jordan, et al., *Texas: A Geography,* 240.

6. Lewis E. Hill, "Industry, Transportation, and Finance," in Lawrence L. Graves, ed., *Lubbock: From Town to City* (Lubbock: West Texas Museum Association, 1986), 56.

## FOR FURTHER READING

"Cities and Towns." In *Encyclopedia of the Great Plains*, edited by David J. Wishart, 149–89. Lincoln: University of Nebraska Press, 2004.

De León, Arnoldo. *San Angeleños: Mexican Americans in San Angelo, Texas.* San Angelo: Fort Concho Museum Press / Mulberry Avenue Books, 1985.

———. *Racial Frontiers: Africans, Chinese, and Mexicans in Western America, 1848–1890.* Albuquerque: University of New Mexico Press, 2002.

Miller, Char. "Sunbelt Texas." In *Texas through Time,* edited by Robert Calvert and Walter Buenger, 279–309. College Station: Texas A&M University Press, 1991.

Olien, Diana Davids, and Roger M. Olien. *Oil in Texas: The Gusher Age, 1895–1945*. Austin: University of Texas Press, 2002.

Sledge, Robert W. *A People, a Place: The Story of Abilene*. Buffalo Gap, Tex.: State House Press, 2008.

Timmons, Wilbert H. *El Paso: A Borderlands History*. 2d ed. El Paso: Texas Western Press, 2004.

Veselka, Robert E. *The Courthouse Square in Texas*. Edited by Kenneth E. Foote. Austin: University of Texas Press, 2000.

CHAPTER 11

# The Political Culture of West Texas

*Sean P. Cunningham*

In the period after the Civil War West Texans for the most part voted for Democratic candidates. At present, from the later twentieth into the twenty-first century, the situation is very different: Republican candidates often dominate in state and national elections. Emphasizing broad issues and memorable personalities, this chapter provides an interpretive synthesis of the region's shifting political culture.

On January 20, 2009, just hours after attending Barack Obama's inauguration as the 44th President of the United States, George W. Bush boarded a plane and flew from Washington, D.C., to Midland, Texas. Shortly after his arrival he delivered the first speech of his career as former commander-in-chief. As he had done so often during his tenure in the Oval Office, Bush used the occasion to draw nostalgically upon his West Texas heritage. "The values that Laura and I learned here in West Texas have guided us," he told his audience. "This is the place where people treat each other with decency and respect . . . and where character counts an awful lot." Accepting the warm welcome of his Midland supporters, Bush praised the region and its people while admitting that, although it had been a "joy" to serve his nation as president, "nothing compares to a West Texas sunset." No one present that day could doubt that the often vilified world leader had returned home and was finally among friends.[1]

Bush's intent during this first post-presidential appearance may not have been to explain the political culture of West Texas, but as is often the case in the world of politics, intent matters less than perception. His stop in Midland that day in a sense completed a full circle: it was from Midland that he had begun his own inaugural journey to the White House eight years before. On January 18, 2001, just weeks after Texas Speaker of the House (and fellow West Texan) Pete Laney had introduced him as the nation's official president-elect, and unable to foresee the chaos and controversy that would plague his administration over the next eight years, Bush described his rise to the presidency as an adventure rooted in a "spirit of possibility . . . as big as the West Texas sky." Sporting a white Stetson hat, he promised the audience of some 10,000, who had assembled in Midland to see him off to Washington, "I'm going to take a lot of Midland and a lot of Texas with me up there. . . . It is here where I learned what it means to be a good neighbor, at backyard barbecues or just chatting across the fence. It is here in West Texas where I learned to trust in God."[2]

To both these Midland audiences, eight years apart, Bush communicated volumes about how conservative Texans, especially in West Texas, have viewed and continue to view the world around them. Such perspectives inform the culture of West Texas politics—where the quintessentially western values of rugged individualism, faith, family, and perseverance have long been ingredients for political success. But despite the prevailing winds of modern conservatism that have shaped West Texas political culture over recent decades, the region's political history, and its corresponding identity, is more complex.

This chapter is about some of the stereotypes and complexities that have defined the political culture of West Texas. It provides an interpretive synthesis of that political culture, not a comprehensive political survey. It illuminates several of the issues, personalities, and images that position West Texas within the broader political history of the state and nation. From this standpoint, rather than seeing West Texas politics as the exclusive product of one issue, idea, or impulse, it is more accurate to say that the political culture of West Texas has been affected by the interwoven and often complementary themes of inclusion and exclusion, race and ethnicity, economics and demography, and an ideological worldview, rooted in an imagined past, that conveniently perceives the giant side of Texas conveniently more western than southern.

With some important exceptions this ideological worldview, for most voting West Texans, has long been shaped by conservatism, the sources of which are varied and abundant. The region has always been more sparsely populated, at least by Anglos (non-Hispanic whites), than other parts of Texas. The situation has contributed to and reinforced a political culture that prioritizes notions of individuality, antistatism, and stereotypically western conceptualizations of the frontier, adventure, self-sufficiency, and survival. Some historians have seen in West Texas a form of hyperconservatism, whereby the only acceptable responsibility of government is to protect private business interests by preserving the free market against burdensome regulations. At least rhetorically, and at least by the voting Anglo majority, government intervention typically has been resisted or flatly opposed. Even West Texans' response to an issue as essential to the region as groundwater conservation has been driven, in large part, by an impulse to retain local control and avoid state or federal intervention.

West Texas farmers who broadly denounce government intervention must nevertheless tread lightly, considering the heavily subsidized and regulated nature of federal agriculture policy in the region since at least the 1930s. Yet self-regulation has not always worked very well in West Texas, particularly for racial and ethnic minorities. One thing it does accomplish is the preservation of a perception that individualism and independence are at the forefront of West Texans' political value system. Such attitudes remain prevalent in popular depictions of West Texas. Examples include the 1989 CBS television miniseries *Lonesome Dove* and the long-running musical *TEXAS*, which can still be enjoyed almost nightly every summer at the Palo Duro Canyon State Park Amphitheater. These spectacles communicate to West Texans—as well as to the "foreigners" from around the world who are exposed to such images—that the people who settled the region carved out a life for themselves fueled by sheer grit and determination, fighting off hostile Indians while resisting the advancing and intrusive reach of both state and national governments. This commitment, loosely conceived and oft-repeated in popular culture, reinforces many West Texans' sense of political conservatism as inherently protectionist and preservationist.

Not surprisingly, these conservative impulses have also fueled a common hostility toward outsiders, loosely defined. It was a lesson that even the young George W. Bush, today certainly the region's most well-known conservative political figure, had to learn the hard way. In 1978, when he waged his first campaign for public office, seeking a congressional seat from the Nineteenth District, he was defeated by Kent Hance, a conservative Democrat (and future Chancellor of Texas Tech University). In a campaign full of intrigue, Hance ran the following radio advertisement, questioning the regional bona fides of his GOP opponent:

> In 1961, when Kent Hance graduated from Dimmitt High School in the 19th congressional district, his opponent George W. Bush was attending Andover Academy in Massachusetts. In 1965, when Kent Hance graduated from Texas Tech, his opponent was at Yale University. And while Kent Hance graduated from the University of Texas Law School, his opponent—get this, folks—was attending Harvard. We don't need someone from the Northeast telling us what our problems are.[3]

For Bush in 1978, not being perceived as authentically West Texan might well have made the difference between winning and losing. The product of a Connecticut family and an Ivy League education, he seemed far less West Texan in 1978 than did his opponent. Given a choice between two relatively conservative candidates, voters (primarily in Lubbock, Midland, Odessa, and the surrounding areas), chose a Democrat who seemed more homegrown.

The concept of the "outsider" further informs the volatile dynamic of inclusion and exclusion that animates the ideological worldview of most conservative West Texans. The history of Texas Tech University, the region's dominant institution of higher education, provides a prominent example. The very first controversy arose in 1923 over its prospective location—a contest Lubbock won over several other competing West Texas communities. Perhaps the most dramatic recent equivalent has been the athletics realignment that allowed the school into the Big XII Conference in the mid-1990s, a decision made possible primarily thanks to the influence of then Lieutenant Governor Bob Bullock, who, probably even more than former Texas Governor Preston Smith, was the most politically influential Texas Tech alumnus of the late twentieth century. Texas Tech's ongoing fight for funding, recognition, and inclusion on a par with the state's two wealthiest and most prominent public universities—the University of Texas at Austin and Texas A&M University—stands as a microcosm of the broader fight waged by West Texans throughout the twentieth century: a fight to be recognized and included in state politics. Many West Texans are particularly sensitive to the politics related to the Permanent University Fund (PUF), which pumps West Texas oil revenues into the coffers of the UT and A&M systems.

The "outsider" dynamic of inclusion and exclusion is also plainly apparent in terms of race and ethnicity. Racial and ethnic issues have not shaped the politics of West Texas to the same extent that they have in East or South Texas—or in the rest of the American South, for that matter. At times in those regions, race has functioned as an almost singularly definitive component of state and local political culture. But in West Texas, demographics have had a mitigating effect. As late as the early 1960s, African Americans in West Texas comprised less than 3 percent of the state's black voting population. That statistic did not change very much in the decades after the 1960s, despite passage of the Voting Rights Act of 1965. Unquestionably, that act and the Civil Rights Act of 1964 stand together as significant breakthroughs on the path toward social, cultural, economic, and political inclusion for African Americans and other minorities, both nationally and in West Texas. However, the impact of these laws in West Texas was comparatively weaker than in other parts of Texas or the South, simply because of the relatively smaller black presence in the region. Nonetheless, the broader implications of Washington's efforts to legislate racial equality, at the very least, accelerated the migration of some West Texans out of the Democratic Party. Although it is still clear that in various ways race did play an important role in shaping the political culture of West Texas, historians may often have oversimplified and overemphasized the racial dynamics of that migration from the party. Neil Foley's analysis of racial and ethnic currents in the region's long-term history is particularly noteworthy in this context. as it demonstrates how racial and ethnic stresses intersected with issues of labor, immigration, and farm subsidization over time. His work reveals that racial and ethnic stereotypes have influenced political inclinations in the region—both subtly and overtly—for as long as Anglos have lived in West Texas.

The political career of Lawrence A. Nixon (1883–1966) offers a compelling example of the extent to which race shaped politics in West Texas during the first half of the twentieth century. During the 1920s, Nixon—an African American physician and civil rights advocate who had moved to El Paso in 1907—filed a series of legal challenges to state laws governing ballot access in Democratic primaries. By winning decisions in 1927 and 1932, Nixon paved the way for the far more sweeping victory that came for minority voting rights through *Smith v. Allwright* (also a Texas case, from Harris County), decided by the United States Supreme Court in 1944. In short, though occasionally overstated and not always fully understood within a uniquely West Texan context, race was and remains a critical component of the region's dynamics of inclusion and exclusion, and therefore of West Texas political culture more broadly.

Oil also contributed to the region's conservative political culture. Gushers and boom towns concurrently reinforced a stereotype of the region as more western than southern. Oil booms in West Texas further exposed concerns over self-regulation, democratic access to economic and political opportunity, and the region's image as a dusty, lifeless place. During the first years of the twentieth century, numerous West Texas boom towns were forced to respond to issues of rapid population growth, fears about crime, and the diversification of employment opportunities open to job seekers who were attracted to the region's vibrant economy. These communities responded in different ways, but each chose to embrace forms of regulation, usually local and discriminatory. As the Texas Railroad Commission began to assert greater influence and authority over the oil industry during the early twentieth century, the ability of small West Texas towns to self-regulate was undermined, even though the connection to larger market forces circularly reinforced locals' desire for local control—social, economic, and political.

Shaped in part by a somewhat mythologized but powerful impression of the region's history and informed by notions of nostalgia, exclusion, and race, conservatism has long dominated the political culture of West Texas. Perhaps the best reflection of this sense of an authentic, West Texas political conservatism is found in the life of J. Evetts Haley (1901–95). Haley grew up on West Texas ranches, was educated in Midland and later in Canyon at what was then West Texas Normal College (now West Texas A&M), and quickly became an influential historian, working for the Panhandle–Plains Historical Society. He later published several highly regarded studies on ranching, ranchers, and the West Texas cattle industry. In the 1930s, Haley also became an active and outspoken voice of opposition to Franklin D. Roosevelt's New Deal. He even served as chairman of the Jeffersonian Democrats of Texas—a hyperconservative faction of the already predominantly conservative Texas Democratic Party. Though he and the Jeffersonian Democrats rallied a loyal following, the faction ultimately achieved little. FDR lost some support among West Texas conservatives when he decided to run for a third term in 1940, but events overseas and continued economic troubles at home, mixed with the fierce loyalty that most West Texans still felt toward the Democratic Party, ensured that Texas would remain in Roosevelt's pocket in 1940, and again in 1944.

Haley remained politically active throughout the 1940s. His agenda was often bathed in anti-Communism as he worked to rid Texas of subversive influences, particularly from what he thought of as the secular, ivory towers of higher education. Despite having staged an unsuccessful bid for the governorship in 1956, the West Texas arch-conservative is probably best remembered, at least politically, for *A Texan Looks at Lyndon,* his scathing indictment of Lyndon Johnson, published in 1964 to coincide with the presidential campaign of that year. Ever conservative, but also insensitive to the political necessity of rationality and perceived moderation, Haley was one of West Texas's loudest and most consistently ideological voices. Throughout his life as a scholar, a rancher, and a political activist, Haley, though rarely if ever expressing the sentiments of a majority of voting West Texans, passionately articulated many of the antistatist tenets that informed both the farthest right wing and the simplest strands of mainstream, West Texas conservatism.

Reviewing Haley's life, one is also struck by his consistent use of populist, antielitist rhetoric. Whether battling intellectuals in academia or

172 POLITICAL AND ECONOMIC LIFE

bureaucrats in Washington, his writings and speeches effectively employed a powerful antiestablishment ethos. Because this ethos was malleable enough to conform to a variety of political contexts, it helped shape West Texas political culture throughout the later twentieth century.

Texas politicians have also long taken advantage of the region's antiestablishment proclivities. Like Haley in later decades, Jim "Pa" Ferguson (1871–1944), first active in the 1910s and governor of Texas 1915–17, often spoke of faceless, ivory tower intellectuals as an enemy to the common folk in West Texas. Populist rhetoric, such as that styled by Ferguson and Haley, held tremendous sway over the region's voters, so much so that it is sometimes tempting to see in Haley's life or in Ferguson's rhetoric a microcosm of West Texas politics.

It should also be noted, however, that populist, antiestablishment rhetoric has often been used in West Texas for less than conservative ends. Even a cursory overview of the history of politics in West Texas reveals that although most West Texans have long been committed conservatives, variations and exceptions have popped up from time to time, often paralleling state and national trends. This willingness to deviate from strictly conservative ideologies might be explained by seeing West Texas conservatism less as an ideology than as a practical and preservationist inclination. West Texans' pragmatic, no-nonsense approach to life has historically permeated their conservatism and allowed for occasional support of liberal variations.

For example, following the Civil War, federal troops intervened on Anglo settlers' behalf by warring with and expelling the region's Native American population after local efforts and resources were widely accepted to be unequal to the challenge. Later, conflicts between ranchers and farmers forced some West Texans to reconsider their Democratic loyalties in favor of the Populist movement, which had originated in Central Texas and became a major third-party force during the early 1890s, especially in the Great Plains counties. Affected by falling crop prices, deflationary monetary policies, perceived railroad monopolies, and an overall anxiety that stemmed from national industrialization, many West Texans flirted with opposition to the conservative state Democratic Party, seeking leadership that would reinforce local control over the economy. Put differently, there have been times when the conservative, West Texas worldview has made plenty of room for government intervention in a variety of forms.

The willingness of many West Texans to break from conservative Democratic antistatism was not an insignificant shift. As West Texans endured the political evolution that took the state away from populism and through progressivism, the reform that West Texans most obviously supported, and did so at the ballot box and through calls for regulation, was the issue of prohibition. Support for "dry" legislation came in large part from the strength of West Texas churches, the Baptist and Methodist denominations

*Harry Truman, Bess Truman, and Buford Jester, Fort Stockton, 1948, on Truman's Whistle Stop Campaign for U.S. president. (Courtesy Southwest Collection, Texas Tech University)*

primarily. Support also came from small and short-lived West Texas chapters of the Ku Klux Klan. Less often motivated by race—which was an issue noticeably absent from the region's most mainstream political rhetoric— Klan chapters had sprung up across West Texas during the 1920s, advocating a "100 percent Americanism" that remained suspicious of government but did not oppose the regulation of vice and morality.

Just a few years later, West Texans, like almost all Texans, became less concerned with Prohibition, ratified in 1920, and far more concerned with economic survival. Many farmers across West Texas welcomed Franklin D. Roosevelt's New Deal subsidy programs of the mid-1930s, especially as the Dust Bowl droughts of the decade seemed to scatter all hope into the prevailing winds. Virtually all West Texas communities benefitted in at least some way from New Deal agencies like the Civilian Conservation Corps (CCC), the Works Progress Administration (WPA), and the Rural Electrification Administration (REA). Lubbock, for instance, used the political and fiscal fruits picked from New Deal vines to make tremendous strides toward urbanization and modernization. The New Deal funded public parks, electrification, and street and highway improvements, all of which enabled greater access to other parts of the state, both physically and, as far as political influence was concerned, ideologically and intellectually as well. In other words, in this era West Texas cities like Amarillo, Lubbock, Midland, and El Paso grew increasingly connected to state and national politics as state and federal appropriations, accompanied with state and federal regulations, more commonly began to appear across the region. At the same time, Democratic loyalties were reinforced and a willingness to embrace government intervention was made more acceptable across smaller West Texas communities whose very survival had been threatened by the twin calamities of drought and depression.

After the exceptional times that reshaped the nation in the 1930s and 1940s, West Texans remained generally conservative and Democratic throughout the 1950s and 1960s. Eventually, however, social, cultural, and economic instability at the national level contributed to the willingness of many West Texas conservatives to break from tradition and increasingly support Republican candidates. This trend was widely mirrored at the state and national level. Republican presidential candidates began to visit

West Texas more regularly after Dwight D. Eisenhower's success there in his bids for the White House in 1952 and 1956. Such exposure added a measure of credibility to the nascent, local GOP chapters across West Texas, thus aiding the development, though still slow, of a viable and local Republican Party. In 1962 Ed Foreman (1933–) became only the third Republican since Reconstruction to win a seat in the United States House of Representatives, claiming victory in the Sixteenth District, which represented a vast region that stretched in places from El Paso to the southern Permian Basin. Although Foreman served only one term, his election presaged future GOP success at the local level across West Texas.

The rise of modern conservatism was a political force in West Texas that compelled even the most well-established of public officials to reexamine their political positions. For part of five decades, the most prominent representative of West Texans' political interests in Washington was George Mahon (1900–1985). College-educated in Abilene, Mahon briefly practiced law in Colorado City in Mitchell County before serving four years as district attorney for the state's Thirty-second Judicial District. In the 1930s, when the Great Depression and the New Deal were at high tide, Mahon leaped into the world of West Texas politics, running and winning as a Democrat for the newly created Nineteenth U.S. Congressional District in 1934. Mahon's long legislative career included various stints on several influential committees until 1964, when he was named Chairman of the House Committee on Appropriations, a position he held until his retirement in 1978. At the time of his retirement he was the longest-sitting member of the U.S. House of Representatives and one of the most influential congressmen in the nation.

As an elected West Texas Democrat, Mahon understood the importance of balancing ideology with pragmatism. First elected during the Great Depression, he had little choice—like virtually all elected Texans—but to run as a Democrat. Doing so meant supporting the national party, particularly as the New Deal was attempting to bring relief to the thousands of West Texas farmers Mahon represented. He never billed himself as an ardent New Dealer, choosing, as he put it, to remain above the partisan fray, supporting those programs he deemed worthy of support and opposing those he did not. Maintaining this balance between independence and loy-alty immunized Mahon against charges from far right–wingers like Haley, who saw in the New Deal an ideological war against "Americanism." For Mahon, supporting New Deal legislation was a reasonable, logical, and practical decision aimed at providing relief and recovery for his constitu-ents. No doubt he was also very aware that power in Texas was, at the time, distributed exclusively through the Democratic Party. When occa-sionally courted by conservative Republicans, he always refused to switch parties. Becoming a Republican, he said, would mean forfeiting influence.

Guided by his pragmatic philosophy, Mahon kept a relatively unchal-lenged hold on his congressional seat from the Nineteenth District for most of his career. Still, the strains of national political tumult, as well as the growing viability of the GOP in West Texas, began to catch up with the Democratic loyalist during the 1960s and, especially, the 1970s. Mahon's ability to toe the Democratic line was eventually undercut as conservative West Texans grew increasingly fearful and hostile to the trends of the 1960s, including the perceived militancy of the Civil Rights Movement, opposition to the war in Vietnam, and perceived liberaliza-tion (often couched as moral relativity) of social and cultural norms. Throughout the 1960s Mahon remained hawkish on Vietnam and openly supported President Lyndon Johnson's approach to the Cold War in Southeast Asia. At the same time, he also struggled to find a voice on issues of race, integration, and equality. For instance, his stance on public school desegregation—he was against it—moderated over the course of the 1960s as national trends dictated greater acceptance of change. Such gradual modifications did not alienate Mahon from West Texans; they largely agreed with him. Yet, ever the party loyalist, Mahon angered many of his West Texas constituents when he backed George McGovern over Richard Nixon in 1972.

By the mid-1970s, placing party loyalty ahead of ideological conviction no longer guaranteed success for Democratic candidates in West Texas. The Republican presidential primary of 1976 was also a critical turning point in the history of the region's politics. That year, Ronald Reagan chal-lenged Gerald Ford for the Republican Party's presidential nomination. Reagan lost that bid but won the Texas primary in a landslide, winning

100 percent of the state's delegates, including, obviously, all of those from West Texas. Reagan's coattails proved to be a very challenging obstacle for George Mahon, who in that year won his last bid for reelection in a razor-thin contest against GOP challenger Jim Reese.

Reese's strategy against Mahon reflected both the region's long-standing conservative proclivities as well as the tumultuous political atmosphere of the late 1970s. He made no effort to engage Mahon on specific issues but carefully and simply depicted himself as an authentically West Texan and pro-Reagan conservative. On the rare occasion that he actually referenced Mahon, Reese was always brief and far more focused on the national Democratic Party's encroaching liberalism than on his opponent.

Mahon adjusted his strategy accordingly. He chose not to focus on his experience in Washington or on his Democratic affiliation but rather on his experience as a Sunday school teacher at a United Methodist Church in Lubbock, his advocacy for the death penalty, his calls for tougher crime laws, and his support for the elimination of federal welfare programs. When the dust settled, Mahon won what would be his last term in Congress, claiming the smallest majority of general election votes of his career.

Despite Reese's challenge in 1976, Mahon's career stands as an instructive reflection of both the pragmatic and ideological nature of West Texas politics. Widely respected and admired, Mahon brought national influence to West Texas. Highlights of his career in service to West Texas include the establishment of Reese Air Force Base in Lubbock and what is now Webb Air Force Base in Big Spring, funding for and construction of Interstate 27 (which connected Amarillo and Lubbock), and regular advocacy for legislation that allowed area farmers to enjoy increased protection and prosperity in a global marketplace. Still, for most of his career and with some notable exceptions, Mahon resisted the temptation, often indulged by representatives from other districts nationwide, to endorse or lobby for pork barrel projects that might have benefited his home district. A pragmatic conservative, he typically represented his district well.

Since the 1970s, West Texas politics has grown far more Republican. Such trends reflect the recognition among conservative candidates that

Ronald Reagan's capture of the White House in 1980 brought a new era of Republican credibility and power to West Texas. Younger West Texans, less tied to the traditions of the Democratic Party than their parents, began to break party ties more easily until, by the 1990s, West Texas politicians like Republican Larry Combest were winning campaigns virtually unopposed. When Combest retired in 2002, vacating the same congressional seat once held by Mahon and Hance, Lubbock businessman Randy Neugebauer won a special election against more than a dozen aspiring candidates, virtually all of whom were conservative Republicans of one stripe or another. Two years later, Neugebauer demonstrated the newfound power of Republican loyalties in West Texas when he won a full term representing a realigned Nineteenth District by defeating the twenty-six-year incumbent Democrat from Abilene, Charles Stenholm. The loss ended Stenholm's political career. Some pundits blamed that loss on the Republican-controlled Texas legislature's controversial push to redistrict the statewide congressional map. Regardless, Stenholm's defeat was but another painful loss for Texas Democrats in what had become an overwhelmingly Republican section of West Texas.

Pete Gallego's election to the Texas House of Representatives in 1990 represents one important exception to this general trend. The first Hispanic to represent the state's Seventy-Fourth District, which covers a broad swath of the Trans-Pecos, Gallego also became the first minority to chair the Texas House Democratic Caucus, a position he held from 1995 to 2001. He remained in office, later for the Twenty-Third District, until he won a seat in the U.S. House of Representatives in 2011. A liberal, and far more representative both of his West Texas constituents and the modern Democratic Party than most of his predecessors, Gallego has provided West Texas Democrats with a beacon of hope. As the Hispanic population of West Texas increases, liberal politicians like Gallego will almost certainly enjoy greater success, especially in Far West Texas communities like El Paso. Whether liberal Democrats become a viable voice across the rest of West Texas remains to be seen, though again, demographics and the politics of district realignment will almost certainly be an issue.

Other stories and examples undoubtedly exist that could further illuminate the nature of West Texas political culture. Specific political personalities, controversial issues, notable progressive exceptions to the rule of conservative dominance, and more evidence of an enduring conservative predisposition in West Texas could literally fill a tome of many hundreds of pages dedicated to the region's politics. As the population of West Texas grows smaller, particularly in proportion to the rest of the state, the need for candidates to represent bigger and more diverse districts— where agriculture, water policy, and funding for public schools will surely remain of central importance—becomes more necessary and more likely. As such, another wave of ideological and partisan adjustment may reshape the region's political landscape during the first decades of the twenty-first century. Whatever the future holds, the central themes of its history remain clear. The political culture of West Texas reflects a colorful and diverse past that, with important and notable exceptions, has reflected the persistence of overwhelming loyalty to the party that best convinces the voting majority of its conservative bona fides.

## NOTES

1. *Midland Reporter-Telegram*, January 21, 2009.
2. *Midland Reporter-Telegram,* January 18, 2001.
3. As quoted in *New York Times*, July 27, 2000. For more on Bush's 1978 congressional campaign see Sean P. Cunningham, *Cowboy Conservatism: Texas and the Rise of the Modern Right* (Lexington: University Press of Kentucky, 2010), 203–205.

## FOR FURTHER READING

Barr, Alwyn. *From Reconstruction to Reform: Texas Politics, 1876–1906*. Dallas: SMU Press, 1971.
Brown, Norman D. *Hood, Bonnet, and Little Brown Jug: Texas Politics, 1921–1928*. College Station: Texas A&M University Press, 1984.
Cunningham, Sean P. *Cowboy Conservatism: Texas and the Rise of the Modern Right*. Lexington: University Press of Kentucky, 2010.
Davidson, Chandler. *Race and Class in Texas Politics*. Princeton: Princeton University Press, 1990.

Foley, Neil. *The White Scourge: Mexicans, Blacks, and Poor Whites in Texas Cotton Culture.* Berkeley and Los Angeles: University of California Press, 1997.

Gould, Lewis. *Progressives and Prohibitionists: Texas Democrats in the Wilson Era.* Austin: University of Texas Press, 1973.

Green, George Norris. *The Establishment in Texas Politics: The Primitive Years, 1938–1957.* Norman: University of Oklahoma Press, 1979.

Hine, Darlene Clark. *Black Victory: The Rise and Fall of the White Primary in Texas.* Millwood, N.Y.: KTO Press, 1979.

Key, V. O. *Southern Politics in State and Nation.* Knoxville: University of Tennessee Press, 1949.

Olien, Roger M. *From Token to Triumph: The Texas Republicans Since 1920.* Dallas: SMU Press, 1982.

Worster, Donald. *The Dust Bowl: The Southern Plains in the 1930s.* New York: Oxford University Press, 1979.

## CHAPTER 12

# The Varied Economy of West Texas

### Stephen Bogener

The economy of West Texas has been dominated since the days of early Anglo settlement by agriculture, military activities, petroleum, and, more recently, by tourism. The region's natural environment and geography, major determinants of how the economies of its several subregions have developed, constitute a significant theme in the history presented here.

T he economic history of West Texas, shaped in major ways by the region's geography, is as varied as the huge land itself. From the limestone hills of the Edwards Plateau, through the Chihuahuan Desert scrubland of the Trans-Pecos, across the extensive flatness of the storied Llano Estacado, over the Rolling Plains stretching west from Fort Worth, in the Canadian River–dominated Texas Panhandle, and along the oil-rich Permian Basin, the region is a vast, seemingly endless country whose economy has changed over time and whose economic past has adjusted to meet changing needs. Much of West Texas is part of what the Navajos called the Horizontal Yellow, a landscape of yellowed grasses stretching in four directions and encompassing New Mexico, Texas, Oklahoma, parts of Colorado, Kansas, Arkansas, and Louisiana. Sun, wind, and water shaped West Texas long before the region's latest peoples developed its natural resources and altered its economic activities.

The Edwards Plateau, lying west of San Antonio and Austin, is a good example. The southernmost extension of the Great Plains, it stretches from the Colorado River west to the Pecos. The region lacks deep soils for farming except along valleys in its far northeast sections and near Eldorado, where cotton fields exist but where grain sorghum predominates as feed for the region's livestock. Despite its aridity, isolation, and thin, rocky soil, sheep and goat raisers have found the area optimal for their needs.

The wool and mohair industry in Texas dates to the sixteenth century, when Spanish soldiers and missionaries brought the first sheep and goats to Texas for food and breeding stock. Anglos (non-Hispanic white settlers) who began arriving in the nineteenth century introduced merino sheep, known for their fine wool; these were bred with the hardy Spanish churros, which by that time had spread throughout the Southwest. In the 1850s, George Wilkins Kendall took a leading role in this enterprise, establishing a sheep ranch near Boerne and promoting his newfound success in wool growing in the area. As the Civil War began to curtail cotton raising in the southern states, New England textile mills shifted production increasingly to the manufacture of wool cloth, and Texas prospered as a result. In the 1880s and 1890s, Thomas Frost and Charles Schreiner introduced warehousing and marketing systems for storing and selling the wool collected from the many ranchers on the Edwards Plateau, making San Antonio and later Kerrville preeminent distribution centers. Sheep and wool production soared into the 1880s, when the state held nearly 7 million sheep.

Concurrent with wool production after the Civil War, mohair production began in earnest after ranchers introduced Angora goats to the state, particularly on the uplands of the Edwards Plateau, a region containing the best browse for Angoras in the United States. In the twentieth century, Texas became a leader in the wool and mohair industry, producing 20 percent of the nation's wool and 90 percent of its mohair. The introduction of new breeds of sheep and goats coincided with the advent of more efficient, scientific processing methods, and San Angelo in Tom Green County replaced Kerrville as the leading wool and Mohair market.

San Angelo was founded soon after the establishment of Fort Concho in 1867, when Bartholomew J. DeWitt purchased a half-section of land directly across the North Concho River from the fort and built a trading post. It was an inauspicious beginning, as the new frontier town soon attracted saloons, prostitution, gambling, and other objectionable forms of entertainment. Sheep and cattle ranching soon supplanted the economic impact of the fort (it was abandoned as a military post in 1889). This thriving livestock industry, plus the coming of railroads in the 1880s and 1890s, made San Angelo a leading cattle market in the Lone Star State and paved the way to its eventual status as the largest market for sheep in the United States.

World War I and World War II stimulated a sagging market for wool, with a peak in production in 1943. Mohair production peaked in 1965, and, tariffs and subsidies notwithstanding, goat raisers increasingly faced tough foreign competition. Nevertheless, by the 1990s wool and mohair output accounted for some $65 million annually in Texas. A decade later, in the early years of the twenty-first century, the 150-year-old wool and mohair industry in Texas had declined significantly, but the state has remained the national leader in growing these important products.

The Trans-Pecos and Big Bend subregion is one of the driest, hottest, least populated, most sun-drenched places in North America, and it is more akin to the American Southwest than it is to eastern parts of the state, including the rest of West Texas. El Paso aside, the population averages one person per square mile in Far West Texas. Although Juan de Oñate passed through the area in 1598, its isolation, Apache and Comanche resistance, and aridity restricted settlement until well after Texas became a part of the United States.

At the foot of Guadalupe Peak, along today's New Mexico southern boundary, lies a series of dry lake beds once packed with salt, historically a highly sought commodity. Viewed as public property by the Spanish, who ruled the region until 1836, these ancient saline lakes ninety miles east of El Paso provided an early economic stimulus to Anglo settlements in the region as competing groups sought to privatize the site. Its importance led to competition and even to violence, in the Salt Wars of the late 1860s and 1870s.

Beginning in the late nineteenth century, extensive cattle ranching began to dominate the region. Given the scant forage available, animal population densities, like the human population density, have remained very low, dispersed across vast ranch properties averaging 20,000 acres (average ranch size is 1,200 acres elsewhere in the state). In an area larger than South Carolina, cowboys on horseback still ride fences and chase cattle today as they did in frontier times.

Because of inadequate, unpredictable rainfall, irrigated agriculture has been the rule rather than the exception in scattered locations along the Rio Grande, the Pecos River, and their tributaries. Dams and prior claims to waters in New Mexico have forced Trans-Pecos irrigators increasingly to rely upon pump technologies to pull waters to the surface from deep aquifers. In isolated stretches from Dell City to Van Horn, and just to the west and east of Fort Stockton, watered oases of grapes, tomatoes, chilies, onions, alfalfa, pecans, and cotton rise incongruously from a seared landscape of creosote and cactus. Nearby, as if competing with the cactus and desert scrub, large, black pump jacks bob incessantly like so many reptilian dinosaurs, bringing dark crude oil to the land's surface.

The petroleum industry has long played a role in the West Texas economy. Exploration began around the opening of the twentieth century. By the 1920s, attention from other parts of the state had shifted to the Permian Basin. Some early discoveries included one in Mitchell County in 1920, but strikes near Big Lake in 1923 guaranteed commercial quantities of crude oil. Successive discoveries in Howard, Glasscock, and Pecos counties and near McCamey, Kermit, and present-day Iraan bolstered a shift by wildcatters and established exploration companies in the region.

The Yates field discovered near Iraan became one of the most prolific oil and gas fields in the world. Located at the time in nearly inaccessible terrain, the field's outflow soon outpaced managers' ability to store the product. By 1928, huge quantities of crude (reckoned at millions of barrels) migrating from poorly cased deep wells rose to the surface of the Pecos River and began to flow freely into nearby canyons. By July 1929, wells on 15,000 acres were yielding astonishing amounts of crude. In September, only a few hundred yards down canyon from the discovery well, a new well set a world record by producing more than 200,000 barrels per day. In 1929, on the eve of the Great Depression, that field produced more than 41 million barrels of oil.

*Presidio Mining Company in Shafter, Presidio County, ca. 1910. A silver mining operation, it remained open until the 1940s. (Courtesy Southwest Collection, Texas Tech University)*

Farther west, significant mineral extraction in the Trans-Pecos included the mining of sulfur, talc, fluorspar, silver, and quicksilver (mercury). The mining of quicksilver in the Big Bend country had begun with its discovery in the mid-1880s. The village of Terlingua sprang up near the Mariposa quicksilver mining camp but eventually moved ten miles east to the Chisos Mining Company camp, where the tiny community remains today.

Eventually forgotten after production slowed, Terlingua became a ghost town after World War II. In the 1960s and 1970s the old mining town experienced a resurgence of sorts when in 1967 the Chili Appreciation Society christened the village Chili Capital of the World for its annual chili cook-off. With its proximity to Big Bend National Park and Big Bend Ranch State Park, Terlingua became the entertainment capital of southern Brewster County. In 2012, the local population numbered about 267 inhabitants.

North and east of the Trans-Pecos country lie the Texas High Plains, or Llano Estacado. Encompassing 32,000 square miles of sun, grass, and sky, the Llano Estacado is larger than New England, taking up a good portion of northwestern Texas and eastern New Mexico. The southern extension of the High Plains that comprise the western area of the Great Plains, the Llano, an enormous semiarid mesa sloping ten feet per mile toward the southeast, is one of the largest tablelands in North America and part of what was long known as the Great American Desert. Canyons cut into this endless horizon of yellow grass and blue sky.

The perimeter of the Llano Estacado is marked on the north by the southern escarpment of the Canadian River valley and on the east by the edge of the caprock escarpment. Southern stretches of the Llano are not so obvious, gradually sloping into the Edwards Plateau near Big Spring. To the west, the Mescalero Escarpment east of New Mexico's Pecos River valley stands as a historic sentinel to the caravans of human activity that have passed this way over many millennia. Although Paleo-Indians and, later, Apaches and Comanches made vital use of its resources, to Europeans and later Americans the Llano was often a transitory place, something to cross to get to somewhere else.

As for many areas of frontier North America, the history of the Llano Estacado is a story of resource extraction and exploitation. A glaring, unfortunate example, at least from a modern point of view, is the decimation of the vast herds of American buffalo, *Bison bison*, an animal commodity sought by white settlers and eastern markets for its hide and tongue. By the 1880s, owing in part to a U.S. military policy to destroy the herds and in part to their economic value, few of the animals remained on the Llano Estacado or elsewhere across the plains. Surviving marginally in small herds on open lands owned by area ranchers, bison eventually drew greater attention as the natural conservation movement grew in the later twentieth century. Today, in the early twenty-first century, a remnant of the great southern bison herd lives at Caprock Canyons State Park, headquartered in Briscoe County.

Before the arrival of Anglo settlers in the 1880s, the wide-open spaces of the Llano Estacado had served as a prime grazing land for millions of bison, providing a way of life for a succession of American Indian peoples and, eventually, for *ciboleros*, Spanish and Mexican bison hunters who made their way east from Taos and the Mora Valley in New Mexico. They charted the Spanish place names of the Llano and nearby breaks off the caprock that we know today, among them Mescalero, Tule, Blanco, Las Lenguas, Casas Amarillas, Agua Corriente, Brazos, Cita, Frio, Tierra Blanca, Palo Duro, and Muchaque, to name only a few examples. They also traded with the Comanches everything from *aguardiente*—"Taos Lightning"—to horses and human captives in places like Cañon del Rescate (Ransom Canyon) just east of present-day Lubbock; Coyote Lake, one of the largest natural salt lakes on the High Plains, ten miles southwest of Muleshoe; and Silver Lake, or Laguna Plata, in the northwest corner of Hockley County, where a historic spring provided waters for Casas Amarillas, or Yellow House Draw.

The near extinction of the bison opened the Llano Estacado and its flanks to thousands of cattle on far-flung ranches. Early prominent cattlemen such as Charles Goodnight and Oliver Loving, for example, saw much merit in the Llano. Following Loving's death and the removal of the Comanches from that area, Goodnight in 1885 established the JA Ranch in the well-watered Palo Duro country of the Texas Panhandle. Named for John Adair, Goodnight's newfound Scottish business partner and provider of capital, the ranch eventually encompassed 1,385,000 acres in Randall, Armstrong, Donley, Briscoe, and Swisher counties.

In the 1880s eastern and foreign investors flocked to opportunities available on the Llano's sweeping grasslands. The storied Espuela (Spur), Matador, and JA ranches encompassed huge portions of unsettled land. But the largest of the great ranches, the XIT, dwarfed all others, covering 3 million acres and extending 220 miles north to south along the eastern New Mexico border. In exchange for this vast rangeland of virgin grass, Chicago and London investors in the XIT had paid cash that funded the construction of the Texas State Capitol building in Austin, to replace the one that burned in 1881. Completed in 1888, the massive building cost the Chicago investment syndicate $3.75 million. Investors thus paid slightly more than $1.00 per acre for the largest ranch in the world at the time

Farmers and farmer-stockmen, relative latecomers to the High Plains, followed the megaranchers. They brought with them a strong will to survive in what seemed a harsh and unforgiving environment. Proud and stubborn, they also brought along a conviction that they were destined to succeed on the Llano. A series of land laws in the 1880s and afterward, plus the state's unabashed courting of railroads, opened up the vast territory of the Llano Estacado to these lean, hard "nesters," as cow punchers and cattlemen derisively called them.

By the last decades of the nineteenth and the beginning of the twentieth century the large ranching syndicates had lost their holdings. A series of factors—barbed wire fencing technology, overgrazing, a glut in the cattle market, range wars, an unprecedented drought, winter storms, political pressure, shifting land laws, and the coming of railroads—combined to reduce the size of West Texas ranches like the XIT, Matador, Slaughter, and Spur that were controlled by "foreign" investors from Chicago, London, and Edinburgh.

When XIT Ranch officials began withdrawing from the cattle business in 1901, George Littlefield emerged as a major force in events unfolding on the Llano Estacado. He purchased the 312,000-acre Yellow House (southern) Division of the XIT in Lamb and Hockley counties. Erecting what was then the world's tallest windmill, which stood 130 feet and projected high above the escarpment of his headquarters in Yellow House Draw, Littlefield established the Littlefield Lands Company and within a decade had sold more than 60,000 acres to farmers.

Anglos who started trekking up the Llano's eastern caprock in the late nineteenth century chose watered canyons in which to live, but those who came later braved the elements out on the open plains. Windmills helped. By the 1890s wooden frame houses and windmills stood as the tallest features on the plain, defiantly erect in contrast to the yellow grasses surrounding them for miles. The advent of windmills allowed ranchers to fence their lands and to water their cattle from earthen, wooden, and, later, steel "tanks" (holding ponds).

But farmers needed more, especially on the southern portion of the plains, where cotton had become the main crop by the 1920s. As springs were tapped out, farmers discovered what has been called "the land of underground rain." The Ogallala Aquifer stretches from Texas north to South Dakota. Its waters were a godsend to former dryland farmers, especially because state law allowed them to pump as much water as they wanted from beneath their land. As irrigation systems increased in number in the mid-twentieth century, cotton agriculture on the Llano Estacado expanded, helped by government subsidies, crop insurance, and chemical fertilizers, pesticides, and herbicides. In 2000, cotton growing generated $10 billion annually in the area around Lubbock.

Lubbock, long called the "hub of the plains" by the local chamber of commerce, sits in the middle of the largest cotton patch in the United States and represents 25 percent of the entire nation's production. More than half of the cotton produced in Texas comes from a twenty-five-county area surrounding the city. In 1928 the region planted 1,666,500 acres of cotton. At its peak in 1981, farmers devoted more than 4.5 million acres to the white fiber. In the first decade of the twenty-first century, farmers planted between 3.52 and 3.89 million acres annually.

In addition to irrigating cotton, some growers in the area, taking advantage of government support programs and the new market for biofuels that emerged in the late twentieth century, turned to crops far more dependent on irrigation than cotton. As large plants for converting vegetable matter into ethanol appeared, many farmers signed lucrative contracts, committing themselves to producing tall stands of corn watered by efficient center-pivot irrigation systems. Except for the circular shape of the stands watered by these systems, cornfields near Nazareth, Olton, and Lazbuddie in 2014 made the area look more like Iowa than the semiarid grasslands of the Llano Estacado.

But there is more to the story. Farming has never been easy in West Texas, including the Llano's High Plains. Pioneer farm families in rural sections of Texas were often isolated, often lacked proper equipment, and often existed at the mercy of natural elements—some agricultural land received less than twenty inches of rainfall per year. As a result some twentieth-century settlers have resembled victims of the Great Depression and the Dust Bowl depicted in the imagery of Dorothea Lange, Russell Lee, Arthur Rothstein, and John Steinbeck. It was not always a pleasant tale. But many second- and third-generation High Plains farmers moved toward an easier lifestyle, particularly in the 1920s and 1930s with the new availability of gasoline tractors, the extension of electricity to rural areas, and the accessibility of many modern appliances.

Meanwhile, the economy of the Llano Estacado received a boost from military activities, particularly in the World War II era. In the 1940s two air bases for training pilots were established on the Southern Plains, and

Lubbock became a military town. One of the bases, South Plains Army Air Field (today's Lubbock Preston Smith International Airport), was the site of glider training during the war. Military officials had determined that if pilots could manage the winds over the Llano Estacado, they could fly over anything, including the beaches at Normandy.

Areas of the Texas Panhandle east and south of the Llano Estacado have also seen a diversity of economic activity. The huge cattle ranching operations that arose in the Llano Estacado, such as the XIT, the JA, the T-Anchor, and the LS, extended down the slopes bordering the high flat-lands and into outlying areas as well. But beginning in the 1880s the arrival of the railroads, including the Fort Worth and Denver City (FW&DC) and the Santa Fe, along with changing land laws, encouraged a rise in farming in these lower areas.

By the 1920s and 1930s, large feedlots for cattle on the way to market had become established in these areas as well, an industry that has since generated billions of dollars and employed thousands of workers in the Texas Panhandle. Many of the cattle feeding factories are located directly in the middle of draws and creeks along the margins of the Llano Estacado, like Tierra Blanca, whose waters once fed the wildlife oasis of Buffalo Lake, eight miles east of present-day Canyon. Runoff from the feedlot eventually contributed to closure of the lake as a popular recreation site, but the lake bed and surroundings have since been preserved as a wildlife refuge. Beef production and feedlot "finishing" have remained important to the Pan-handle economy. Today, in 2014, Amarillo is the epicenter of the largest cattle-feeding region of the country.

Farther north, particularly above the Canadian River, farmers plowed millions of acres of native bluestem and grama grass, replacing them with a variety of hard winter wheat called Turkey Red, from the steppes of Russia, introduced to the United States in the late 1800s. Early success with this important strain led the Panhandle to become one of the largest wheat-producing areas of the country. Today, in 2014, Panhandle farm-ers, especially in eastern portions of the area, continue to raise enormous amounts of wheat.

Petroleum extraction has also been important to the Panhandle economy. An oil and gas field 120 miles long and about 20 miles wide, covering 1.5

million acres, stretches across seven Panhandle counties. Mainly situated north of the Canadian River, the Panhandle Oil and Gas Field, one of the largest such fields in the United States, reaches from Wheeler in the east to Dumas in the west. Opened in 1921 with a small well in Carson County, the large field by 1926 had created an enormous boom for several Panhandle towns, but especially for Amarillo, which became the headquarters for a number of oil companies, pipeline operations, trucking firms, and other oil-related businesses. In 1926 its companies pumped 25 million barrels of black crude from Panhandle Field wells.

The American military-industrial complex has also played a key role in the Texas Panhandle, especially around Amarillo. In 1942 the U.S. Army constructed the original Pantex Ordnance Plant on 16,000 acres near the city. Plant workers packed conventional artillery shells and bombs in support of the World War II effort. The plant closed briefly after the war but reopened in 1951, by then equipped for the production of nuclear weapons as well as containing a nonnuclear component assembly. By 1960 Pantex had begun a partnership with Lawrence Livermore National Laboratory in the development of high explosives and nuclear weapons assembly. Between 1965 and 1975 the Atomic Energy Commission centralized the nation's operations for weapons modification and assembly and high explosives at Pantex, where workers put together thousands of weapons. Since 1991 the weapons plant has operated in reverse, dismantling weapons retired from the stockpile by the military and placing the leftover plutonium in temporary storage.

Their entrepreneurial spirits relatively unfazed by national economic fluctuations, Lubbock on the Llano Estacado and Amarillo in the Panhandle moved steadily into the twenty-first century. Anchored by the resources of Texas Tech University, multifaceted health care and medical facilities, and agricultural enterprises, Lubbock reflects the can-do attitude of its earliest settlers. Amarillo, on Interstate Highway 40, has experienced rapid growth in recent years. The closure of Amarillo Air Force Base in the mid-1960s temporarily set back the city's economy, but Bell Helicopter, Tyson Foods, and the Pantex weapons facility joined with banking and the cattle and feedlot industries in sustaining a robust economy. West Texas A&M University in nearby Canyon, Amarillo College, and Texas Tech

University in Lubbock combine to offer vocational and professional training for Panhandle residents and businesses.

East of the Llano Estacado and southeast of the Texas Panhandle, the Rolling Plains of Texas lie in the north central portion of the state and include parts of more than twenty counties. The western portion of the region, the area just below the eastern caprock of the Llano Estacado, is broken country. The Cross Timbers and prairie areas of Central Texas border the eastern and southeastern portions of the Rolling Plains. To the south lies the Edwards Plateau.

The area is largely rolling country, with rivers flowing west to east, and the bulk of its lands are devoted to cattle ranching. Some sections are dedicated to cotton, sorghum, wheat, and milo. The Rolling Plains saw appreciable discoveries of oil in the 1940s, providing yet another infusion of monies into the area's economy. Urban centers on the Rolling Plains are the mid-sized cities of Abilene and Wichita Falls.

Pioneers arrived in the Wichita Falls area soon after 1870, when many people purchased school lands, sold to raise funds for education, to start cattle ranches, the early mainstay of the economy. The Fort Worth and Denver City Railroad arrived in Wichita Falls in September 1882, thus securing the town's long-term existence. Additional railroads built between 1884 and 1911established Wichita Falls as a regional transportation and distribution center. During World War I, Call Field, built south of the city, served as an Army Air Corps training center, adding to the city's population of 40,000 and bringing new dollars to the local economy.

During the same era oil discoveries changed Wichita Falls and surrounding area. After a small well produced in 1910, discoveries in the Electra oilfield in 1911, followed by major finds near Burkburnett in 1918, led to a full-scale oil boom in Wichita County. By 1940 production had reached 320 million barrels, topping all other counties in the state. Oilfield product manufacturing, crude oil refining companies, and speculators had flocked to Wichita Falls in response, a trend that persisted through the 1940s.

Developments in other industries and in agriculture also have marked the Rolling Plains economy in the Wichita Falls area. Agriculture, especially cotton production, took on major importance, particularly in the first two decades of the twentieth century. World War II saw the development of Sheppard Field, an Army Air Corps base established north of Wichita Falls that added hundreds of jobs and millions of dollars to the local economy. The facility began operations in 1941, specializing in pilot training, aircraft maintenance training, and basic training. It was deactivated in 1946 and opened again as today's Sheppard Air Force Base in 1950. During the Korean War, Sheppard served as a training center for pilots and aircraft mechanics. The local economy grew from $43 million in the middle 1950s to $280 million by the 1980s.

Abilene, the informal capital of the Rolling Plains, is named after the Kansas cattle town. It rose to prominence when local ranchers and speculators persuaded officials of the Texas and Pacific Railroad to build their line across northern Taylor County, thus bypassing the original county seat of Buffalo Gap. In the 1870s cattlemen had begun to graze their herds on lands previously occupied by millions of head of bison. Promoters of Abilene boomed the town vigorously and by 1881, when the railroad came through, they had laid out lots and started building businesses and a church. In 1883, residents incorporated the town and made it the new county seat.

Abilene boosters attracted additional rail connections to the city, but the next landmark of major economic growth came during World War II, when the federal government in 1941 established Camp Barkeley, a military training facility that served some 1.5 million soldiers, southwest of the city. The Tye Airfield, soon Abilene Army Air Field, was established nearby in 1942. Camp Barkeley was dismantled in 1945. The airfield, however, was decommissioned in 1946 and used for National Guard training until city leaders courted Washington officials for a new airfield at the time of the Korean conflict. The construction of the new military installation was pumping millions of dollars into the local economy by 1952. In 1956, when completed, it took the name it has today, Dyess Air Force Base.

In addition to the military presence, Taylor and adjoining counties in the Rolling Plains in the Abilene area saw their economies infused with monies from the expansion of oil exploration, drilling, refining, and service industries, especially after World War II. Oil production greatly affected several communities, including Snyder, Sweetwater, and Abilene.

Abilene has also long been known for its church-affiliated institutions of higher education. In 1891, the city pushed for the establishment of a Baptist school, Simmons College, now called Hardin-Simmons University. Abilene Christian University, founded in 1906, and McMurry University, a Methodist-affiliated school established in 1923, also provide quality college education to area residents. The schools have also been a boon to the local economy.

Viewed broadly, an economic history of West Texas reveals a number of common threads woven through the huge region's past and into its present. Agriculture, for example, both livestock and crop agriculture, dominated the early history of West Texas and its subregions. Railroads were vital to the larger region and its emerging cities in the late nineteenth and early twentieth centuries. For nearly a century now, petroleum, its production, and its many related businesses, have been an economic dynamo for much of West Texas, and in 2014 the high cost of gas and oil have produced a renewed boom in cities, such as Midland and Odessa, where oil drilling, pipeline operations, and other petroleum-related industries have seen spectacular renewed growth. Manufacturing has been an important but secondary enterprise in West Texas. And, water or the lack of it in an arid and semiarid land, remains a vital key to understanding the economy, especially its agricultural sectors.

In the early twenty-first century both new concerns and new opportunities have emerged in West Texas. The concerns centered on the declining availability of water. The opportunities arose in connection to the growing use of alternative sources of energy, particularly wind energy. Whatever the challenges, West Texas will continue to be an important part of the state and nation's larger economy. Natural resources, agriculture, national and state parks and recreational facilities, and a strong industrial and military background all attest to a vital and vibrant economy built upon historical foundations.

## FOR FURTHER READING

Caffey, David L. *The Old Home Place: Farming on the West Texas Frontier*. Austin: Eakin Press, 1981.

Carlson, Paul H. *Amarillo: The Story of a Western Town*. Lubbock: Texas Tech University Press, 2007.

———. *Texas Woollybacks: The Range Sheep and Goat Industry*. College Station: Texas A&M University Press, 1982.

Cool, Paul. *Salt Warriors: Insurgency on the Rio Grande*. College Station: Texas A&M University Press, 2008.

Flores, Dan L. *Horizontal Yellow: Nature and History in the Near Southwest*. Albuquerque: University of New Mexico Press, 1999.

Gracy, David B., II. *Littlefield Lands: Colonization on the Texas Plains, 1912–1920*. Austin: University of Texas Press, 1968.

Holden, William Curry. *Alkali Trails: Or, Social and Economic Movements of the Texas Frontier, 1846–1900*. Dallas: Southwest Press, 1930; reprinted Lubbock: Texas Tech University Press, 1998.

Jordan, Terry G. *North American Cattle Ranching Frontiers: Origins, Diffusion and Differentiation*. Albuquerque: University of New Mexico Press, 1993.

Olien, Roger, and Diana Olien. *Oil Booms: Social Change in Five Texas Towns*. Lincoln: University of Nebraska Press, 1984.

Ragsdale, Kenneth B. *Quicksilver: Terlingua and the Chisos Mining Company*. College Station: Texas A&M University Press, 1976.

Sledge, Robert W. *A People, a Place: The Story of Abilene*. Vol. 1, *The Future Great City, 1881–1940*. Buffalo Gap: State House Press, 2008.

Weaver, Bobby D., ed. *Panhandle Petroleum*. Canyon: Panhandle–Plains Historical Society, 1982.

# Chapter 13

# Agriculture, Ranching, and Rural Life in West Texas

*M. Scott Sosebee*

One of the more popular topics in West Texas history is the large-scale open range cattle raising that was a hallmark of the later nineteenth century. This chapter gives an overview of that history but also offers far more than a traditional look at ranching and rural life. In a fresh approach, the author brings the ranching and agricultural story of West Texas into the twentieth century, explains the important role of smaller ranches, and describes how farmers and farmer-stockmen have played a significant part in the larger narrative.

Because of a business setback, Henry C. "Hank" Smith on a November day in 1878 loaded his family's possessions onto a wagon and set out to an uncertain future. He left behind a successful hotel and freight enterprise in Fort Griffin, Texas, to recoup an investment in another man's failed dream. At age forty-two, he had never operated a ranch, but the vagaries of life now forced him to try his luck at raising stock in Blanco Canyon, a place at the time virtually unknown to Texans. He was sure that his life had taken a turn for the worse.

A month after his arrival in Blanco Canyon, Smith's brooding had dissipated. In letters to Fort Griffin he extolled the canyon's potential for raising stock, its abundant game, and its lush valleys. He encouraged settlers in west central Texas to make homes on the plains, and he began to envision a land capable of large profits. Eventually Hank Smith's Cross B Ranch would cover more than 3,000 acres, and on it he raised cattle, sheep, and hogs.

Smith became a wealthy man, but he operated what constituted a small enterprise in West Texas. The sprawling Matador Ranch, the Espuela ranching operation, and the Kentucky Cattle Company each covered hundreds of thousands of acres. Other huge ranches, such as the XIT, the JA, and the Pitchfork, exploited the lush West Texas grasslands. The idea of a western cattle kingdom began to emerge.

But cattlemen were not the only ones who tried their luck on the plains of West Texas. Closely following the huge herds of cattle came farmers with their hoes and plows ready to open a new region for cultivation. By the mid-twentieth century, market crops, such as wheat, grain sorghum, and cotton, dotted land once teeming with cattle. West Texas became indelibly identified with agricultural pursuits.

"West Texas" conjures images of cowboys, dust storms, tornadoes, and table-top flatlands stretching to the horizon. If pressed, most people will associate West Texas with agriculture—snow-white cotton fields, roaming cattle spread across an endless landscape, and farmers operating their large tractors deep into a clear night. That present-day image evolved slowly, though, starting in the mid-nineteenth century. Like West Texas agriculture itself, the notion moved forward with fits and starts and changes and transformations.

In the early to mid-nineteenth century, pioneers viewed West Texas and its grasslands with curious wonder or sometimes as an obstacle to cross on the way to great fortune elsewhere. They worried too about Comanche and Apache attacks, which may have slowed settlement west of the black prairies of Central Texas. By the 1850s, however, disease had greatly diminished the Indian presence in Texas, and United States Army operations had weakened the Comanche hold on lands they had long dominated in West Texas. As Indian families moved from the region, Euro-American settlers—soon known as Anglos—migrated into and beyond the Cross Timbers area of Central Texas and onto the eastern reaches of the Rolling Plains. The Civil War only slowed the process.

But the war did disrupt settlement. Comanches, taking advantage of the wartime drain on manpower toward needs in the eastern states, along with military shortages in Texas, increased their raids and pushed the leading edge of settlement back almost one hundred miles. After the war, United States Army units moved in to reestablish a strong presence along the line of western settlement, which then ran from Jacksboro, county seat of Jacks County, to near the Rio Grande at Laredo, in Webb County. Nonetheless, Comanches, Kiowas, and Apaches slipped across the vastness of West Texas to outmaneuver the ill-supplied and sometimes ill-trained federal troops.

This situation began to change in the early 1870s, when a new generation of federal officers arrived in Texas. These included the Fourth Cavalry's Ranald S. Mackenzie, Benjamin Grierson of the all-black Tenth Cavalry, and William R. Shafter with his black Twenty-fourth Infantry. Their troops pursued Indian families everywhere across West Texas. They burned villages, slaughtered Indian ponies, and destroyed material possessions that warriors needed to defend themselves and their families.

Also about 1870, after a new tanning process caused a dramatic boom in demand for bison hides, bison hunters took tens of thousands, ultimately millions, of the animals that Indians needed to live. By 1873 the herds on the central Great Plains had dwindled, and hunters turned to the southern herds in Texas. Soon they had destroyed most of them, leaving the Southern Plains Indians dependent upon the federal government for survival.

Cattlemen, arriving after the army and the bison hunters had cleared the plains of West Texas, inaugurated the romantic era of the western range cattle industry. During the Civil War, Texas cattle markets had collapsed. Cattle went untended, but these animals also increased in number. At the close of the conflict perhaps as many as 5 million unbranded cattle roamed the South and Central Texas prairies.

At the same time, new, lucrative markets opened in the North. People everywhere were demanding fresh meat, and large slaughterhouses opened in Chicago, Cincinnati, and elsewhere to supply it. Enterprising Texans, some destitute and aimless after the war, rounded up stray and wandering herds in the state and drove them to railheads in Missouri and Kansas, where buyers from northern slaughterhouses waited to purchase Texas cattle. Trail drivers hired young men—almost literally "cow boys"—to drive herds to Sedalia, Missouri, and to Abilene, Wichita, and Dodge City in Kansas. From 1866 to 1880 more than 3 million Texas cattle made the trek north.

Thus three things—extermination of bison, displacement of Indians, and exodus of cattle to northern markets—created favorable conditions for extending ranching into West Texas. Quickly, cattlemen such as C. C. Slaughter, Charles Goodnight, and A. H. "Shanghai" Pierce staked out land on the public domain, usually near a source of water, and grazed their animals on the free range. Ownership of the land was not necessary, although many protected their "range" with force. When the state began to sell its public lands in the 1880s, enterprising cattlemen bought range land on which they grazed their animals, or leased pastures to other stockmen.

*(Left–right) Murdo Mackenzie, Alexander Mackey, and N. Johnstone, 1892, senior management of the Scottish-owned Matador Land and Cattle Company. (Courtesy Southwest Collection, Texas Tech University)*

Cattle became big business on the West Texas plains and expanded to the Big Bend and Trans-Pecos regions.

A ranch representative of these new developments, which became the Matador Land and Cattle Company, was originally a partnership between H. H. Campbell, who operated the ranch, and A. M. Britton, a Chicago banker who financed the operation. The partners bought rangeland in the 1870s and by the early 1880s had established the largest operation in West Texas. With a good water supply, an abundance of plains grasses, and high beef prices, the ranch prospered. Despite the profits, Britton determined to sell. British venture capitalists had become interested in American cattle operations, and in Dundee, Scotland, he found a group eager to invest in the western livestock industry.

Upon buying the ranch, the Dundee merchants incorporated their property as the Matador Land and Cattle Company. Campbell continued to manage the massive ranch, which by then counted more than 1.5 million acres and more than 400,000 cattle. In 1890 reorganization of the Matador placed Scotsman Murdo Mackenzie in charge of company holdings. Mackenzie further expanded the ranch, extending its holdings from Texas through the western Great Plains to Canada, and diversified its operations. A. M. Britton, in the meanwhile, had established another livestock operation, the Espuela Land and Cattle Company.

The "land and cattle company" business model came to dominate the range and created more such massive operations as the Matador. Each employed dozens of wranglers and "waddies" (cowboys), and over time they squeezed out many smaller ranches. Hank Smith, for example, found his Blanco Canyon range surrounded by the Matador, the Kentucky, and other operations.

In the 1880s many large companies began to fence their range holdings with a new and highly effective technology, barbed wire. They also introduced purebred stock. With these two improvements, the open range tradition soon came to a close, and by the beginning of the twentieth century ranching had become a meticulous and virtually scientific enterprise.

Sheep represented a second component of the ranching industry. They did not carry the prestige or romance of cattle, but they were profitable. Although sheep had been present in West Texas since the time of the first

Spanish colonists, the movement of the sheep industry paralleled that of cattle. It came out of the South Texas brush country and into the Hill Country. George Wilkins Kendall and Charles Schreiner ran sheep on their lands west of San Antonio. From there, operations spread throughout the Edwards Plateau and onto the northwest Texas plains. Hank Smith raised sheep with his cattle, as did other West Texas cattlemen.

Like cattle enterprises, West Texas sheep operations grew significantly after the Civil War. In the mid-1870s the region witnessed a sheep boom, and sheep operations expanded through the Trans-Pecos region. *Texas Historic Livestock Statistics* reported that in 1885 there were 62 million sheep in Texas, a good portion of them in flocks in West Texas. The Edwards Plateau became the center of sheep production and helped Texas become and remain the leading sheep producing state in the nation.

Close behind sheep herders and cattlemen came farmers. The semiarid plains of West Texas had every capability for supporting stock operations, but a land of little water should have been no place for the hoe and plow. Such an obstacle did not stop land-starved farmers of the late nineteenth century. When news of potential new lands reached eastern farmers, the natural barriers of West Texas could not restrict a mass movement of families intent on breaking the land for cultivation.

The desire to move beyond the western edge of settlement may have captured these farmers' attention, but they quickly found that cultivation in portions of West Texas constituted a tough new adventure. For the most part, eastern Texas received adequate rainfall; crops grew well, and a farmer could manage a somewhat comfortable subsistence. But as Walter Prescott Webb made clear in *The Great Plain* (1931), the history of the lands west of the 98th meridian, (roughly, the Balcones Escarpment) has been marked by the search for an adequate water supply.

Such a detail did not deter farmers from moving into the West Texas plains. Beginning in the 1870s and 1880s, railroads provided a cheap mode of transport to the western lands. Texas's rail lines initially connected widely separated towns and cities in-state and then expanded to connect Texas to intercontinental lines that reached the rest of the nation. The Texas and Pacific Railroad crossed Texas from east to west, entering the state near Marshall and continuing through Dallas and Fort Worth to El Paso. The

Texas and Pacific linked with the Southern Pacific Railroad, which followed a more southerly route from east to west, near Sierra Blanca in Far West Texas. Other important lines included the Fort Worth and Denver City Railroad (FW&DC), which connected the Panhandle with the remainder of the state and nation, and the Gulf, Colorado, and Santa Fe, which also reached into West Texas.

A symbiotic relationship developed between railroads and farmers. Railroads needed customers and people; farmers needed a way to ship their products to market. Thus rail companies sold some of their land, tracts that had been granted to them by the state, to families eager to establish farms. As both railroads and farmers needed communities to serve as shipping and supply points, farmers and railroad leaders pushed for town development along the rail lines. Many West Texas towns and cities, among them Abilene, Odessa, Amarillo, and Big Spring, owe their existence to railroads, and other established towns, such as Lubbock, Pecos, and San Angelo, developed into cities only after the arrival of the rails.

Farmers entered West Texas full of bright optimism. For many, it was their first opportunity to own land and break from the tenant farming system that strangled enterprise in other agricultural areas of Texas. Often the harsh reality of the western plains crushed their optimism. Farming in West Texas could be a difficult life. It proved quite different from most farmers' previous experience. The lack of trees meant homes for first arrivals had to be built from sod or were simply "dugouts" literally excavated into hillsides. The soil was poor and unsuitable for most crops, and too often uninvited snakes and other nuisance animals shared the settlers' crude dwellings.

Unpredictable weather added to these woes. Drought was a constant partner to West Texans. Rain, when it came, too often fell in large amounts in too short a time. Violent thunderstorms with high winds might devastate a homestead. Summers were hot. Winters were often cold and bitter, and blinding blizzards could rage for days.

If weather was not enough, vast swarms of locusts that blackened the sky descended on the plains, consuming everything in their path—crops, tools, and even implements and utensils. Fire, usually spawned by lightning, could sweep across the prairies and destroy all in its path. West Texas farmers often lived on the edge of financial solvency, and any natural disaster added to their precarious situation.

Nonetheless, the farmers persevered. They met the heat and the cold head on, and they developed ingenious ways to handle drought, prairie fires, blizzards, and sandstorms. They solved the lack of available water by drilling wells and erecting windmills, which became the most important and most identifiable feature on the West Texas plains. Windmills gave farmers a water source, allowing them to irrigate crops, to plant fruit trees, and in general to help brighten the farmstead.

West Texas farm families not only carved out a life for themselves in an otherwise harsh environment, they built up their farms and founded towns. They formed social networks, organizations of all kinds, and city and county governments. By 1900, most of West Texas was a checkerboard of fully functioning counties with permanent settlers, although some areas on the Llano Estacado's South Plains and in the Trans-Pecos had to wait until the twentieth century for full settlement.

As the population swelled with farm families and townspeople, even stockmen, generally regarded as rugged individualists, joined with farmers in town formation and in establishing permanent roots on the land. Farmers and ranchers achieved something of a partnership in West Texas: stock operations became farm customers, and both welcomed the formation of new town sites as supply depots. Ranch owners sold land to farmers and served as a capital base in a region that lacked lending institutions.

While most West Texas farmers of the nineteenth century practiced a subsistence lifestyle, a number of agriculturists decided to enter the produce market. Cotton became the favorite crop. As its cultivation spread through the western Cross Timbers area and into the Rolling Plains, Texas by 1890 became the leading cotton producing state, and more than half of that cotton was grown by poor tenant and small-plot farmers—a pattern that became prevalent in parts of West Texas.

Mechanization also increased, especially after 1890, allowing West Texas farmers to cultivate more land with less labor. The development of the mechanical stalk cutter in the 1880s and the mechanical planter made planting cotton and other crops easier. The invention of the riding cultivator made farming on the West Texas plains less labor intensive. The development of new, horse-drawn machinery went hand in hand with the adoption of such row crops as cotton, grain sorghums, corn, and in some places peanuts.

New dryland farming techniques, a result of increased scientific study of the mechanics of farming, brought even more land under the plow. Land, such as the area near present-day Lubbock and west of the Pecos River, which just a few years previously had almost precluded crops, became viable for farmers who utilized these modern methods, a development that attracted even more migration to West Texas. Mechanization and dryland farming techniques transformed a virtually unoccupied plain into a region of comfortable production within a matter of decades.

For stockmen too, new technology and new ideas led to change in the early twentieth century. In the late nineteenth century, large ranching operators had begun to improve their stock with purebred animals, fenced ranges, and scientific practices. Somewhat later, pesticides eliminated noxious plants, and new agricultural methods allowed rangeland to be reseeded with drought-resistant and more nutritious grasses. After 1900 the Progressive Era brought widespread emphasis on professionalization and scientific research and also encouraged new techniques of range management and land reclamation.

But hardships did not disappear. A severe drought in 1895 drove many marginal operators out of business. More droughts followed in 1909 and 1910. These, combined with one of the coldest and most destructive winters on record in 1910, made ranchers' costs rise while prices plummeted. A brief uptick in beef, mutton, and wool prices during World War I provided only temporary relief.

In face of economic peril, the ranching business transformed itself to survive. Many of the most extensive stock operations resorted to selling off large sections of land. The famed XIT sold its Southern (Yellow House) Division in 1901 to George Littlefield. By 1912 the XIT had ceased cattle operations altogether and had divided or sold most of its holdings, sometimes for as little as $30 an acre. The mighty Matador Land and Cattle Company also pieced off some of its holdings, and the Kentucky Cattle Company began to liquidate its land plot by plot.

In effect, by the 1920s the era of the huge land and cattle companies had begun to close. Littlefield could not turn a profit on his South Plains holdings and sold out. Others, such as C. W. Post's Curry Comb, C. C. Slaughter's Running Water, and the remnants of the Espuela operation, all but disappeared. Other ranches, such as the Mallet, the Pitchfork, and the Spade, continued to raise stock on reduced land. Although smaller stock operators purchased property from the large landholders, farmers bought the majority of the land, and much of West Texas, outside the arid and thin-soiled Big Bend and Trans-Pecos areas, shifted to farm-based rather than stock-based agriculture.

National events also dramatically influenced the transformation in the West Texas livestock industry. Prices and markets collapsed after World War I, which placed great burdens on stock operations already saddled with large debt. From 1920 to 1929 ranches lost almost one-third of their total value within the state. West Texas ranchers, with heavy investments in water wells, fencing, and sprawling physical complexes, were hard hit. Adding to the trauma was the increase in global production of beef. Argentina and Australia began to produce an abundance of beef at prices in many cases much lower than American production costs.

Prices and stock production enjoyed a slight increase in the late 1920s, but then hope crashed during the Great Depression of the 1930s, when the total valuation of stock operations declined by more than half. Plummeting prices and shifts in consumer demand, along with another devastating drought—Dust Bowl conditions that extended deep into the Texas Panhandle—brought disaster to West Texas livestock producers. President Franklin D. Roosevelt's New Deal legislation offered aid to depressed ranchers. Federal agencies helped to increase access to credit, provided direct monetary payments, and assisted with disease and predator eradication. Still, the amount of ranch land in West Texas declined and ranchers' incomes faltered.

World War II actually reinvigorated West Texas ranching fortunes. From the outbreak of the conflict in Europe in 1939 through the end of hostilities in 1945, stockmen achieved unparalleled success. As employment in the nation improved in support of the war effort, consumption of meat increased, and the market for wool production also climbed.

The period of readjustment before the war also helped West Texas stock raisers enhance techniques and practices that enabled them to compete with foreign competition. West Texas ranchers looked forward to a much more prosperous postwar future.

The first half of the twentieth century also brought much change to West Texas' farmers. More land came into cultivation. In fact more land in West Texas came under cultivation after 1900 than before the turn of the century, as farmers benefited from the breakup of the large stock operations. Railroad expansion continued into the early 1900s, bringing more rural folk to the region. Between 1907 and 1909, C. C. Slaughter sold most of his holdings to farmers. Cattleman George Littlefield sold parts of his acreage for farms, and he also sold lots to build the town of Littlefield, which became a central shipping and supply depot. By the 1920s farmers, not cattlemen, dominated West Texas agriculture.

Many farmers produced cotton, although grain also formed a good portion of cultivation. Until the 1930s, East Texas remained the most abundant area of cotton production, but in each succeeding decade West Texas producers dramatically increased their acreage and harvest. West Texas farmers gathered a little less than 80,000 bales of cotton in 1880, but in 1930 they harvested more than 1 million bales, more than 25 percent of the state's total output.

New varieties of cotton also stimulated production. Texas Storm-proof, the predominant cotton grown in eastern Texas, did not fare well in the climatic and soil conditions of the western side of the state. But agricultural scientists developed Mebane Triumph in the early 1900s, which did well in soils and growing conditions below the caprock. Further experimentation produced the Westex variety that after 1920 became the preferred cotton on the High Plains.

Unfortunately, the same economic conditions that hindered the livestock industry brought damage to West Texas farm operations. Relatively high commodity prices during World War I and immediately thereafter led West Texas agriculturalists to take on debt to further mechanize production and to increase land holdings. When commodity prices collapsed early in the 1920s, many farmers faced spiraling mortgage payments while their income declined. West Texas farmers did not experience foreclosure rates equal to some other plains states, but the number of failed farms rose by almost 15 percent during the decade.

As indicated above, the Great Depression profoundly affected West Texas farmers. A combination of devastating conditions, mostly economic but also natural, forever altered the farming landscape. The worldwide economic depression of the 1930s caused commodity prices to fall to depths many could not imagine, and it also dried up credit outlets, took away vital national and international markets, and caused many West Texas farmers to lose their livelihood. The disastrous and prolonged drought that gave rise to the Dust Bowl afflicted farmers as much as it had stockmen.

The negative consequences of years of overcultivation and the resulting loss of native grasses and soil nutrients became evident during this drought. Soil on the plains was thin and now lacked a natural anchor element, and when the parching winds swept across the region, they produced enormous and devastating dust storms after 1932. These massive storms obscured the sky for days at a time. Between January and April 1935, visibility fell to zero seven times in Amarillo. In March of that year Lubbock experienced a dust storm that lasted three days and dumped as many as seven inches of fine dust in some rain gauges.

New Deal agricultural initiatives, such as the Agricultural Adjustment Administration (AAA), the Civilian Conservation Corps (CCC), the Farm Credit Administration, and later the Commodity Credit Corporation, provided limited relief and eventually saved a number of West Texas farms. The New Deal program that perhaps had the most long-lasting benefit was the Rural Electrification Administration (REA). The REA gave many rural West Texans access to electricity for the first time, which allowed them to modernize farms with new amenities and reduce labor in terms of cost and size.

Although more dramatic in other regions of Texas, the Great Depression also helped end sharecropping and greatly reduce tenancy in West Texas. Uncertain economics related to the depression caused many farm families to quit and move to cities to find work. Landowners, who benefitted more directly from New Deal programs, reoccupied tracts at the expense of tenants. Conversely, liberal credit programs, subsidized with federal funds, allowed many former tenants to purchase their farms instead of renting them.

World War II completed the conversion to modern farming practices. The international necessity to supply food and other commodities
encouraged West Texas farmers to return to maximum and, in many
cases, record production, while also facing a severe labor shortage. The
solution came with greatly increased mechanization, on a scale much
larger than in the late nineteenth century. The number of West Texas
farms decreased, but production grew.

A related change occurred. The need for greater food production to
supply a rapidly growing population, combined with new techniques
and mechanization, led farmers in East and Central Texas to diversify
production from cotton to grains, sorghums, tomatoes, onions, and
other food products. East Texas began to raise more cattle than West
Texas. At the same time, new technology made irrigation in West Texas
cost-effective, which made cotton crops more viable there. West Texas
farmers, particularly those on the High Plains, began to raise a greater
percentage of the state's cotton—a trend that continued throughout the
twentieth century. At the dawn of the twenty-first century, West Texas
grew a majority (60 percent or more) of the state's cotton crop. In the
years leading up to the present, 2014, signs of climate variation, with later
spring frosts, have led the region's farmers to adapt to change once again,
seeking crops more tolerant of cold.

The postwar period also witnessed the beginning of a change in the
business of agriculture. As larger, more mechanized farms became the
norm, capital expenditures and the large tracts needed to turn a profit
became more than most small, family farms could sustain. The mechanical cotton picker meant that cotton became most profitable on large,
professionally managed tracts. Cotton also became big business, one that
depended on global marketing and corporate management. West Texas
farmers became either employees of, or contractors for, large, multina-
tional agricultural consortiums. Farming became an industry, the farm
the factory floor, and the farmer the industrial laborer.

The West Texas stock industry also changed during the postwar years.
Red meat consumption and prices soared in the United States. Ranchers,
like crop-raising West Texans, became dependent on federal subsidies
and governmental manipulation of the global market. Federal oversight

and regulation also increased. Foreign competition became keener, particularly from South American operators.

Faced with such conditions, West Texas stock operations transformed yet again. Some operators who had withstood the ravages of the 1920s, the Great Depression, and the Dust Bowl years did not survive the new era of global competition and federal intervention. They either reduced their holdings or sold out altogether. Other ranch managers reconfigured their operations into publicly held corporations associated with large agribusiness firms.

Today, in 2014 and for the future, water availability remains a major concern for farmers and ranchers in West Texas. For decades the region's agriculturalists have been able to tap into the underground aquifer reserves to sustain crops and help feed the world. After more than a century of sustained agriculture these immense water sources, such as the vast Ogallala Aquifer, are dwindling with little chance of recharge. Urban populations in Lubbock, Abilene, Midland, and San Angelo are competing with the agricultural industry for these water supplies. If the water becomes irretrievably depleted, most of the industry will dry up or adopt dryland techniques.

In 2014 change and transformation was already taking place to confront this growing concern. Reeves, Pecos, and Ward counties, located in Far West Texas, are home to the famed Pecos Cantaloupe variety, but declining resources have shrunk the cantaloupe crop. The number of cattle in West Texas is also declining, and the stock industry may not again reach the levels achieved in the 1970s. West Texas farmers continue to grow cotton and remain the leading producers of the fiber in the state, but low prices, environmental concerns, rising costs, and global market competition have caused many cotton farmers to abandon the business of agriculture.

Despite such seemingly dire twenty-first century conditions, the news is not all gloomy. On the High Plains and in the Trans-Pecos country, cultivation of grapes for the wine industry has increased. Former cotton farmers now raise peanuts, sunflowers, and sorghum crops with success. Goat meat production is becoming more important in many regions of the Rolling Plains, with most of the product exported to foreign markets.

Tomatoes, a big business in some of the mountain regions of the Big Bend, are now largely grown in enclosed hothouses that utilize less water than field cultivation. Innovations in irrigation may hold new promise in helping stem the loss of valuable water resources, and new crop varieties that require less water may prove hardy enough to survive the often harsh West Texas environment.

Whatever the future may bring, the history of West Texas agriculture has demonstrated one unique feature: the region's agriculturalists are tenacious—some would say stubborn—and surely they will find a way to maintain an industry and a way of life that has persevered through many transformations and shifts in often rapid succession. Agriculture will remain a vital economic and social factor in West Texas for a long time to come.

## FOR FURTHER READING

Carlson, Paul H. *Texas Woollybacks: The Range Sheep and Goat Industry.* College Station: Texas A&M Press, 1982.

Dale, Edward Everett. *The Range Cattle Industry: Ranching on the Great Plains from 1865 to 1925.* Norman: University of Oklahoma Press, 1930; reprinted 1960.

Green, Donald E. *Land of the Underground Rain: Irrigation on the Texas High Plains, 1910–1970.* Austin: University of Texas Press, 1973.

Hamalainen, Pekka. *The Comanche Empire.* New Haven: Yale University Press, 2008.

Jordan, Terry G. *Trails to Texas: Southern Roots of Western Cattle Ranching.* Lincoln: University of Nebraska Press, 1981.

Pearce, William M. *The Matador Land and Cattle Company.* Norman: University of Oklahoma Press, 1964.

Rathjean, Frederick W. *The Texas Panhandle Frontier.* Austin: University of Texas Press, 1973.

Reisner, Marc. *Cadillac Desert: The American West and Its Disappearing Water.* New York: Viking, 1986.

Skaggs, Jimmy M. *Prime Cut: Livestock Raising and Meatpacking in the United States, 1607–1983.* College Station: Texas A&M Press, 1986.

Worster, Donald. *Dust Bowl: The Southern Plains in the 1930s.* New York: Oxford University Press, 1979.

Part IV

# SOCIETY AND CULTURE

The five chapters that complete this volume cover dynamic aspects of the social and cultural history of West Texas. The region has produced a large number of successful writers, including, among others, Elmer Kelton, Louise Erdman, and A. C. Greene. It has been a cradle of development for seemingly countless musicians, including Buddy Holly, Bob Wills, Marty Robbins, Tanya Tucker, Ralna English, and, not least, Roy Orbison. Its religious practices, Roman Catholic under Spanish rule, then dominated by evangelical Protestantism in the era of Anglo settlement, continue to support conservative Christian traditions. The region also has a long-standing reputation for support of public education. The large number of parks and recreation areas in West Texas, many of them state and national parks preserving terrain of exceptional natural value, draw visitors from far beyond the region.

In fresh and singular ways, chapters 14 and 15 treat the literature of West Texas, broadly defined, its music, and the people who have created them. The authors of these innovative approaches to their subjects describe the region as a place that has produced many fine writers and musicians, some remarkable literature, and much beautiful music. In unique ways, chapters 16, 17, and 18 cover big and highly significant material—education, religion, and recreation—in sharp and vigorous perspectives.

Collectively, the five chapters represent a large amount of new material, modern ideas, and fresh interpretations.

# CHAPTER 14

# Literature and Finding West Texas in the Poets of Place

*Andy Wilkinson*

Wilkinson, himself a poet, musician, songwriter, and playwright, reminds us that creative expression takes many forms. He reviews the poetry of West Texas, defined broadly, and also considers the region's more traditional genres as part of a poetics of place. Building on an observation made by Wallace Stegner, he establishes his own notions and hypotheses about West Texas poets—liberally conceived—and their relationship to the region's varied landscapes. His vision includes conventional forms of literature (fiction, narrative history, journals, poetry itself) but also performance art (dance and song) and visual art (petroglyphs, painting, and photography).

Wallace Stegner's pronouncement that "no place is a place until it has a poet" is itself poetry, an armful of meaning in a handful of words.[1] We understand it straightway—about place and about how place comes about without making the mistake of definition. Find the poets, Stegner suggests, and West Texas can be found through them.

Yet these poets of place cannot be defined either, for poets fit into boxes no better than places do. Should we look for poets who write about the place, or for poets from the place, or for poets who qualify both ways?

Should we look only to published, recognized works, or will poems in the oral or folk traditions satisfy? And what, exactly, is a poet?

The word "poet" springs from the Ancient Greek word *poiēsis*, "to make." Classical thought divided the works of mankind into two realms. The first of these is philosophy (science, in contemporary terminology) which concerns itself with the practical uses of things. Poetry, *poiēsis*, the second realm, has as its purview the true making of things. In this sense, poetry does not refer only to what today we call verse, but rather is the spirit that underlies all the arts. If we stick with this older, fundamental distinction, we can search for the poets of West Texas by describing rather than by defining them.

As with science, the primary description of art is that it is a process rather than a product, not an achievement but a constant work in progress. We expect the process of science to yield consistent, replicable results, but in art we expect that a consistent process will yield unique results. By extension, the notion of place is the same, a thing always changing, never immutable, and never clearly defined. Organic, growing from within, place cannot be limited by the definitions and maps and surveys of geographers, historians, or politicians.

Unlike science, art is not didactic. Fundamentally based in story, not theory, it cares more about questions than answers. Whereas science invites confirmation, art, by its acceptance of the inevitability of mystery, invites participation, its process a conversation that allows, even demands, that others share in the creation of the narrative. Said another way, art shows, it does not tell. In the same way, place evinces itself only to participants, not through signs and borders created to benefit outsiders.

Unlike science, art is not progressive. Science is based on a rigorous and constant testing of the null hypothesis, a testing that relentlessly narrows the gap between what is known and what is able to be known by building on a shared communal knowledge. Art, in contrast, never proceeds by rejection but instead moves in a constant seeking of balance, a balance that is equally abstract and concrete, a balance that is ascertained equally by intuition and analysis. And though art carries no ideal of certainty, when the word "beauty" is substituted for the word "balance," art has the certainty of the ideal.

Place, likewise, is an aesthetic achievement, a product of those same balances of concreteness and abstraction, of clear-eyed appraisal and the ache of intuition. In the passage leading up to his observation about place and poet, Stegner points out that the poet's knowledge of a place involves "the senses, the memory, the history of a family or a tribe . . . the knowledge of place that comes from working in it in all weathers, making a living from it, suffering from its catastrophes, loving its mornings or evenings or hot noons," a knowledge that is only the province of insiders.[2] He notes, moreover, that being inside or outside is not a matter of residence but one of essence: the outsider's allegiances and understandings lie always elsewhere and remain always temporary, but the insider is of the place, inseparable from it, more owned than owner. Poetry—even by a very accomplished poet—may through origin or accident be *from* a place, and yet not be *of* it. The same might be said of the poet.

The poets of place, then, it can be said, have insider aesthetics. Embodying the balance of art, a balance that is the same as beauty, they are not critics. Though they may point out and even dwell upon the faults, difficulties, and shortcomings of their chosen places, they nevertheless embrace them, one and all. For the outsiders, whatever beauty a place might have is but a facade over its intrinsic flaws. But for the poets of place, whatever the flaws, there is an underlying beauty. It is these insiders whom Stegner meant, the voices whose songs are required to make the place. And they are the poets we seek here.

As we have already eschewed definition in favor of description, what follows are some examples of specific West Texas poets—poets in the broad sense described above—those with insider aesthetics. Neither exclusive nor exhaustive nor comprehensive, these examples instead mark a beginning, a recommendation to the reader who looks not for the art of West Texas, but for the West Texas of art.

Over the 12,000 years since the era of the last ice age, as people have traveled the length and breadth of West Texas in the changing seasons of its springs and autumns, the histories and the legends of their tribes and homelands were danced and sung around the millions of their campfires. This and other kinds of performance constitute the most immediate poetry. Watching the making as it unfolds, the audience finds it impossible to confuse process with product, or to conflate the two. That immediacy also makes the experience primal and accessible. Song and dance come spontaneously to children and, among adults, encounter no cultural or linguistic barriers. So it is all but certain that performers were the first poets of West Texas.

Sadly, we have no record of this poetry, but its traces are strong. It may be found in modern powwow dances, such as those at the Comanche Nation Fair in Oklahoma, or around the neon campfires in any West Texas honky-tonk on almost any weekend. These poets' melodies may be found in the old fiddle tunes of Elijah Cox, Jess Morris, Eck Robertson, and Uncle John Wills. Their rhythms are the underpinning of the 1950s rock and roll of Buddy Holly and Roy Orbison. Their stories form the basis of the cowboy songs collected by Jack Thorp and by John Lomax, the country music of Tommy Hancock and Waylon Jennings, and the contemporary singer/ songwriter ballads of Mac Davis, Butch Hancock, Jimmie Dale Gilmore, Joe Ely, Terry Allen, and Cary Swinney. Their passion survives in *corridos* and in the Tejano of El Grupo Milagro and The Hometown Boys.

Visual poetry has less immediacy than performance poetry. We feel what we feel, but we see what we learn to see. It is the first level of abstraction, in which line and color and form stand for the thing itself. Choosing from them, the visual poet consciously makes a representation of the place.

Some record of the earliest West Texas visual poetry remains in its proliferation of rock art (petroglyph) sites, most notably in the pictographs along the Lower Pecos River, where a unified style persisted from 6,000 years ago into the late nineteenth century. Though we lack the certain knowledge to be able to ascribe insider aesthetics to their makers, they nevertheless possess a palpable poetry that has moved modern artists to incorporate their images into contemporary pieces. The sculpture of Bill Worrell is a notable example.

In contrast, with one possible exception, the first visual representations by Anglo-Americans who began to appear in West Texas in the nineteenth century, especially after Spain ceded the region to the United States, clearly lack the insider's perspective. From 1839 to 1854 a half-dozen expeditions crossed West Texas with the aim of establishing well-watered trails suitable either for pioneer travel or the laying of an east–west railroad. Half of these companies brought along artists to document their journeys. Two of the expeditions—one led by United States Army Lieutenant Amiel W. Whipple along the 35th parallel in 1853 and the other by Andrew B. Gray in the same year in a survey for the Texas Western Railroad Company—chose European artists who worked diligently to represent the land in distinctly Old World fashion. The exception came with a third railway survey in 1853, when Captain John Pope chose Harry S. Sindall, who has been described as a mysterious but exceptionally talented oil painter and watercolorist who did his work *en plein air,* that is, on site.[3] Pope himself had an insider's perspective, seeing as he did beyond the landscape's natural barriers to the possibilities of West Texas. Even though we know almost nothing more about Sindall, it is not much of a stretch to conclude that Pope picked someone with an appreciation of place likely to equal his own.

Several good examples of visual poets with insider aesthetics have followed Sindall's brief envisioning of West Texas. Perhaps the most important of these is Frank Reaugh, an outsider-turned-insider. Born in Illinois before the outbreak of the Civil War, Reaugh moved with his family to Texas in 1876, first to Terrell, then to the Dallas suburb of Oak Cliff, where he lived out his life, dying there in 1945. In 1880 he began a series of annual painting trips, first going horseback with trail drives and later, when the droving days were over, by automobile. He painted with pastels *en plein air*—on site, as had Sindall with his watercolors—completing literally thousands of exquisite pastels over his long career, returning time and again to his favorite locations in West Texas: Tule and Palo Duro canyons, Margaret's Peak, Comanche Peak, and the Double Mountains. Though he is best known for his paintings of longhorn cattle, it is the brilliant luminescence and vibrant hues of these captured landscapes that reveal an insider's exuberance for this place.

Like Reaugh, Harold Bugbee was born elsewhere (Lexington, Massachusetts, in 1900) before moving to Texas with his family as a teenager. They wound up on a ranch near Clarendon, where he would die almost fifty years later. Again like Reaugh, the young Bugbee understood that he was witness to a vanishing way of life and set out to record it in sketches and paintings. By the early 1920s he had earned recognition among West Texans as one of their own, becoming a fixture in the regional art scene.

His works are spread throughout the Texas Panhandle in public and private collections.

Visual poets can work in film as well as in paint. Born in north Texas in 1886 at the close of the trail drive era, Erwin E. Smith spent summers on his uncle's ranch near Quanah. Formal study in art school allowed him to bring a painter's eye to the photographic documentation of cowboy and ranch life, and over only a few years, 1905 to 1912, before turning to other interests, he built a body of work that still stands as some of the best visual poetry of a particular way of life in West Texas—and the American West as a whole.

Wyman Meinzer, in contrast, did not come to photography through art. Raised on a ranch near Benjamin, where he still lives, Meinzer was introduced to the camera through his university studies in range and wildlife management in the early 1970s. Though he went on to complete his degree, he chose to make his career as a landscape photographer, marrying a scientific understanding of the natural world to an artist's eye for its dramatic beauty.

So far as is known, the first nonnative to see West Texas was also the first to capture it in the written word. Álvar Núñez Cabeza de Vaca traveled through in 1535 near the end of a remarkable journey that had begun seven years earlier after a shipwreck on the east coast of Florida. Upon returning to Spain in 1537 he wrote an account of his experiences that included descriptions of the land he had traversed and observations about the native peoples he had encountered. Though it was both poetic in tone and sympathetic in sentiment, it lacked the allegiance and the sense of beauty that are required before a work of poetry can be considered a poetry of place.

The same can be said for the next four centuries' worth of diaries and journals kept by the Euro-Americans who crossed West Texas. A few approached Cabeza de Vaca's sentience—Pedro de Casteñeda, who chronicled the Coronado expedition (1540–42), and Albert Pike in his *Prose Sketches and Poems Written in the Western Country* (1834) foremost among them—but most brought with them the prejudices and frames of reference characteristic of the explorers, colonials, and tourists that they were.

*Author Elmer Kelton, San Angelo, 1990s, one of the most accomplished and successful western novelists in America. (Courtesy Monte L. Monroe)*

A smaller number of writers also began to incorporate West Texas into works of fiction, but these early works likewise lacked the poet's perspective. Alexander Le Grand, born in Maryland, created an entire fictional narrative of an expedition on the High Plains in the late 1820s, and Albert Pike who came west from Massachusetts in 1831, wrote, in addition to his early *Prose, Poems and Sketches,* journals and songs all set in West Texas or northern New Mexico. By 1848 a novel, Charles Wilkins Webber's *Old Hicks, the Trail Guide,* had appeared. Though the story unfolds in a mythical valley on the upper Canadian River, that is simply a useful device for the author's version of what was at the time a popular notion: the modern, civilized man entering into an untouched paradise. In its day, though, *Old Hicks* was favorably compared with Herman Melville's *Omoo* (1847), a novel in the same genre.

Fiction works set in West Texas first began to fit our description of poets of place in the twentieth century. Dorothy Scarborough, who lived in Sweetwater for five years as a small child, produced *The Wind* in 1925.

Larry McMurty grew up punching cows on his family's ranch near Archer City on the eastern edge of West Texas. His first novel, *Horseman, Pass By*, published in 1961, later became the movie *Hud*, and a long series of West Texas works has followed—most notably *The Last Picture Show* (1971) and its sequels. The year 1971 also saw *A Way of Knowing*, a novel by Nolan Porterfield, who grew up in Draw, near Lamesa, and is best known for his definitive biographies of Jimmie Rodgers and John Lomax. There followed. a couple of years later, what may be the quintessential West Texas novel from its quintessential native son, Elmer Kelton's *The Time It Never Rained* (1973).

Drawing from the same vein as the diarists and journalists of the Spanish *entradas* and explorations of previous centuries, a number of contemporary writers of nonfiction have written extensively about West Texas. Among them are the narrative historians J. Evetts Haley, J. Frank Dobie, Paul H. Carlson, and John Miller Morris. An historian who doubles as essayist, Dan Flores, has produced two very important works about the region: *Caprock Canyonlands* (1990) and *Horizontal Yellow* (1999). Memoirs, too, have helped flesh out the place that is West Texas, most notably A. C. Greene's *A Personal Country* (1969), Sandra Scofield's *Occasions of Sin* (2004), and Elmer Kelton's *Sandhills Boy* (2007).

Let us rest our brief exploration with two straightforward and essential examples of West Texas poets of place in which "poet" is used in the popular sense and whose works are suffused with both insider aesthetics and the wind and grit of the land itself.

Born in Lubbock in 1934, Walt McDonald was raised there in the center of what he calls hardscrabble country. After service as an officer and pilot in the U.S. Air Force, he collected a doctorate in writing from the University of Iowa before spending a long and storied career as a professor, first at the Air Force Academy and then at Texas Tech University, all the while building a prolific body of work that numbers almost two dozen published collections of poems and hundreds of magazine and journal credits.

Buck Ramsey (1938–98), born on a farm just east of New Home, Texas, grew up in the Amarillo area, coming of age in the ranch country on the north side of the Canadian River breaks near the community of Middle Well. He worked as a cowpuncher, journalist, and performer, spending most of his adult life in a wheelchair after a horse wreck ended his cowboy career. His poetry flowered later in life when he took up with what has been called the cowboy cultural renaissance, a movement sparked by the Elko gathering of cowboy poets and singers that began in 1987. He is best known for his long epic poem *Grass*.

West Texas has indeed had its poets. They have been recording their efforts from not long after humans first arrived in the region. They have worked in such genres as literature, painting, drawing, sketching, and photography, and one can find this place West Texas through them.

## NOTES

1. Wallace Stegner, *Where the Bluebird Sings to the Lemonade Springs: Living and Writing in the West* (New York: Random House, 1992), 202–205.

2. Stegner, *Where the Bluebird Sings,* 202–205.

3. See John Miller Morris, *El Llano Estacado* (Austin: Texas State Historical Association, 1997).

## FOR FURTHER READING

Carr, Joe, and Alan Munde. *Prairie Nights to Neon Lights: The Story of Country Music in West Texas.* Lubbock: Texas Tech University Press, 1995.

Dobie, J. Frank. *The Longhorns.* New York: Bramhall House, 1951.

———. *The Mustangs.* New York: Bramhall House, 1952.

Flores, Dan. *Caprock Canyon Lands.* Austin: University of Texas Press, 1990.

———. *Horizontal Yellow.* Albuquerque: University of New Mexico Press, 1999.

Folkins, Gail. *Texas Dance Halls: A Two-Step Circuit.* With photographs by J. Marcus Weekley. Lubbock: Texas Tech University Press, 2007.

Greene, A. C. *A Personal Country.* New York: Alfred A. Knopf, 1969.

Kelton, Elmer. *The Time It Never Rained.* New York: Doubleday, 1973.

Kirkland, Forrest, and W. W. Newcomb, Jr. *The Rock Art of Texas Indians.* Austin: The University of Texas Press, 1967.

McDonald, Walt. *Rafting the Brazos.* Denton: University of North Texas Press, 1988.

———. *Whatever the Wind Delivers.* Lubbock: Texas Tech University Press, 1999.

Morris, John Miller. *El Llano Estacado.* Austin: Texas State Historical Association, 1997.

Paredes, Américo. *A Texas-Mexican Cancionero: Folksongs of the Lower Border*. Urbana: University of Illinois Press, 1976.

Porterfield, Nolan. *A Way of Knowing*. New York: Harper's Magazine Press, 1971.

Price, B. Byron. *Imagining the Open Range: Erwin E. Smith, Cowboy Photographer*. Fort Worth: Amon Carter Museum, 1998.

Ramsey, Buck. *Grass*. Lubbock: Texas Tech University Press, 2005.

Stegner, Wallace. *Where the Bluebird Sings to the Lemonade Springs: Living and Writing in the West*. New York: Random House, 1992.

Weismann, Donald L. *Frank Reaugh: Painter to the Longhorns*. College Station: Texas A&M University Press, 1985.

# CHAPTER 15

# The Giant Side of Music

*Curtis Peoples*

The author, a musician and songwriter, describes West Texas musicians and songs that illustrate the sense of place often pervading the region's music, and applies a broad perspective to his theme. Much of the narrative here covers country music, but other genres are not neglected.

Texans value music and, as if to emphasize the point, over time scores of nationally recognized musicians have called the state home. Indeed, because of such performers and songwriters, in recent years a new genre called "Texas Music" has emerged in contemporary popular media. Very few states can claim such a phenomenon. Moreover, Texas seems to have more songs written about it than any other state except, perhaps, Virginia. The place has been immortalized in such songs as "The Yellow Rose of Texas," "Deep in the Heart of Texas," and "Waltz across Texas." Like other states, Texas has an official song: "Texas, Our Texas," although, not surprisingly, some people misidentify the state song as "The Eyes of Texas."

Although geographically large and comprised of various natural and political subregions and subareas, the state in an unusual development seems to enjoy few songs about East, South, or North Texas. One can find numerous songs, however, about West Texas—the "giant side" of the state.

Within West Texas, publicists, cultural historians, local policy makers, music industry professionals, and people living throughout the large region often praise its musical vitality. People are constantly revisiting, discussing, and writing about the meaning of the region's music and its connection to the place. Despite a historically scant population, the greater West Texas region has been a catalyst for creativity, especially in music. It has produced innumerable musicians. Many have become famous, and some have even pioneered new musical trails.

West Texas music has become important enough to the state's culture that the 76th Texas Legislature designated Lubbock and West Texas the "Music Crossroads of Texas." This formal resolution recognizes that area musicians have made a significant contribution to Texas culture and, as it states, have "provided listeners with countless hours of entertainment, contributing to the soundtracks of our lives."[1]

Many well-known musicians have originated from West Texas or at some point in their lives called the region home. Bob Wills and Woody Guthrie remain two of the most celebrated of them. Wills, "The King of Western Swing," is one of the region's more accomplished musicians. He grew up in Hall County and in 1929 began developing his popular music style in Fort Worth. He rose to fame after moving to Tulsa, Oklahoma. Upon refining their sound, Bob Wills and the Texas Playboys, as his band was called, moved west to California, where Wills appeared in films and his group played dances that drew large crowds. A prolific songwriter, Wills is perhaps best known for his popular "New San Antonio Rose."

Oklahoma native Woody Guthrie lived in Pampa, Texas, between 1931 and 1937. During those years of the Great Depression and the Dust Bowl in West Texas, Guthrie found inspiration to pen many of his most admired songs. His experience culminated in the 1940 RCA Victor album *Dust Bowl Ballads*, which features such memorable songs as "Blowin' Down This Road" and "So Long, It's Been Good to Know Yuh (Dusty Old Dust)," among others. Woody Guthrie and Bob Wills remain among the earliest West Texas songsters.

West Texas has been home to countless additional musicians, including Buddy Holly, Don Williams, Jimmy Dean, Mac Davis, and the incomparable Roy Orbison. Snuff Garrett, Tanya Tucker, Waylon Jennings, Joe Ely,

Lee Ann Womack, Virgil Johnson, Donnie Allison, Mary Jane Johnson, David Gaschen, and others have also called the region home. Because the region is both a place and a frame of mind, and because so many musicians have contributed to that tradition, the emphasis here has been limited to songs written about West Texas and related elements of the large territory, a place comprised of wide-open spaces, prairies, deserts, rivers, valleys, and mountains. Songs and folklore featuring such elements of the place have existed since humans first arrived. Indeed, the West Texas environment has shaped the music, and in turn the music to a limited extent has helped to shape the region.

Popular music recordings illustrate the influence. Lyrics and songs are not simple signifiers of the relationship linking place, music, and identity, but rather they represent a complex set of issues. Furthermore, not all songs written about "place" are successful; song structures or artistic performances might not work well.[2] In other words, the overall musicality of a song and its presentation must be exceptional for the song to endure.

Nonetheless, a survey of songs and lyrics shows how songwriters and recording artists view West Texas and related elements of the place. There are, for example, songs about one of the prettiest towns you have ever seen, Abilene; the old West Texas town of El Paso; or the Texas High Plains, where busting the Hub (Lubbock) for the Golden Spread (the Texas Panhandle) along the Amarillo Highway, are typical.

Numerous writers from various genres use the term "West Texas," but it is most associated with country music. Some popular recordings that use the West Texas theme include Brad Paisley's "Clouds of Dust," Garth Brooks's "Cowboy Bill," Kenny Rogers's "Saying Goodbye," Lyle Lovett's "West Texas Highway," Kimmie Rhodes's "West Texas Heaven," Taylor Hicks's "West Texas Sky," the Dixie Chicks' "West Texas Wind," Nanci Griffith's "West Texas Sun," and Gene Autry's "Way out in West Texas." West Texas native and prolific songwriter Butch Hancock penned many such songs. His "West Texas Waltz" and "Dry Land Farm" are two that easily illustrate the region in lyric.

Music about place, however, does not rely solely on lyrically based songs. The aesthetics of instrumental music can evoke visual images of place. For instance, if one hears a traditional Irish or Russian instrumental composition, it is relatively easy to feel some resonance linking the song to its associated place.

Doug Smith's instrumental piece "West Texas" is such a song; it resonates with local West Texas impressions. A passionate West Texan, Smith initially composed "West Texas" in the late 1980s; it appears on his album *Hope* (1998). Along with his passion for the region, Smith imparts his insider aesthetics into the song. He creates an instrumental musical landscape that seems as big as the West Texas sky. The song brings to mind images one might see flashing by the window from a car traveling down a West Texas highway—pump jacks, jackrabbits, coyotes, dust devils, tumbleweeds, tornados, mesquite, horses, and cattle. The song's pulse is that of a dirty blue jeans and worn-out-boot-stomping beat. Listen to the song, and you hear Smith's foot pounding the piano's sustain pedal, as the song's melody builds to an edgy rhythm culminating in the lead section with a sound akin to a tornado. Smith has composed other instrumentals evoking West Texas, including "Tumbleweed Rag," "Buffalo," "Strippin' Cotton," "Acuff Shuffle," and "Flatland Train."

Of course, many songs exemplify West Texas as a whole. Equally, many songs are about the towns, cities, and other elements within the region. The soundtracks of such intimate spaces further reveal West Texas.

El Paso lies farther west than any other major city in West Texas, and it is one of the region's oldest communities. As with any large city, many musicians have called El Paso home, including Vikki Carr, Jimmy Carl Black, Adam Fredric Duritz, Cedric Bixler-Zavala, Al Jourgensen, and Tom Russell, and there are others. Perhaps the most famous El Paso musician is Bobby Fuller, who headed the Bobby Fuller Four. The band had two hits: "I Fought the Law" and "Love's Made a Fool of You." The former, written by fellow West Texan Sonny Curtis, brings to mind the gun-toting outlaw, an image sometimes associated with the region's pioneer and early ranching past. Many groups have recorded the song, including the punk group The Clash, who had a great deal of success with their rendition. Other songs about the city include Trace Adkins's "Snowball in El Paso," Kinky Friedman's "Asshole from El Paso," The Gourds' "El Paso," and Elton John's "All the Way Down to El Paso."

The large, old city is also the namesake for one of the most popular West Texas songs of all times, Marty Robbins's "El Paso." First released on Robbins's *Gunfighter Ballads and Trail Songs* (1959), the piece is about a cowboy in love with a Mexican girl. He guns down a rival and escapes the city, only to return and face his death in the arms of his love. Once again the gunfighter-outlaw theme appears. The song topped both the pop and the country music charts and in 1961 won the Grammy Award for the Best Country and Western Recording. It is Robbins's most famous song, and numerous artists have covered the ballad.

Robbins's sequel to "El Paso" was a song titled "San Angelo," for a city located in the southern heart of West Texas, near the central part of the state. "San Angelo" is also about an outlaw and his lover, but in this song both the gunfighter and his girl die in the streets of the city. Texas music artists Aaron Watson and Mark David Manders also have songs titled "San Angelo." Watson's song is about a brokenhearted man who finds love again. Manders sings about a hard-living man trying to leave the city.

Jazz musician Jack Teagarden lived in San Angelo, and country music star Ernest Tubb operated a live music radio program there on KGKL. Tubb wrote "Swell San Angelo" about a big-hearted city where they raise "sheep, cattle and cotton," and although they "may not have a world of gold," they "got love right in [their] souls." In 1947 the movie *Hollywood Barn Dance* featured the song.

Dennis Linde also lived in San Angelo. He wrote hit songs for Elvis Presley, the Dixie Chicks, Tanya Tucker, Don Williams, and others, including Roger Miller's "Tom Green County Fair"—the county in which San Angelo is located. In recent years San Angelo's Los Lonely Boys achieved worldwide fame and won a Grammy Award.

Northeast of San Angelo is Abilene—the Key City of West Texas. Several notable musicians have called Abilene home, notably Slim Willet, who composed the odd-metered hit song "Don't Let the Stars Get in Your Eyes" as well as "I'm a Tool Pusher from Snyder." Other musicians from Abilene include Lee Roy Parnell, who has had a number of top ten country songs in his long career, and the popular and award-winning country artists Larry Gatlin and the Gatlin Brothers.

According to music historian Joe Specht, Abilene is a city found in numerous songs simply because "it rhymes."[3] Artists who have used just the name "Abilene" for a song title include Sam "Lightnin'" Hopkins, David Alvin, Sheryl Crow, Ian Moore, and George Hamilton IV. Hamilton's song is the most famous written about Abilene. Once, some doubt existed about whether the song was about Abilene, Texas, or its namesake in Kansas, but the song now is most associated with the Texas city. The ballad tells of freedom of space, hospitality, and serenity, three enduring traits often associated with West Texas.

Many writers have used Abilene as a main theme of a song, or as a brief reference. Besides George Hamilton's song, the best-known song referencing Abilene, for Texans at least, must be Gary P. Nunn's Texas tribute "London Homesick Blues." Nunn wrote it while touring with Michael Martin Murphey in England, and it first appeared on Jerry Jeff Walker's *Viva Terlingua* (1973). In 1977 the PBS television series *Austin City Limits* adopted "London Homesick Blues" as the theme song for its closing credits—a tradition that lasted twenty-four years, helping to make it a patented (West) Texas country anthem celebrating country music from Amarillo to Abilene.

Northwest of Interstate 20 lie the High Plains of Texas. The area encompasses parts of both the Llano Estacado and the Texas Panhandle. Numerous musicians have lived in the area, and several of its towns and cities have been popularized in song. Possibly the earliest recorded song about a West Texas town is Phil Baxter's "I'm a Ding Dong Daddy (from Dumas)." The song transpired after Baxter stumbled upon Dumas in his travels. He spent some time in the town and penned the song within in a year after his departure. The song gained national attention after Phil Harris, bandleader of the *Jack Benny Radio Show,* recorded the song. In the late 1930s Bob Wills and his Texas Playboys likewise had success with a rendition of the song. It even inspired the call letters of the Dumas Radio station KDDD, which came on the air shortly after World War II.

Leaving Dumas, one can take U.S. 87 south to a city that is commemorated in numerous recorded songs, Amarillo. Many notable musicians have called Amarillo home, including the famous fiddler Eck Robertson. A pioneer of the Texas fiddle style, he is credited with playing on the first commercial country music recordings in 1922. Other musicians who lived in Amarillo are Buddy

Knox, Jimmy Gilmer, Eddie Reeves, The Nighthawks, and Susan Gibson. In the early 1990s Gibson wrote the huge hit song "Wide Open Spaces," which appeared on the Dixie Chicks' album of the same title in 1998.

The most famous song written about the Panhandle city is the rodeo ballad "Amarillo by Morning," by Amarillo's own Terry Stafford (with Paul Fraser). Stafford recorded the song in 1973, and George Strait covered it in his album *Strait from the Heart* (1982), through which it gained enormous popularity. Although it did not reach number one on the country music charts, it is widely considered to rank among the best country songs of all-time. Several other songs in widely different styles briefly mention the city, such as Johnny Cash's "I've Been Everywhere," Bob Dylan's "Brownsville Girl," and Nat King Cole's "Route 66."

*Tommy Hancock and the Roadside Playboys, 1949, at the original Lubbock Cotton Club, among the first venues in West Texas to welcome entertainers and patrons from all ethnic groups. (Courtesy Tommy and Charlene Hancock)*

Four additional songs that have Amarillo in the title are worth mentioning. Neil Sedaka's "Is This the Way to Amarillo?" tells of a man on the road longing to get back to the city and his sweet Marie. Sedaka used Amarillo because it rhymes with pillow. Emmylou Harris and Rodney Crowell's song "Amarillo" is about a woman who has lost her man to several dire influences: Amarillo, pinball, and Dolly Parton and Porter Wagoner on the jukebox. Alan Jackson's "Amarillo" portrays a man telling a young love, who is leaving town to go to Hollywood, that if she ever gets back to Amarillo, he will be waiting. The country group McBride and the Ride and country artist Jason Aldean have both released the song "Amarillo Sky," about a farmer carrying on the tradition of his father and grandfather and praying that his dream does not run dry underneath the Amarillo sky.

And, of course, there is Terry Allen's "Amarillo Highway." Like Nunn's "London Homesick Blues," it has become something of a West Texas anthem. The song features towns like Plainview, Idalou, and New Deal. It was created in 1970, after Allen had spent the day with fellow writer David Hickey in a horrible sandstorm in Idalou. Both the Maines Bothers and Robert Earl Keen released versions of the song, making it very popular. It first appeared on Allen's *Lubbock (On Everything)* (1979), an album filled with numerous references to Lubbock and things associated with the city.

Lubbock has been a music powerhouse for years. Musical groups and individuals who have called Lubbock home include, among many others, the Lubbock Texas Quartet, Drugstore Cowboys, Sons of the Pioneers, Buddy Holly, Mac Davis, The Heartbeats, Bobby Keys, The Flatlanders (Jimmy Dale Gilmore, Butch Hancock, and Joe Ely), the Maines Brothers, Pete Orta, the Hometown Boys, Grupo El Milagro, Pat Green, and Richie McDonald. Not many songs exist about Lubbock, but some are notable. Trisha Yearwood's "Hello, I'm Gone" is about a woman leaving Dallas who breaks down in Lubbock. Aaron Watson wrote "Lonely Lubbock Lights," not about the infamous lights seen in the Lubbock sky on August 25, 1951, but about driving down the road and seeing "no love in sight, just those lonely Lubbock lights."

Terry Allen's album *Smokin' the Dummy* (1980) contains the song "The Lubbock Tornado (I Don't Know)," regarding one of the most significant events in Lubbock's history, and indeed the state's, a severe tornado that hit the city in May 1970. The song recounts how the massive tornado "throwed around that Panhandle town, till it couldn't throw it around no more, and tiny creatures went flying, right out of prairie dog town." In the end, it killed twenty-six people, injured hundreds, and left a path of destruction of fifteen square miles between downtown and the city's airport. The greatest destruction occurred in the predominantly Hispanic Guadalupe sector. The devastation inspired Agapito Zuniga to write a heartfelt *corrido* titled "Desastre de Lubbock, Texas," telling how "the tornado began in the American neighborhood, but all the disaster occurred in the Mexican neighborhood."

Although a number of popular songs about Lubbock have appeared over the years, two have received a majority of widespread attention. Mac Davis, one of the city's most successful musicians, who penned many hits during his career, commemorates the city in his well-known song "Texas in My Rear View Mirror." Released in 1980, the song begins with a restless teenager yearning to go to Hollywood to pursue his dream of becoming a famous musician—like Lubbock's hometown musical great, Buddy Holly. Then comes the main chorus and the famous line: "I thought happiness was Lubbock Texas in my rear view mirror." Most people clearly identify the line with the song and, for some reason, many think it means that Davis (whether as composer, or as the character in the lyrics) is contemptuous of Lubbock. Yet by the end of the song a clear affinity for Lubbock becomes apparent: the young fellow wants to be buried there, someday, in his denim jeans.

In 2006 the Dixie Chicks, with lead singer Lubbock's own Natalie Maines, released "Lubbock or Leave It," which pokes some fun at the city. The song describes some of the city's less inspiring attributes, such as the lack of trees, the twenty-six-mile Loop 289 beltway, and the enormous Lubbock Preston Smith International Airport. But it also references Buddy Holly and the city's relationship to the Bible Belt.

Lubbock and many other communities in West Texas continue to produce new and talented musicians. In addition to some of those mentioned above, successful musical artists who have come from West Texas include Guy Clark, Jimmy Torres, Carolyn Hester, Buck Ramsey, Charlie Phillips, Joe King Carrasco, Cary Swinney, Bob Montgomery, Billy Walker, Tommy Allsup, Delbert McClinton, Tony Guerrero, J. D. Souther, Tommy and Charlene Hancock, Ralna English, Andy Wilkinson, and Floyd Tilman. The list is far-reaching and continues to grow.

Many popular recorded songs reveal something of the historic West Texas identity. The music often evokes long-established regional images of varied landscapes, towns and cities, farming and ranching, long highways, the sky, the wind, the weather, love, tragedy, and comedy. Often inspired by gospel and blues music, most of the music is historically rooted in the Anglo country repertoire and modern rock and roll. However, the region has also been home to vibrant strains of Tex-Mex, Latino, and other Hispanic popular genres. In 1968 San Angelo's Tony "Ham" Guerrero joined Little Joe (Hernandez) and the Latinaires and in 1973 formed Tortilla Factory, which mixed various musical genres to create a Latin Soul sound. The group received a Grammy nomination in 2009. Lubbock's Grupo El Milagro was a 2004 Grammy nominee for the best Tejano album. In 1996 the Hometown Boys were the first Hispanic group inducted into the West Texas Walk of Fame. The following year, pioneers of Chicano music Los Premiers were also inducted. Other West Texas Walk of Fame inductees include accordionist Pete Morales in 2002 and Agnes Morales of the New Variety Band in 2005. These well-known figures represent music traditions firmly established in West Texas, which continue to thrive and draw an ever-wider audience.

Modern West Texas remains a ranging territory of urban and rural environments, a wide array of peoples, and, as it turns out, a place that continues to produce new music. But, within the region's emerging music genres, such as hip-hop, one still hears the strong, traditional connection to West Texas as place and life within its borders. Although songs and folklore about the area date back for centuries, the advent of technology and recorded music helped popularize the region.

Many songs about West Texas reached high positions on music charts. They helped to promote the diverse territory to the world. Songs about West Texas reveal a conventional history and mystique and at the same time a modern transformation. No doubt, established and budding song-writers will continue to produce strong new material about the giant side of Texas.

## NOTES

1. John Connell and Chris Gibson, *Sound Tracks: Popular Music, Identity, and Place* (New York: Routledge, 2003).

2. "Bill HCR 65 Legislative Session 76 (R) History," *Texas Legislature Online*, http://www.legis.state.tx.us/BillLookup/History.aspx?LegSess=76R&Bill=HCR65 (accessed 27 August 2013). The resolution recognizes some of West Texas's better known musicians, including Jimmie Dale Gilmore, Butch Hancock, Roy Orbison, Buddy Holly, Tanya Tucker, Joe Ely, Natalie Maines, Billy Walker, The Maines Brothers Band, Sonny Curtis, Darren Norwood, Ronna Reeves, Andy Wilkinson, Johnny Ray Watson, Mac Davis, Bob Wills, Guy Clark, Waylon Jennings, Jimmy Dean, The Crickets, Pat Green, Terry Allen, and the Gatlin Brothers.

3. Joe W. Specht, *The Women There Don't Treat You Mean: Abilene in Song* (Abilene, Tex.: State House Press, McMurry University, 2006), 10.

## FOR FURTHER READING

Carney, George, ed. *The Sounds of People and Places: Readings in the Geography of American Folk and Popular Music.* Lanham, Md.: Rowman and Littlefield; University Press of America, 1994.

Carr, Joe, and Alan Munde, *Prairie Nights to Neon Lights: The Story of Country Music in West Texas.* Lubbock: Texas Tech University Press, 1995.

Connell, John, and Chris Gibson. *Sound Tracks: Popular Music, Identity, and Place.* New York: Routledge, 2003.

Gilmore, Mikal. "West Texas Music, from the Outside." In *Honky Tonk Visions on West Texas Music: 1936–1986.* Lubbock: The Museum at Texas Tech University, 1986.

Hartman, Gary. *The History of Texas Music.* College Station: Texas A&M University Press, 2008.

Knight, David B. *Landscapes in Music: Space, Place and Time in the World's Greatest Music.* Lanham, Md.: Rowman and Littlefield, 2006.

Oglesby, Christopher J. *Fire in the Water, Earth in the Air: Legends of West Texas Music.* Austin: University of Texas Press, 2006.

Peña, Manuel H. *The Mexican American Orquesta: Music, Culture, and the Dialectic of Conflict.* Austin: University of Texas Press, 1999.

Specht, Joe W. *The Women There Don't Treat You Mean: Abilene in Song.* Abilene, Tex.: State House Press, 2006.

Zelinsky, Wilbur. *The Cultural Geography of the United States.* Englewood Cliffs, N.J.: Prentice Hall, 1992.

CHAPTER 16

# Public Education in West Texas

*Gene B. Preuss*

During the late nineteenth century and through much of the twentieth, changes and challenges to public education in West Texas were affected by events at local, state, and national levels. The ways in which West Texans reacted to those developments in turn influenced the course of public education beyond the region.

I n 1911 Zell Rodgers SoRelle was born in the Texas Panhandle town of Clarendon. She attended Clarendon schools and Clarendon Junior College and then enrolled in West Texas Normal College at Canyon. "I graduated from high school in 1929," she recalled in an interview in 1973, "and I went to college a year and a summer, and then started teaching."[1] She taught at the one-room Bairfield School near Clarendon. Like many other small, rural schools in West Texas, the little school did not survive the Great Depression. The building could seat twelve students, but when SoRelle taught there she only averaged five students; one year she had only one pupil.

The novelty of a teacher instructing a single student attracted the attention of *Ripley's Believe it or Not*, and national attention brought notoriety to the Bairfield School. "I had letters from all over the United States," said SoRelle. "I had two or three proposals." Whether or not she responded to any of the proposals, she soon found a spouse: "I quit at the Christmas break and got married, and I forgot who took over, but I believe that little school closed the very next year after that because there were no students—the ranchers moved away and I think there were just no students."

Today, the Bairfield School is on display at the National Ranching Heritage Center at Texas Tech University in Lubbock. It is an example of what often happened to small, community-built one-room schools. Sometimes called old-field schools, they were often established in old, fallow fields no longer useful for cattle or farming. After the students in an area were old enough to leave school, families with younger children moved the school building to another old field nearer to the next generation of students. The Bairfield School was named after the last family that moved the building to their property so that their children could go to school close to home. Its modest history illustrates one of the challenges of public education in West Texas.

Not many years before SoRelle taught at the Bairfield School, the eminent historian Frederick Jackson Turner explained that the concept of the frontier was "the distinguishing feature of American life," whereby the nation continually created itself anew. In his article "The Significance of the Frontier on American History," he wrote that at the frontier—"the meeting point between savagery and civilization"—those institutions important to American society were recreated with each successive wave of settlement.[2] Yet settlers on the West Texas frontier did not create a new vision of the conventional public school system. Instead, as with the Bairfield School, the tried and true, existing institution was simply transported to extend public education to serve new settlers.

West Texas communities of course benefited from developments in the state school system that originated in the late 1880s. And, likewise, they struggled with the rest of the state to find solutions to the challenges that confronted public education through the twentieth century. Just as in other parts of the state, three major questions came to dominate public education in West Texas: Where does the responsibility for schooling lie? Who should have access to educational opportunity? And how will schools be funded equitably?

The story of public education in Texas is a halting one, revealed in fits of activity followed by intervals of neglect or opposition. The story of state-supported public education usually begins with the School Law of 1854; in fact, however, little organization and implementation of public schools took place as a result of that legislation. Most people considered education a parental responsibility. The majority of parents taught their children at home. Perhaps a teacher would move to town and set up a school for the few who could afford to pay tuition. Wealthier parents might hire private tutors or send their children to boarding schools outside the state. Parents in rural areas might pool their monies to attract a teacher, and their children would attend school for as long as the teacher stayed. In most cases, the only qualification for teaching was the ability to write, read, and "factor" numbers.

The Civil War distracted Texas leaders from devoting much attention to the state's public schools, but during Reconstruction lawmakers passed constitutional provisions to establish a state educational system. The Freedmen's Bureau and missionary organizations also created schools for the children of poor whites and former slaves. Yet Redeemers—former Confederate leaders—soon dismantled the Reconstruction system of schools.

Nevertheless public school proponents continued to stress the importance of free schools for Texas children. In 1884 the legislature again provided a basis for a public education system by creating the office of state superintendent of schools, instituting a property tax, and creating the Permanent School Fund. At the same time, Anglo settlement moved into western Texas, and farmers, business owners, bankers, and builders appreciated the importance of state-supported public schools in attracting more families to the western part of the state. By the time Texans were able to take advantage of the land and opportunity that the western counties provided, questions about who bore the responsibility for education were already being resolved. Yet Texas lawmakers continued to struggle with questions about access and equitable funding, problems that West Texas educators also faced.

Sparse settlement in West Texas exacerbated these concerns. Some scattered settlements had existed in the western part of the state prior to the Civil War. El Paso was long a military outpost, and some farmers had moved beyond the Hill Country despite the environmental challenges and prior claims on the land asserted by Native Americans, who then occupied much of West Texas.

In the 1880s cattle ranchers, attracted by the region's rich grasslands and inexpensive land prices, moved into West Texas. At the same time, railroads began to stretch westward across the region. The lines further encouraged western settlement by enticing farmers to move onto agricultural land near the new tracks and shipping nodes. Concomitantly, an increased military presence to control any Comanche threat, along with the reduction of bison herds, attracted still other pioneers to the frontier as rangelands opened for grazing and settlement.

San Angelo exemplifies the population growth and importance of education in communities near military outposts. In the 1870s children in the area attended school at Fort Concho. By 1876 the area boasted three schools, which students paid tuition to attend. A tax-supported public school opened in 1883. In 1889, in an area not far from San Angelo, settlers in the area of Lipan Flat donated their own money to build the Lipan school, also known as the Little School, for their children. The community's founder, John Bunnell, remembered the importance of the school. "After the schoolhouse was rebuilt, it became a social center," he stated. The rural schoolhouse became the nucleus of the budding community. "People we had heard of, but [had] never seen, began to take part in the social activities," he recalled.[3] Later, after a windstorm destroyed the building, residents held a barbecue fundraiser and soon built a larger schoolhouse. Settlers continued to move to the area, and by 1903 San Angelo's population had grown large enough to support an independent school district.

In 1875 the Texas legislature had enabled the creation of independent school districts in towns and urban areas, but rural areas continued to convene schools on an "as needed" basis. If enough school-aged children lived in an area, parents could petition for an ad hoc committee to create a school and call for a teacher. The temporary nature of rural schools made it difficult to secure permanent teachers, and salaries were often low. Many West Texas schools hired very young women as teachers, who may have only recently graduated high school.

Ethel Moore Fulton's story illustrates the inexperience of many such young women. "My father got the school for me," she wrote.

I finished high school at the age of seventeen, took the teachers' examination. . . . I came into Brownfield on Wednesday afternoon. I
rode the train from Lubbock. It was snowing. It was night. My daddy
had told me to stay at the Hill Hotel. . . . All the cowboys from the surrounding towns had come down there to celebrate Thanksgiving and
they didn't have a room for me, and I was absolutely scared to death.

Fulton's luck soon improved:

[Someone] told me the lady who keeps the telephone office sometimes keeps a woman, so this lady had a room and let me stay there.
The snow was deep the next morning, and I had to stay there in this
room and go back down to the hotel for my meals. It was Saturday
before they could come in from Scuddy [School]. Mr. Jim Cunningham came in. I met him over at Judge Price's office and we signed the
contract, and got my trunk in his old Hupmobile. I never had seen
a prairie dog, and just couldn't wait to see my first prairie dog as we
drove out from the old Dick Brownfield house and out toward Old
Lamesa Road. It was quite an experience for a little girl who had never
been off anywhere.[4]

Inexperienced and low-paid teachers aside, rural schools provided a
substantially different education than permanent, better-funded schools in
districts with a larger population and a more substantial property tax base.
The differences between schools in small rural communities and those in
larger towns and urban areas became a special focus for education reformers during the Progressive Era.

In the late nineteenth and early twentieth centuries, these reformers created organizations at local, state, and national levels to address common
concerns, including educational issues. In 1893, for example, members of
the Child Culture Study Circle in El Paso encouraged the school district
to create the first free public kindergarten in Texas. One of the group's
founders, Olga Bernstein Kohlberg, was active in numerous women's
groups and social improvement causes around El Paso. She also served as
a vice-president for the Texas Federation of Women's Clubs, which lobbied for a number of school reforms in the early decades of the twentieth

century. The Texas Congress of Mothers and Parent-Teacher Associations, founded in Dallas in 1909, is another example of local groups that pooled their resources to found a statewide organization to lobby lawmakers in support of reforms in public education.

In 1911 the state legislature passed the Rural High School Law, which classified rural schools along the same lines as independent school districts. First-class schools would have at least two teachers, a four-year program, and an eight-month school year. Second-class schools would have the same requirements as the first-class schools but have a three-year program. Third-class schools would have at least one teacher, at least a two-year program, and hold class for at least seven months of the year. The law also allowed consolidation of smaller, less efficient schools, greater curricular authority for rural school administrators, and new regulations for teacher certification.

In 1915 Governor James Ferguson, who had campaigned on a rural improvement platform calling for a "Million Dollar Appropriation for Rural Schools," signed a compulsory attendance law. The influence of Progressive reforms in Texas also became further evident when in 1918 Annie Webb Blanton became the first woman elected to the office of

*West Texas schoolroom in session, ca. 1915. (Courtesy Southwest Collection, Texas Tech University)*

state superintendent of public education. As superintendent, she oversaw several additional reforms benefiting rural West Texas schools, including a free-textbook law, teacher certification requirements, and increased teacher salaries.

These reforms benefited West Texas, where school enrollment grew rapidly in the early twentieth century. For example, Lubbock High School's first graduating class was in 1909. The next year, enrollment in Lubbock schools reached almost 500 pupils, taught by twelve teachers. By 1913 the number had increased to 681 students and fourteen teachers. In 1919 twenty-eight teachers taught more than 1,000 students. By the start of the next school year, Lubbock schools had employed forty instructors and counted more than 1,300 pupils. Lubbock's rapid growth challenged the school district to provide additional teachers and facilities. Moreover, in 1920 Lubbock opened schools for Mexican American students, and also schools for African American students, and in 1922 the district built schools in the northwest, southwest, and southeastern wards of the city. While other West Texas communities may not have grown as rapidly as Lubbock, even rural districts gained from the new school laws.

As public school populations in West Texas increased, the need for higher education also grew. In the Texas Panhandle the Methodist Episcopal Church established Clarendon College in 1898, which until 1926 operated largely as a two-year college. Additional colleges opened in the early twentieth century to serve the rising population's increasing demand for educational opportunities, especially for schoolteacher training but also for other education beyond high school.

In the 1890s the state legislature had created normal schools to provide teacher training. Such schools opened in Huntsville (Sam Houston Normal School), Denton (North Texas State Normal School), and San Marcos (Southwest Texas State Normal School). In 1909 West Texas Normal School opened in Canyon, just south of Amarillo; a former state superintendent of public education, Robert B. Cousins, served as its president from 1910 through 1918. In 1916 the legislature passed a law to certify junior colleges; in 1920 the College of the City of El Paso became the first public junior college in the state (it later merged with the Texas School of Mines). In 1922 Wichita Falls opened a junior college, the second municipal college in the state. Responding to pressure from West Texas leaders and civic groups for a large university in West Texas, the legislature in 1918 approved West Texas Normal School's affiliation with Texas A&M. When controversy ensued, the legislature reversed its approval.

The newly formed West Texas Chamber of Commerce now lobbied for a large university. After much wrangling over the nature and location of such an institution, Governor Pat Neff in 1923 signed a bill authorizing Lubbock as the site of a new major university. Classes began at Texas Technological College two years later, and by the 1930s, West Texans could take graduate-level instruction in either Lubbock or Canyon.

In the early 1920s the number of women enrolling in higher education nationwide increased; soon women represented almost half of the country's college students. Women in West Texas soon took advantage of the region's educational opportunities. Maria Elena Garcia of El Paso enrolled in the College of Mines at a time when few Mexican American women attended college. "We must have been a very advanced family ideologically, because I went to college," she stated. "I remember when my mother sent me to high school that these friends of mine told Mama, 'That's wasted money. What is she going to serve her husband? Algebra? Chemistry? . . . How is she going to iron his shirts?' And then my mother said, 'Well, who said she's going to get married?'"[5] Her father also supported her continued education: "She's going to school as long as she's interested in it," he told family members. "When she isn't interested in it, she can quit." During the Great Depression of the 1930s, Maria Elena's father lost his job. As she had already taken the student teaching course in college, she applied at the El Paso school district for a teaching position:

> So I went and made my application, and they told me, "Sorry," they couldn't employ me because there was no place for me. But I was going to get a job regardless. I was there for two weeks every morning and every afternoon. I just sat there and waited for Mr. A. H. Hughey. . . . So Hughey would come in and say, "Hello," and he would leave and say, "Good-bye." Finally, he must have said, "Get that girl out of my sight. Give her a job." So I went to Aoy School. And when I signed the contract, I was seventeen, so my mother had to come.

Maria's teaching assignment provided support for her family while her father was out of work, a powerful example of how much these early educational opportunities for women could accomplish.

Stories like those of Maria Elena Garcia, Ethel Fulton, and Zelle SoRelle illustrate that educated young women could find work as teachers in West Texas. But many also learned that their position could also be tenuous, especially as the region experienced economic hardships during the 1930s. SoRelle remembered that during the Great Depression teachers in West Texas faced uncertainty:

> Things were a little bit hard with all the teachers. You had to take vouchers. Then you had to take those vouchers to the bank, and then they had to be discounted, I remember the bank at Clarendon was awfully nice to me, they didn't discount very much . . . I think about $4 or $5. I believe my salary was around $90 or $95 [monthly] . . . and that was a BIG salary. . . . I was paid from September to May, then I had no salary from May to September.[6]

The Great Depression affected communities across West Texas in various ways. In a general sense the economic crisis together with the onset of Dust Bowl environmental conditions drove numerous people from farms, and many small communities lost their schools. Some communities disappeared altogether. Small rural schools especially were forced to shut their doors as families left farms or teachers moved to cities. In 1937 the *Report of the Results of the Texas Statewide School Adequacy Survey*, a WPA-sponsored study, emphasized that school systems needed to be more efficient and encouraged the consolidation of small rural schools. Consolidation was not a new idea, considering that many schools were already closing; in this respect the report only acknowledged what was already occurring. And when the United States entered World War II, smaller schools continued to decline as more people moved into urban areas and male teachers enlisted in the military.

The postwar years at last brought sweeping changes in public education. The Servicemen's Readjustment Act, or G.I. Bill of Rights, passed by the U.S. Congress in 1944, provided educational opportunities for former military personnel. The law led to increased enrollment in colleges and universities and teacher-training programs. In addition, the "baby boom" following the war soon led to rapid growth in public school enrollments.

In 1949 the Texas legislature passed the Gilmer-Aikin laws, a major revision of the Texas school system. The laws replaced the elected state superintendent of schools with a commissioner of education appointed by an elected board of education, guaranteed all Texas teachers a minimum salary of $2,000 annually, encouraged school consolidation, and required that all schools offer classes through the twelfth grade. Groups that supported the Gilmer-Aikin legislation, such as the Texas State Teachers Association, emphasized low teacher salaries as an important issue. Several of the legislators who drafted and voted for the bills were former teachers and recognized that too many school teachers were leaving Texas classrooms for other jobs. Lubbock representative Preston Smith, who later became governor of Texas, was one of those who supported raising teachers' salaries. When constituents asked how he stood on the issue of the teacher pay raise, Smith replied, "How many of you here have ever known a school teacher to get rich on what the state paid him? And who else in your community had more influence in raising your child than a school teacher?"[7]

African American teachers across the Lone Star State particularly benefited from the Gilmer-Aikin laws. For the first time they were guaranteed a salary equal to that of white teachers. Throughout the 1940s the NAACP had supported a number of efforts by educators across the South to challenge their local school boards for equal pay. The strategy was successful in some areas. Where it was not, the Commission on Democracy in Education, organized by the Colored Teachers State Association of Texas, sought legal recourse to address pay inequity. Although the commission enjoyed some successes, challenging individual school districts remained time-consuming.

Overall, the Gilmer-Aikin legislation changed the landscape of public education in Texas overnight, and West Texas felt the change. One former teacher at Lubbock's Dunbar High School, the segregated school for African American students, recalled how his father, who also had been a teacher, had struggled to earn a living in the classroom, and what a difference the reform had made:

> The biggest change that I noticed [about the Gilmer-Aikin laws] was the salary [increase]. Because, see, my father made as little as seventy-five dollars a month teaching and working seven months out of the year. And he had to do other things to maintain his family during the five months that he didn't teach. And he also went to school. Then when he came to Slaton, he made a big increase in salary from seventy-five dollars to ninety dollars a month. And when I finished my first job under Gilmer-Aikins, I made $2,405 a year, and that was a fantastic salary. Of course, he benefited from it, too. He just thought it was fantastic.[8]

The change in West Texas public education aligned the region's schools with trends affecting schools across the nation. They specifically succeeded in addressing some of the issues of public education funding that had concerned educators for the first half of the century.

Events beyond West Texas further affected the region's schools in terms of access to education. Most importantly, legal decisions following World War II signaled the end of de jure segregation. At the beginning of the twentieth century, the majority of the state's Mexican American and African American population lived in South or East Texas, respectively, yet by the middle of the twentieth century the state's demographics had begun to change. Although there had always been numbers of African Americans and Mexican Americans who called West Texas home, immigration from Mexico during the Mexican Revolution (1910–ca. 1920), as well as the general shortage of agricultural workers during and after both World War I and World War II, had increased opportunities for Mexican migrant farmworkers. These laborers followed a route known as the Big Swing, beginning in South Central Texas and following the harvests into West Texas. Ranching also attracted Mexican cowboys, sheepherders, goatherds, and shearers to the region.

As the Hispanic and African American populations increased, the League of United Latin American Citizens (LULAC) and the National Association for the Advancement of Colored People (NAACP) challenged segregation in West Texas schools. Although, historically, laws had mandated separate schools specifically for African American children, Mexican American children, because they spoke Spanish, were often segregated as well, in schools of their own. Most segregated schools provided only elementary classes, because they did not anticipate minority students' staying in school beyond the fifth grade. Few schools, except in the larger districts, offered high-school coursework for black or Hispanic students.

After Mexican American students won a case in Central Texas in 1948, the state school superintendent issued a directive against arbitrary segregation of students. But school systems still avoided immediate integration, through such steps as language tests. When the U.S. Supreme Court issued its decision on school desegregation in *Brown v. Board of Education of Topeka* in 1954, West Texas schools were faced with a more serious challenge to traditional segregation practices.

Several West Texas districts simply attempted to avoid integration. In 1955 the Texas Citizens Council in Big Spring tried to argue that the Gilmer-Aikin laws mandated segregation because, according to the legislation, school funds were to be distributed on a segregated basis. Ultimately, this line of reasoning proved unsuccessful. But segregationists found other ways to ignore integration. In 1956, when three African American students attempted to enroll in Mansfield High School, near Fort Worth, hundreds of anti-integrationists converged on the tiny town and protested. Governor Allan Shivers encouraged opposition to the *Brown* decision, and conservative West Texas rancher and historian J. Evetts Haley ran for governor that year on a segregationist platform.

In 1957 the state legislature passed House Bill 65, allowing communities a local-option vote on desegregation of schools. Another bill, HB 231, which allowed school boards to assign students to schools, resulted in schools districts' integrating Mexican American students with African American students. Because Mexican Americans were legally considered white, the bill allowed schools to claim that they had become integrated, while avoiding the spirit of the law. In 1958 Amarillo only had one African American student enrolled in a desegregated school, and in Lubbock only six black pupils were in integrated schools. There were in fact more than 1,000 school-aged African American children in Amarillo and twice that number in Lubbock.

Abilene school officials, in an effort to comply with federal requirements, had tentatively agreed to desegregate students at the newly installed Dyess Air Force Base, but because the school was on state property, not federal land, they were able to delay the integration. In 1962, after Texas Attorney General Will Wilson declared HB 65 (the local-option rule) unconstitutional, Abilene school officials at last proceeded with integration. When President Lyndon B. Johnson signed the Elementary and Secondary Education Act of 1965, the increased federal involvement in public schools further eroded segregation in the public schools. Ultimately, in *United States v. Texas* in 1971, U.S. district court judge William Wayne Justice ordered the Texas Education Agency to take responsibility for the desegregation process throughout the state.

Also in the 1970s, Mexican American families in El Paso challenged the city's education authorities on the system's practices regarding access to Hispanic children. In the 1976 decision *Alvarado v. El Paso Independent School District*, the judge ordered the school district to recruit more Mexican American teachers and to institute desegregation practices, including busing. As a result of the judicial decrees, schools throughout West Texas began meeting desegregation requirements for Mexican American and other Spanish-speaking students.

Although the African American population was relatively small in West Texas cities, desegregation did not occur quickly or evenly. Amarillo desegregated in 1972. The city's population was 144,000 with a school enrollment of 28,000, of which 6 percent were African American. Lubbock's population of 179,000 included 33,000 school-aged children, with 11 percent black; the school system desegregated in 1978. It was another four years before Odessa, with 157,000 residents and 24,000 students, of which 6 percent were African American, desegregated its schools. Although West Texas school integration did not lead to the protests or threats of violence that had occurred in Mansfield, racial tension contributed to the murder of an African American student by a white classmate at Lubbock's Dunbar High School in September 1971.

Desegregation of institutions of higher education in West Texas did not attract as much resistance as it did at the grade school level. Integration at the junior colleges in Big Spring and Amarillo was uneventful. In 1955

Thelma White mounted a successful legal challenge to gain admission at El Paso's Texas Western College, and thus to all Texas state colleges, for African American undergraduate students. Twelve students enrolled following White's victory, although she did not attend the El Paso school, remaining instead at New Mexico A&M at Las Cruces. In the movie *Glory Road* (2006) Hollywood memorializes Texas Western's integrated men's basketball team, coached by Don Haskins, that won the NCAA tournament over the top-ranked Kentucky Wildcats (an all-white team) in 1966.

Despite decades of reform, questions of educational access and equity did not go away, but the question of quality changed the nature of those older issues when they resurfaced at the end of the twentieth century with the information age and the advent of virtually universal global communications. By 2010, a generation of educators had already begun to address new and ongoing concerns about the availability of quality educational opportunities for all students and about whether schools could be funded in such a way as to afford every student access to important and necessary educational opportunities. The resurgence, and evolution, of these core issues in public education—responsibility, access, and funding—affirms their complexity and lack of simple legislative solutions.

In 1991 the state legislature had enacted a short-term funding solution nicknamed the Robin Hood Plan. It took property taxes from wealthier districts and redistributed the monies to poorer districts. West Texas schools that had once benefited from oil revenues faced a decline after oil prices crashed in the mid-1980s, but they were able to recoup lost revenue with Robin Hood funds a few years later.

Toward the end of the next decade wind farms began springing up across rural West Texas. Giant wind turbines stretched across the landscape and by 2010 had made the state the number one producer of wind-powered electricity in the nation. Areas of the state with large numbers of wind turbines are again property-rich, but, because of their sparse population and low school enrollment, their property tax dollars will be redistributed to poorer districts across the state, an unintended wrinkle in the Robin Hood Plan. Here again, the region's variable economic fortunes seem to deny any easy answers to questions about school funding equity, educational access, and quality. Although federal courts have mandated that states find a permanent solution to equitable school financing, a solution has eluded Texas lawmakers.

West Texas public schools were not "recreated" on the frontier. Instead West Texans viewed public education as means to attract more settlers to the area and eagerly incorporated the institutions of public education in eastern states into their frontier communities. West Texas educators often avoided earlier debates over whether public schools should be established, if education should be a parental or state responsibility, or even whether public funds should be allocated toward education. Thus a history of public schools in West Texas must focus not only on how state and national educational developments affected educational institutions in the region, but also on how those wider influences shaped the region's contributions to public education in the state as a whole.

## NOTES

1. Zell SoRelle, interview by Duncan Muckelroy, March 8, 1973, Oral History Collection, Southwest Collection/Special Collections Library, Texas Tech University, Lubbock.

2. Frederick Jackson Turner, "The Significance of the Frontier on American History," in *The Frontier in American History* (New York: Henry Holt, 1920), 3.

3. Quoted in Otis A. Crook, "Lipan #7 to Wall ISD," unpublished manuscript, 1971, Southwest Collection/Special Collections Library, Texas Tech University, Lubbock.

4. Lester Lee and Ethel Moore Fulton, interview by Katherine Hamilton, February 1, 1972, Oral History Collection, Southwest Collection/Special Collections Library, Texas Tech University, Lubbock.

5. María Elena García Connolly, quoted in *Diamond Days: An Oral History of the University of Texas at El Paso* (El Paso: Texas Western Press, 1991), 59–60.

6. Zell SoRelle, interview.

7. Preston Smith, interview by David Murrah, June 28, 1990, Oral History Collection, Southwest Collection/Special Collections Library, Texas Tech University, Lubbock.

8. William R. Powell, interview by Gene B. Preuss, July 7, 1995, Oral History Collection, Southwest Collection/Special Collections Library, Texas Tech University, Lubbock.

## FOR FURTHER READING

Blanton, Carlos Kevin. *The Strange Career of Bilingual Education in Texas, 1836–1981*. College Station: Texas A&M University Press, 2004.

Cottrell, Debbie Mauldin. *Pioneer Woman Educator: The Progressive Spirit of Annie Webb Blanton*. College Station: Texas A&M University Press, 1993.

Eby, Frederick. *The Development of Education in Texas*. New York: Macmillan, 1925.

Evans, C. E. *The Story of Texas Schools*. Austin: Steck, 1955.

Ladino, Robyn Duff. *Desegregating Texas Schools: Eisenhower, Shivers, and the Crisis at Mansfield High*. Austin: University of Texas Press, 1996.

Preuss, Gene B. *To Get a Better School System: One Hundred Years of Education Reform in Texas*. College Station: Texas A&M University Press, 2009.

San Miguel, Guadalupe. *"Let All of Them Take Heed": Mexican Americans and the Campaign for Educational Equality in Texas, 1910–1981*. Austin: University of Texas Press, 1987. Reprinted, College Station: Texas A&M University Press, 2000.

Shabazz, Amilcar. *Advancing Democracy: African Americans and the Struggle for Access and Equity in Higher Education in Texas*. Chapel Hill: University of North Carolina Press, 2004.

Sraci, Paul A. *San Antonio v. Rodriguez and the Pursuit of Equal Education: The Debate over Discrimination and School Funding*. Lawrence: University of Kansas Press, 2006.

Still, Rae Files. *The Gilmer-Aikin Bills: A Study in the Legislative Process*. Austin: Steck, 1950.

CHAPTER 17

# Religion in West Texas

*David J. Murrah*

The West Texas religious tapestry at first appears to be no different from elsewhere in Texas or anywhere in the South. A majority of religious practitioners today are conservative and Protestant, and in large measure this strong tradition has earned the region its self-designated status as the "buckle of the Bible belt." But as this chapter shows, less prominent Protestant denominations—Quakers, Mennonites, Norwegian Lutherans, and German Lutherans, among others, as well as Catholics and Mormons, have all added texture and, in some cases, controversy to the tapestry.

Religion in some form has been practiced in West Texas for as long as human occupation of the area—12,000 years or more. Native Americans had well-established religious beliefs in place long before Europeans arrived. The West Texas vastness, with its reoccurring natural phenomena of mirages, towering thunderstorms, howling blizzards, and teeming wildlife, must have been a constant inspiration for nature-based worship and remains evocative in the modern age.

Europeans first practiced their version of religion in West Texas from the outset of the historic period in 1541—long before the pilgrims arrived in Massachusetts—when the Spanish explorer Francisco Vásquez de Coronado and his army ascended the plains of West Texas. In 1598, when an advance party of Don Juan de Oñate's expedition reached the Rio Grande in Far West Texas, its leaders celebrated with a thanksgiving service, perhaps the first ever held by Europeans in North America.

New Spain also made some effort to bring Christianity to the nomadic occupants of West Texas, especially after Jumano Indians pleaded with church leaders in 1628 to send religious teachers because they had been taught by a mysterious "woman in blue." In 1629 Father Juan de Salas led an expedition that reached the Jumano villages. By the 1670s some Jumanos had moved to a new mission, Nuestra Señora de Guadalupe, at the present site of Ojinaga, Chihuahua, and to another at Presidio, Texas. And in 1682, after a revolt by Pueblos against the Spanish in New Mexico, missionaries founded San Antonio de la Isleta, at a small settlement that became present-day El Paso, for the Tigua Indians.

In 1683 Juan de Mendoza and Fray Nicolás López went east from El Paso into southern West Texas and established Mission San Clemente, which may have been located near present-day San Angelo, Ballinger, or possibly Menard. There, Franciscan priests baptized more than 2,000 Indians during their six-week stay but abandoned their mission after attacks by Apaches and other tribes.

New Spain made one other major effort to convert West Texas natives. In 1757 Franciscan missionaries established Mission Santa Cruz de San Sabá for Apaches in West Texas. Located near present-day Menard, the site included a mission and presidio (a military garrison). But few Apaches were converted, and the outpost quickly became the target of Apache enemies. In March 1758 approximately 2,000 Indians, including Comanches, Wichitas, Tejas, Bidais, and Tonkawas, attacked and burned the mission, killing the priests and others. New Spain then abandoned its mission efforts on the West Texas frontier, except in the area of El Paso, where Catholic mission work has continued unbroken for centuries.

For another century following the destruction of the San Sabá mission, Comanches and other Plains tribes proved to be an effective barrier to further settlement in West Texas. Euro-American religious practices returned to the region with the arrival of the U.S. military in the 1850s. Chaplains came with units assigned to Fort Mason and Fort Belknap, both of which opened in 1851. Whether the military had any positive religious influence on the region's sparse Anglo settlements in that era is undetermined, but its presence allowed new settlers to begin moving in and to establish their own churches and schools. By 1858, Methodists had built both a church and a school at Fort Belknap.

The first religious service probably held at Fort Concho (established 1867) was conducted by the Ninth Cavalry chaplain, Joaquim Gonzales, in May 1869 at the post hospital. In 1871 the post chaplain, Norman Badger, conducted services in the nearby village (which would become San Angelo), and the post doctor noted that it was "probably the first time that the name of the deity was ever publicly used in reverence in that place."[1] In 1876 Badger also directed the erection of a chapel at the post, one of the first religious structures to be built in West Texas since the San Sabá mission.

In the 1850s as Anglo cattlemen and farmers had begun to make incursions along the eastern approaches to West Texas, established Protestant groups—Methodist, Baptist, and Presbyterian—were in the forefront of promoting religion in newly settled areas. These denominations had all established footholds in Texas as early as 1836, and by 1850 they accounted for three-fourths of all established churches in the state.

Waco became a launching point for religious work. Its first church, a Methodist congregation established about 1850, allowed Baptists and Presbyterians to share the facility for several years. Such cooperation carried through the West Texas frontier years as these denominations, along with the Christian (Disciples of Christ) Church, shared rural schoolhouses, church buildings, Sunday schools, and summer camp meetings for many years.

By 1860 the Methodist Episcopal Church, South, had a membership of nearly 40,000 in Texas, making it the largest denomination in the state. Even though the Civil War dealt a blow to church growth, Methodists responded in 1866 by creating the Northwest Texas Conference, which along with its sister West Texas Conference, embraced three-fourths of the state. The two conferences took the lead in sending circuit riders to the frontier. Supervised by presiding elders under the authority of a bishop, the circuit riding system proved effective for reaching widely scattered pioneer settlements. Participating clergymen would journey, often on horseback without further baggage, along a route from place to place, ministering to the inhabitants, bearing news, and conducting religious services, weddings, baptisms, and other sacraments.

In 1873 Bishop George F. Pierce issued a call for men to serve the frontier mission. "The dainty, the timid, have no business here," he warned. "The rides are long, the fare plain—the exposure in wind and weather very great, often severe—pay scanty. . . . Who will volunteer?"[2] One volunteer to answer the bishop's call was Levi Collins, who began Methodist ministry at Fort Griffin, which had been established in the late 1860s and was then the gateway to the vast West Texas region. By 1880, Methodist records reported 293 members in Taylor and Nolan counties, more than 10 percent of the total population of Near West Texas and the Panhandle.

Baptists also devised an effective ministry through cooperating churches combined as associations to send missionaries to the frontier. One of the first ministers to reach the area via Waco was Noah T. Byars, who had been appointed in 1848 as the first missionary of the Texas Baptist Convention. Byars, who owned the blacksmith shop where the Texas Declaration of Independence had been signed at Washington-on-the-Brazos in 1836, founded five Baptist associations from 1851 to 1876, all of which lay along the southern and eastern fringes of West Texas. He also founded more than sixty churches, including First Baptist, Waco (1851), and First Baptist, Brownwood (1876). By the end of the Reconstruction era, in 1875, Baptists had become the largest denomination in Texas, with more than 2,000 churches and 167,000 members.

Two other groups jumped ahead of the line of settlement and established religious colonies in the heart of the Llano Estacado's South Plains and Texas Panhandle. The first was a colony representing the Methodist Episcopal Church (based in the northern states), established by Rev. Lewis Henry Carhart of Sherman. In 1878 he purchased 343 sections of land and founded the town of Clarendon. He promoted the colony widely and soon attracted settlers from the North and East, including seven retired Methodist ministers. By 1880 the pioneers had built a small church there, for which Carhart purchased a large, cast bronze bell to call the faithful to worship. It was the first house of worship constructed in the Panhandle. The bell still survives, now located at the Lakeview United Methodist Church in Dalhart.

Not far behind Carhart, Paris Cox of Indiana in 1879 acquired a block of land northeast of present-day Lubbock and moved there that fall with four Quaker families to establish the community of Estacado. In 1884 the settlers built a Quaker church—the first house of worship on the South Plains. At its height in the late 1880s the community numbered about 200. In the 1890s, after suffering a locust swarm and drought, most of the Quaker community moved to Friendswood, near Houston. But some of the families moved to the Lubbock area, where they became influential in religious development.

In the 1880s, on the eve of the arrival of railroads in West Texas, two other denominations were poised to help evangelize the region. In 1843 two Presbyterian synods had been organized in Texas. Their work also followed the frontier, and when the Texas and Pacific (T&P) Railroad reached Abilene in 1881, Presbyterians were on hand to organize the city's first church. The Christian Church (Disciples of Christ) also labored on the frontier, but their work slowed in West Texas due to internal strife in the 1870s and 1880s. Ultimately a number of churches separated from the fold to form a new denomination that would later strongly influence religious life in West Texas: the Churches of Christ.

Once the railroads pushed across West Texas, the region began to grow rapidly, and new farms and towns soon dotted the region's wide landscape. Church growth followed closely on the heels of rail expansion. Baptists and Methodists vied to see who would be first, but evangelization was usually marked by a spirit of cooperation, especially among these denominations. Generally, the first denomination to construct a building would share it with other congregations, and nearly all groups shared a union Sunday school.

Baptists and Methodists were also leaders in the development of African American congregations in West Texas, but their white counterparts usually did not include them in sharing facilities. In fact, the Reconstruction era in Texas saw the end of integrated churches in the state, as emancipated African American Baptists and Methodists formed their own denominations and separate churches. One of the first in West Texas was at Jacksboro, where in 1870 residents formed the Mount Pisgah Church associated with the southern-based Colored (now Christian) Methodist Episcopal Church (CME).

The northern-based Methodist Episcopal Church took the lead in forming new churches and conferences for black congregations in Texas through
its support for the African Methodist Episcopal (AME) Texas Conference,
created in 1867. Fort Worth's AME church was founded in 1870. In time,
the city became home to six other AME churches, as well as eleven CME
congregations. Other AME and CME churches still in existence are located
in Amarillo, Wichita Falls, Big Spring, Abilene, Lubbock, Mineral Wells,
Vernon, Stamford, and El Paso. The strong, ultimately majority Baptist
presence in the region (with Methodists second) included African American congregations. By 1875 Fort Worth had two Baptist congregations. In
Wichita Falls, the Mount Pleasant Baptist Church began in 1891. By 1930
Lubbock had six black congregations, including three Baptist, and one each
of Methodist, Church of Christ, and Presbyterian.

Even though some integration of churches began in the 1970s, most
remained segregated. By the 1990s more than forty congregations minis-
tered to the black community in Lubbock. As in the rest of the nation, black
churches in West Texas for generations had assumed a large role in leadership development and in the fight for civic and civil rights that burgeoned
in the decades after World War II.

Meanwhile, other denominations focused on Anglo growth. Christian
(Disciples of Christ) churches were established closely on the heels of Baptist and Methodist in Seymour in 1880 and in Wichita Falls in 1885. By the
1890s the Christian Church was sending preachers to the Panhandle and
to El Paso, where they eventually established churches at El Paso, Lubbock,
Amarillo, and elsewhere. At the same time, many dissident Christian (Dis-
ciple) churches became Churches of Christ. Some of the earliest of these
in West Texas, at first sheltering mainly beneath brush arbors (trees, or
open structures made of poles and branches) were located at Clyde (1886),
Haskell (1888), Childress (1888), Crowell (1890), and Lockney (1894).

A similar dissenting movement divided some Protestant churches when
the holiness revival came to Texas in the 1870s. Preaching a Methodist doctrine of holiness, coupled with emphasis on baptism of the Holy Spirit, its
advocates held camp meetings that attracted hundreds. A woman minister,
Mary Lee Harris, organized holiness churches in 1895 and 1896 near Hamlin and later at Abilene and nearby Mulberry Canyon, as well at Buffalo

Gap, Rising Star, and Merkel. In 1908 these joined with other holiness churches to create the Pentecostal Church of the Nazarene, forerunner of today's Nazarene churches.

A scattering of Episcopal churches also appeared in West Texas about the time railroads arrived, first in Abilene in 1881, then in Big Spring in 1885. The first Episcopal Church in the Panhandle was established at Clarendon in 1889. Others soon followed at Shamrock, Amarillo, Plainview, Canyon, Pampa, Midland, and Lubbock. Slow growth in the denomination kept the area classified as part of a missionary district until 1959, when the Diocese of Northwest Texas was created, and subsequently seated in Lubbock. By the 1980s the denomination in Near West Texas included thirty-four parishes with 8,500 members.

Generally, evangelical Protestants thrived in rural areas of West Texas. There, they utilized schoolhouses and brush arbors for services. Methodists attempted to hold services in every community at least once a month, and other denominations filled in the other Sundays. Union Sunday schools were held weekly; on fifth Sundays there were special celebrations with

*Outdoor baptism, 1895, often seen in many parts of West Texas in the warm seasons. (Courtesy Southwest Collection, Texas Tech University)*

interdenominational services or singings followed by "dinner on the grounds."

Summer camp meetings, long a staple of American frontier life, also helped grow evangelical churches. The first camp meeting in West Texas may have been held at Fort Griffin in the 1870s, when Baptists and Methodists sponsored cooperative revivals that ran from ten days to two weeks. The first camp meeting in the South Plains area was probably held in Blanco Canyon in 1886 in Floyd County, very near the site of the present Plains Baptist Assembly grounds at Floydada. In Lipscomb County in the upper Panhandle, camp meetings began in 1889 under Methodist auspices. Farther west, near Dalhart, rancher W. B. Slaughter in the early 1900s hosted an annual summer revival at his headquarters on Coldwater Creek.

Perhaps the most famous West Texas camp meeting was that begun in 1890 by Presbyterian missionary William B. Bloys in the mountains of Far West Texas near Fort Davis. Initially begun as a two-day meeting to meet local needs, the event remained popular long after other areas of West Texas had stopped the camp practice. Always an interdenominational event, the Bloys camp meeting became a permanent fixture in Texas, hosted by Baptists, Methodists, Presbyterians, and Disciples of Christ. Still held for five days every year, the meeting attracts some 3,000 people annually.

When electricity came to rural areas in the 1920s and 1930s, the summer camp meeting began to fade in favor of denominationally-based revivals. By the 1890s all the Protestant denominations had adopted the practice of semiannual or annual revival meetings, which usually lasted from a week to two weeks. Methodist evangelist Abe Mulkey of Corsicana, with an entertaining style of folksy animated sermons, became a popular and frequent visitor to West Texas. His first tour was in 1893, when he held a ten-day revival in Childress and a shorter one in Mobeetie, where it was reported that there were more than 300 conversions and all the saloons closed.

Although evangelical Protestant groups would continue to flourish in West Texas, other denominations began to establish enclaves, especially after 1905, when abundant rainfall attracted new settlers, eager for land, in greater numbers than ever before. Land promoters often targeted ethnic or religious groups, and as the new settlers moved in, they helped to change the religious complexion of West Texas, sometimes dramatically.

In 1906 Mennonites began arriving in West Texas when a group from the Midwest purchased land in eastern Hale County under the leadership of Mennonite minister Peter B. Snyder. There, they built a schoolhouse, which also served as their church, and by 1909 had a congregation of nearly fifty. The community survived the disastrous drought of 1917–18 but could not sustain itself through the poor agricultural years in the 1920s. Meanwhile, in 1914 two other groups of Mennonites had purchased land near Littlefield in Lamb County. By 1916 approximately 160 had moved from the Midwest to Lamb County and established two churches. However, the severe drought that began in 1917 and the threat of conscription into the U.S. Army soon decimated the new Mennonite colony. Later on, in 1930, a group of forty Holdeman Mennonites settled near Texline, but again drought and then the 1930s Dust Bowl drove the colony away by 1940.

Two more Mennonite colonies developed in the upper Panhandle in the 1940s. In 1943 a group established the Perryton Mennonite Church, and still another group settled the Bethel Mennonite Church at Waka, southwest of Perryton. Eventually, in 1962, the two congregations merged, and today in 2014, the Perryton church continues to operate. Also, in 1975 Holdeman Mennonites returned to Texline and reestablished what has become a thriving community of more than 160 members.

One other large Mennonite colony settled on the Llano Estacado's South Plains. In 1977 Mennonites purchased land in Gaines and Andrews counties near Seminole and began relocating their families from Mexico and Canada. Some, however, were denied entry to the United States, and the federal government ordered forty-three families to return to Mexico or Canada. In 1980 the U.S. Congress intervened, granting legal citizenship to approximately 600 Mennonites. As a result, the colony began to expand, and by 2005 it had grown to more than 5,000, in five churches, making the Seminole colony one of the largest in West Texas.

Ethnic groups of Lutherans began to settle in the region after 1908. At the top of the Panhandle, a settlement of Norwegian Lutherans from the upper Midwest began at Oslo in Hansford County in 1909, and in 1910 they established the first Lutheran church in the area. Another Lutheran church was established in the northern Panhandle at Kiowa Creek near Booker in 1910 by German Russian immigrants, who also started churches at Lipscomb

(1915) and Follett-Darrouzett (1919). On the South Plains, German Lutheran farmers from Indiana founded a church at Rhea in Parmer County in 1910. In 1911 another group, German Americans, established a Lutheran church at Providence, northwest of Lockney in Floyd County.

Catholic work in West Texas also expanded among ethnic groups. At Stanton, Catholics created a German colony beginning in 1881, along with a Carmelite monastery. From there, Catholic ministries began in Big Spring, where a church was built in 1888. Catholics also built a church at Clarendon in 1889. At Amarillo, the first Mass was probably celebrated in 1887 or 1888, but a church was not begun until 1903, two years after the establishment of St. Anthony's Hospital by the Sisters of the Incarnate Word. In Far West Texas, Catholic churches were established in Sierra Blanca, Van Horn, Fort Davis, and Fort Stockton by 1916.

The West Texas Catholic community also grew after 1900 when German Catholic farmers, encouraged by land promoters, began migrating to the region from the Midwest. At Nazareth in Castro County, Mass was first celebrated by new arrivals in 1903, and the new community grew rapidly. Soon further immigration led to strong German enclaves and Catholic work at Waka, Groom, Dalhart, Umbarger, Happy, Olton, Pep, Slaton, Old Glory, Sparenberg, Hermleigh, Roscoe, Littlefield, Perico, Vega, White Deer, and Germania.

The Mexican Revolution of 1910 spurred Catholic growth in West Texas among the Hispanic population. Because of persecution in Mexico, thousands of Catholics fled to the United States. In 1915 the Diocese of El Paso was established, followed by the Diocese of Amarillo in 1927. At its establishment the Amarillo Diocese covered all the area from Junction northward, with twelve priests ministering to 5,000 Anglos and 19,000 Hispanic faithful. As irrigated farms expanded in the region, creating a greater need for workers, immigration from Mexico accelerated and so did Catholic growth in West Texas—to more than 140,000 by the 1960s. In 1961 the Catholic Church created the Diocese of San Angelo to cover the southern part of West Texas, and in 1983 it formed the Lubbock Diocese to cover the South Plains.

Protestant efforts to reach Hispanics in West Texas were meager. In Amarillo a Christian church for Mexican Americans began in 1926. Methodists have always maintained a separate conference for Spanish-speaking churches and, by the 1970s, had established twelve congregations in West Texas. Anglo Baptist churches sponsored missions for Hispanic work, especially during the influx of migrant workers during the federal government's *bracero* program of the 1940s and 1950s, but were reluctant to integrate them into mainstream worship. Unlike Catholic churches, most Protestant churches in West Texas were segregated until well after World War II.

As West Texas cities expanded after 1930, there appeared in all of them a modest number of small churches, most of which were Pentecostal in nature. Many such groups grew out of a reaction among the poor to mainline churches; others were fueled by a new wave of Pentecostalism begun in California in the early 1900s. In 1927 Lubbock had a church called the Full Gospel Tabernacle, and by 1940 the city had six churches serving Pentecostal and similar congregations. In Amarillo and West Texas, Pentecostalism was fostered by a visit in 1934 from California Pentecostal evangelist Aimee Semple McPherson, founder of the Foursquare Gospel Church. By the mid-1950s, there were fourteen Pentecostal churches in Lubbock. Similar growth could be found in other West Texas communities.

Although its beginnings in West Texas were slow to take root, the Church of Jesus Christ of Latter-day Saints (LDS) has become one of the region's newest and most visible denominations. The first LDS family in West Texas was a young couple, Thomas K. and Annie Jones, who moved to Lubbock from Collin County in 1924. A second LDS family, George and Mary Tosh, moved to Lubbock, and by 1926, through the work of LDS missionaries, the two families found each other and began to hold meetings in their homes. Over the next few years, the LDS community grew as Texas Tech attracted professors who were of the LDS faith. By 1928 the little band had held meetings in the Lubbock County Courthouse and later at a funeral home. In 1952 the Lubbock branch was formally organized and the following year constructed its first building.

Meanwhile, LDS groups had begun meeting in Monahans in 1939 and organized its branch in 1941. LDS work in Borger, in Hutchinson County, dates from 1944, starting with a Sunday school; its branch was organized in 1948. Also in 1948 the El Paso area held enough congregations to create the El Paso Stake (similar to a diocese). In 1967 the Lubbock Stake was formed to cover the South Plains and Texas Panhandle. By 1981 other stakes had been created for Odessa, Abilene, and Amarillo. Because of the rapid growth, LDS leaders in Salt Lake City designated Lubbock as the home for its third temple in Texas. Opened in 2002, the Lubbock temple became the focal center for a mission that covers all of Near West Texas and includes more than 10,000 members.

A number of other denominations are represented in churches through-out West Texas. They include Congregational, Seventh-Day Adventist, Sal-vation Army, Christian Science, Jehovah's Witnesses, independent Bible churches, and nondenominational congregations under various names. Lubbock and El Paso host Greek Orthodox congregations. Amarillo is home to a Buddhist temple.

Like Episcopalian missions, Jewish religious institutions tended to fol-low the railroad into West Texas, and synagogues soon appeared. In 1898 civic leaders Ernst and Olga Kohlberg helped to establish Temple Mt. Sinai in El Paso. In San Angelo, Jewish families built a synagogue in 1928 on property secured for that purpose in 1875, very early in the area's history, by local merchant Marcus Koenigheim.

The development of oil and gas fields, coupled with the need to serve military base personnel, prompted further Jewish expansion in West Texas. By the 1920s a Jewish community existed in Wichita Falls, and by 1940 there were synagogues in Amarillo, Lubbock, Borger, and Big Spring. In Breckenridge, merchant Charlie Bender organized Temple Beth Israel, a synagogue that served a wide portion of West Texas. Jews living in Mid-land encountered discrimination from its business community, so several families moved to Odessa, where they established Temple Beth El, in part to serve as a synagogue for Jewish troops at the Midland Bombardier Base.

The vastness of West Texas may have played a role in the establishment of two other sects, these bringing unwelcome notoriety to the region. Begin-ning in 1980, a small and unique sect styled as the House of Yahweh devel-oped a refuge near Abilene. The group was established by a former Abilene policeman, Bill Hawkins, who later changed his name to Yisrayl Hawkins. Described by a newspaper as a "self proclaimed prophet who warns his fol-lowers about the end of time and rails against a dangers and unclean world outside their West Texas compound," Hawkins settled his followers in a 44-acre compound near Clyde, and the group attracted little attention until one of its members was charged with sexual assault and Hawkins himself was accused of bigamy.[3] Hawkins later pleaded no contest to child labor charges, and the bigamy charge was dropped in October 2009.

In 2003, a polygamist group known as the Fundamentalist Church of Jesus Christ of Latter Day Saints (not associated with the mainstream LDS denomination) established an outpost near Eldorado, south of San Angelo. By 2007, several hundred adherents had moved to the area and constructed a temple, but in April 2008, reports of underage marriages prompted Texas authorities to raid the compound and remove more than four hundred children—a dramatic event that drew international attention. Most of the children were returned to their parents, but some individuals either have been indicted or still face indictment in 2014.

As West Texas grew in population after World War II, religious bodies grew proportionately. The 1950s became the Decade of the Church as young parents sought spiritual guidance for their children, and most city churches grew rapidly until the mid-1960s. By that time, approximately one of every three churches in the cities of Midland, Lubbock, and Amarillo were Baptist. In addition, 13 percent were Methodist; 12 percent were Church of Christ, and Presbyterian, Lutherans, Christian Church, and Catholic congregations comprised about 5 percent each. Pentecostal-style churches accounted for a major change since the 1920s, having become the second-largest group of churches, approximately 14 percent. Numerically, in 1965, Baptists in Near West Texas listed more than 300,000 members in nearly 500 churches. Methodists counted approximately 110,000 in more than 300 churches. Catholics (in a slightly larger area that included San Angelo) numbered 140,000. Collectively, the three denominations claimed nearly half the population of West Texas, which at that time totaled 1.1 million.

Since the 1960s, changes in the religious makeup of West Texas have followed national patterns. These have been characterized by a decline in membership among mainline Protestant churches, the emergence of new Pentecostal-style charismatic churches, and the rise of megachurches. Since 1965 Methodists in the denomination's Northwest Texas Conference, for example, have seen a decline of 40 percent in their membership and the closing of more than 100 churches. At the same time, West Texas cities have experienced major growth in nondenominational churches. In Lubbock their number increased from five in 1965 to twenty-two in 2008.

Growth in the megachurch movement has been remarkable. In 2009 the Hartford Institute for Religion Research listed sixteen megachurches (defined as having a weekly attendance of 2,000 or more) in several cities of West Texas—El Paso, Abilene, Amarillo, Lubbock, Midland, and Odessa. Of the seventeen, Baptists counted seven, Churches of Christ claimed two, and Methodists had one. Six were nondenominational; two of the largest of these, Trinity Fellowship and Hillside Christian, both are located in Amarillo.

In addition to spiritual matters, religious institutions have built a number of educational, medical, and retirement facilities across the region. Methodists opened the region's first college at Belle Plain in Callahan County in 1884 and later founded schools at Clarendon, Stamford, Plainview, and McMurry College at Abilene. The Quakers at Estacado established the Central Plains Academy in 1889. Baptists established Abilene Baptist College (now Hardin-Simmons) at Abilene in 1891 and Wayland Baptist College at Plainview in 1910. The Churches of Christ supported the Childers Classical Institute in Abilene in 1906, which was renamed Abilene Christian College in 1920; in later years the denomination also sponsored Lubbock Christian College, founded initially as a junior college in 1957. Holiness churches built Central Plains College at Plainview in 1907 but sold it in 1910 to Methodist investors who renamed it Seth Ward College. In 1911 Nazarene (former Holiness) churches opened Central Nazarene University at Hamlin. Today, in 2014 only Lubbock Christian University, Wayland Baptist University at Plainview, and the three Abilene schools—Hardin-Simmons, Abilene Christian, and McMurry universities—still exist.

West Texas clearly deserves its label as "buckle of the Bible Belt." For nearly five hundred years, hundreds of priests and ministers of all persuasions have worked and sacrificed to produce and serve believers. But religion in the region was an easy sell. Just as forces of nature brought spiritual awe to early man, they also influenced an agrarian society to seek a righteous path. The result has been the placement of many and varied houses of worship in every city and town across the region.

# NOTES

1. Bill Green, *The Dancing Was Lively: Fort Concho, Texas: A Social history, 1867 to 1882* (San Angelo: Fort Concho Sketches, 1974), 75–76.

2. Walter N. Vernon, Robert W. Sledge, Robert C. Monk, and Norman W. Spellman, *The Methodist Excitement in Texas* (Dallas: The United Methodist Historical Society, 1984), 151.

3. "House of Yaweh Hopes All Can Move On, 'Live and Let Live,'" *Abilene Reporter-News*, December 5, 2009.

# FOR FURTHER READING

Camden, Laura L. *Mennonites in Texas: The Quiet in the Land.* College Station: Texas A&M University Press, 2006.

Dillon, Merton L. "Religion in Lubbock." In Lawrence L. Graves, ed., *A History of Lubbock.* Lubbock: West Texas Museum Association, 1962.

Hallam, Anita. *"Hallelujah March": 75 Years of the Church of the Nazarene in West Texas, 1908–1983.* Lubbock: West Texas District of the Church of the Nazarene, 1982.

Mason, Zane A. *Frontiersmen of the Faith: A History of Baptist Pioneer Work in Texas, 1865–1885.* San Antonio: Naylor, 1970.

McQueen, Clyde. *Black Churches in Texas: A Guide to Historic Congregations.* College Station: Texas A&M University Press, 2000.

———. *Monahans Branch: The Church of Jesus Christ of Latter-Day Saints: Celebrating 55 Years.* Monahans, Tex.: Monahans Branch, 1996.

Moore, James Talmadge. *Acts of Faith: The Catholic Church in Texas, 1900–1950.* College Station: Texas A&M University Press, 2002.

Muchado, Daisy. *Of Borders and Margins: Hispanic Disciples in Texas, 1888–1945.* Oxford: Oxford University Press, 2003.

Murrah, David J. *"And Are We Yet Alive?" A History of the Northwest Texas Conference of the United Methodist Church.* Abilene, Tex.: State House Press, 2009.

Rathjen, Frederick W., and Peter L. Peterson. *A Century of God's Grace: A History of Lutheranism in the Texas Panhandle, 1908–2008.* Amarillo: Whitney Russell, 2008.

Vernon, Walter N., Robert W. Sledge, Robert C. Monk, and Norman W. Spellman. *The Methodist Excitement in Texas: A History.* Dallas: United Methodist Historical Society, 1984.

Weiner, Hollace, and Kenneth Roseman, comps. *Lone Stars of David: The Jews of Texas.* Waltham, Mass.: Brandeis University Press, 2007.

# CHAPTER 18

# West Texas Parks and Recreation Areas

*Sharon Morris Bogener*

In some ways West Texas represents a vacation retreat for the rest of the state. Two national parks, many large state parks, several national monuments, state wildlife preserves, historical parks and forts, and national grasslands attest to the unique but enormous recreational opportunities in the region. This chapter considers several of these parks and their history and also explores the shifting ideology and rationale for their existence.

T he natural landscape of West Texas encompasses areas of unsurpassed beauty, with abundant populations of plants and animals, many of which cannot be found elsewhere. State and national parks, wildlife management areas and refuges, monuments, natural areas, grasslands, and recreation areas offer ample opportunities for people to enjoy the magnificent scenery and wildlife that the region has to offer. Much of the beauty and many of the recreational opportunities are associated with natural areas, historical sites, and managed parks.

In Texas perhaps the primary provider of parks and recreation is the state parks system, which in 2014 included ninety-three parks—twenty-three of them in West Texas. In addition, there are two national parks in West Texas: Big Bend National Park and Guadalupe Mountains National Park.

Moreover, West Texas boasts the state's only National Wildlife Refuges—at Muleshoe and at Buffalo Lake near Canyon—as well as the only stretch of nationally designated Wild and Scenic River in the state: a 191-mile stretch of the Rio Grande that in part defines the southern boundary of Big Bend National Park. Both of the National Recreation Areas in the state are also in West Texas: Lake Meredith north of Amarillo, and Lake Amistad near Del Rio. The state counts fifty-one wildlife management areas, several of which are in West Texas, and like parks they offer hunting, hiking, camping, birding, and other recreational activities.

Philosophies governing state parks and wildlife management areas have evolved over the decades since the notion of public preservation of natural areas first took hold. Early parks in Texas focused on automobile travelers and roadside attractions. As automobiles improved and highways modernized, park administration shifted to meet altered needs associated with urban population dynamics and newer trends in recreation. By 2014 the focus on parks and recreation areas had become management

*Roaring Springs, Motley County, 1940s, historically a favorite camping site, watering hole, and recreation area for Indians and for early Anglo settlers. (Courtesy Southwest Collection, Texas Tech University)*

for preservation of unique and beautiful lands and for recreation through numerous activities, including hiking, biking, camping, hunting, boating, historical exploration, photography, that encourage visitors' acquaintance with the natural heritage.

The shifting rationale began with the change in western Texas from frontier to settled region in the early twentieth century. It led many people to see the value of open spaces, and in turn the idea of preserving public lands for relaxation and recreation spread. Such notions had first come to the state in 1913 with the City Beautiful Movement, which had originated in larger U.S. cities; among other initiatives, the movement encouraged the establishment of parks. Plans for larger, state-managed parks grew from these regional indications that increasing urban populations needed parks and rural pleasure grounds; eventually this momentum merged with national ideas and goals regarding land preservation.

In the 1920s the newly created Texas State Park Board began to oversee the acquisition and management of parks. Within just a few years Texas held fifty-one such tracts. Often the sites were too small to provide much more than picnic grounds, but most of the parks were in line with then Governor Pat Neff's desire to create campgrounds for people traveling by automobile.

During the Great Depression in the 1930s, the state park movement gained ground. President Franklin D. Roosevelt's New Deal initiative provided money and manpower through the Civilian Conservation Corps to develop several large state parks in Texas. In West Texas these included, among others, Abilene, Balmorhea, Big Spring, Davis Mountains, Fort Griffin, Garner, Lake Brownwood, Mackenzie, Palo Duro Canyon, and Possum Kingdom.

During the three decades from 1940 through the 1960s, park usage increased in the state, but funding for acquisition and maintenance of parks and recreational areas remained low, and not much was done. In the early 1970s Texas redefined its parks as "spacious areas of outstanding natural or scenic character" that should be selectively developed to provide resource-oriented recreation, that is, to focus visitors' activities on enjoying the various sites' natural attractions. Changes followed and new parks and recreation areas appeared.

Old or new, parks and recreation areas in West Texas may be grouped into four geographic subregions: the Texas Panhandle, the West Texas Plains, the Edwards Plateau and Southwest, and the Big Bend and Trans-Pecos country. Each subregion contains several parks, wildlife areas, grasslands, or recreational areas.

In the Texas Panhandle the first site considered for a park was Palo Duro Canyon, which lies in a unique and beautiful ecosystem, the Caprock Escarpment. The canyon is sixty miles long with walls rising from 600 to 800 feet. Carved by waters of the Prairie Dog Town Fork of the Red River, its striated walls, colored with reds, oranges, lavenders, and grays, are laced with layers of white gypsum. The green tones of various junipers, mesquites, cottonwoods, and hackberry trees provide shade from the intense West Texas sun and add to the beauty of the place. The park encompasses thousands of acres of scenic geological formations, including sandstone and mudstone formations, such as the renowned Lighthouse, that recall feudal castles of past ages.

The awe-inspiring beauty of the canyon had led to calls for a park there as early as 1906. Despite failed legislative efforts, led in 1908 by John H. Stephens, to secure the land to create such a park, the idea persisted. Finally, after extended negotiations, in the 1930s the state arranged a complicated system of loans to purchase almost 17,000 acres at the north end of the canyon and created Palo Duro Canyon State Park. The park has since been enlarged to more than 26,000 acres. Its 300,000 annual visitors can enjoy horseback riding, hiking, and camping. Since the 1960s, during the summer the outdoor musical *TEXAS* has been performed nightly to sellout crowds in the park's amphitheater.

A second park in the Panhandle, Caprock Canyons State Park, was established in 1973. It includes 15,280 acres of scenic badlands in Briscoe, Floyd, and Hall counties. The park's red-rock canyons are brilliantly colored and dotted with juniper, mesquite, and cactus. The less rugged areas feature cottonwoods, plum thickets, and grapevines. A small lake and a variety of grasses lure more than 175 species of birds to the park. Pronghorns share grazing space with the state's largest herd of bison, donated to the park system by the legendary JA Ranch from herds descended from native bison that survived the overhunting of the 1870s.

Caprock Canyons preserves more archeological sites than all other state parks in Texas combined and contains a trailway that was once part of an old, short-line railroad. Acquired in 1992, the trail includes Clarity Tunnel, the last active railroad tunnel in the state. Open to hiking, biking, and horseback riding, the trailway provides striking vistas that showcase the majestic Caprock Escarpment against the ever-changing blues of the Texas sky.

Plenty of other recreational areas exist in the Panhandle. Lake Meredith National Recreation Area, created in 1965 when the Bureau of Reclamation dammed the Canadian River, is a large though now (in 2013) shrinking reservoir with one hundred miles of shoreline and numerous camping spots. Alibates Flint Quarries National Monument, created in 1965 within state lands surrounding Lake Meredith, preserves a ten square mile area along the Canadian River and includes hundreds of prehistoric quarry sites and remains of several small prehistoric Native American villages. Alibates flint, characterized by multicolored banded patterns, is usually maroon and white, although other colors are occasionally found. The flint, important among premodern Indian societies for trade, tools, and weapons, was first used about 13,000 years ago.

Other unique public areas in the Panhandle subregion include the Kiowa and Rita Blanca National Grasslands, McClellan Creek National Grassland, Lake McClellan Recreation Area, Black Kettle National Grassland, and Lake Marvin in the Cibola National Forest and Grassland. These grasslands preserve native short-grass prairie, and also offer multiple-use areas for birding, hiking, fishing, picnicking, and camping. Viewing wildlife in its natural habitat also figures into recreational opportunities at Rita Blanca Lake Park, near Dalhart (the town owns and operates the park), which provides wintering grounds for thousands of migratory waterfowl, including ducks, cranes, and geese. The 7,667-acre Buffalo Lake National Wildlife Refuge near Canyon is also primarily a waterfowl refuge. Thousands of ducks and geese winter there, and more than 275 species of birds have been observed in the area. The lake has largely silted in, leaving a marshland and natural cover for a variety of wetland fauna.

South and east of the Panhandle, the West Texas Plains Area includes several state parks and recreational areas. Three of the parks—Abilene,

Copper Breaks, and Big Springs—preserve areas of scenic beauty. Lake Brownwood, Lake Arrowhead, Lake Colorado City, and Possum Kingdom focus primarily on water-based activities.

Abilene State Park includes 529 heavily wooded acres along Elm Creek. Primarily established for recreation, the park offers a swimming pool, wading pool, volleyball courts, a horseshoe pit, open areas for baseball and other sports, and a recreation hall. Some of the official Texas longhorn herd is housed in the park.

Copper Breaks State Park was acquired in 1970 and opened in 1974. Situated in Hardeman County, the park encompasses almost 1,900 acres of scrubby badlands, a section of the Pease River, shallow ravines, and low hills. The park is named for copper deposits in the area. The red-rock terrain allows for bird-watching, hiking, and equestrian activities, and two small lakes offer boating and fishing. Cynthia Ann Parker, who in 1836 was captured by Indians as a child and eventually became mother of the last great Comanche chief, Quanah Parker, was abducted from her home in Comanche territory near the park area in 1860 and returned to the white community, where she did not thrive and died, some say of grief, in 1870.

Big Spring State Park is dominated by eroded limestone and features early twentieth-century carvings in the soft rock. The spring for which the 382-acre park and adjacent town are named was frequented by people from dozens of Indian societies, as well as early Spanish explorers. Texas acquired the property in 1934, and the Civilian Conservation Corps built its original facilities, including a pavilion, headquarters, residence, and a three-mile drive that loops around the grounds. The park is located in an area where three ecological regions—Rolling Plains, Edwards Plateau, and Llano Estacado—come together.

On the Llano Estacado, three recreation areas exist in or near Lubbock. Mackenzie Park, located within the city, is named for General Ranald S. Mackenzie, a Civil War veteran and western army officer. It was established in 1924 when city developers acquired 138 acres in Yellow House Canyon to create Lubbock's first city–county park. Three years later, when it was enlarged to 542 acres, it became a state park. The Civilian Conservation Corps constructed roads, bridges, and recreation facilities for the park and planted trees. The state park system deeded it back to the city in 1993. In addition to a large golf course, disc golf course, swimming pool, recreation building, and facilities for camping and picnicking, the park contains a small amusement park.

Buffalo Springs Lake Park, a county-owned facility east of Lubbock, offers camping, fishing, boating, and hiking for more than 1 million visitors annually. Special events, including musical performances, powerboat races, and an iron-man triathlon, occur on an annual schedule.

A third significant park in the area is Lake Alan Henry, near Post. Owned by the city of Lubbock, the lake was created by a dam built on the South Fork of the Double Mountain Fork of the Brazos River and has fifty-six miles of rocky and rugged shoreline. The lake is known for bass fishing, boating, and camping, plus year-round hunting opportunities at the adjoining Sam Wahl Wildlife Mitigation Area.

Northwest of Lubbock, the Muleshoe National Wildlife Refuge is the oldest refuge in Texas, with 5,800 acres of prairie and three sink-type lakes. The refuge was established in 1935 to protect migratory waterfowl in the Central Flyway, one of the great migration routes of the North American continent. Birding enthusiasts have observed more than 300 species of birds in the refuge, including hawks, prairie falcons, and golden eagles. Sandhill cranes are the biggest attraction. They arrive in September and stay through February. The cranes roost on the lakes at night and forage in nearby grasslands and agricultural fields during the day.

On the eastern edge of the West Texas Plains are Fort Richardson State Park and Lost Creek Reservoir State Trailway. The 454-acre park preserves historic Fort Richardson, which was established after the Civil War. Although the post was abandoned in 1878, seven of its original buildings still exist: the hospital, officers' quarters, powder magazine, morgue, commissary, and guardhouse, plus a bakery that produced six hundred loaves of bread per day. Adjacent to Fort Richardson lies the trailway, a ten-mile hiking, biking, and equestrian route along Lost Creek that features beautiful scenery, abundant wildflowers, and wildlife.

Nearby Possum Kingdom State Recreation Area is a 1,528-acre park adjacent to Possum Kingdom Lake, reputed to hold some of the clearest, bluest water in the Southwest. Acquired in 1940 from the Brazos River Authority, the park sits amid rugged canyon country associated with the

Palo Pinto Mountains. Although some of the parkland slopes gently to the lake, most of the shoreline consists of steep cliffs. Ash, juniper, mesquite, oak, and redbud trees provide habitat for deer, turkey, raccoons, bobcats, coyotes, and, of course, opossums, the park's namesake species.

In the Edwards Plateau and Permian Basin subregions, state parks dominate recreation opportunities. These include a wide variety of parks and recreation areas. Some, such as Devils River, are primitive and hard to get to; some, such as Monahans, are easily accessible and are accommodating for families with children. All protect various kinds of natural resources.

In San Angelo State Park, four ecological zones converge: Texas High Plains, Rolling Plains, Hill Country, and Trans-Pecos West. Established in 1994, the 12,500-acre park includes the 5,440-acre O. C. Fisher Lake on the Concho River. The area shows evidence of human habitation dating back thousands of years, and seventeenth-century Spanish records indicate that a mission was established at that time to serve the resident Jumano Indians. Much of the land in San Angelo State Park will remain undeveloped to preserve Permian-era fossilized animal tracks and later prehistoric Indian petroglyphs, which can be viewed on guided tours.

Near the park is the Fort Concho National Historic Landmark, the reconditioned remains of a military post active from 1867 until 1889. As early as 1905, local citizens began an effort to persuade the city of San Angelo to purchase the fort as a park, and in 1924 the old military installation became a state historic site. Continued local interest led in 1951 to the purchase of the original headquarters building and the schoolhouse/chapel as well as reconstruction of two of the barracks for enlisted men. In the early 1960s Fort Concho was designated a Texas Historic Landmark. Living-history groups often visit the historic fort to reenact the lives of white infantry and white and black cavalry units on the Texas frontier.

The largest recreation area in the region is Amistad National Recreation Area, one of two national recreation areas in Texas. The enormous, 67,000-acre reservoir features rocky shorelines that offer excellent water-based recreation, including boating, fishing, and water skiing. Amistad in Spanish means "friendship," and this recreational area comprises the United States portion of the international Amistad Reservoir, shared with Mexico, a project started in 1969.

The reservoir is surrounded by a landscape rich in prehistoric rock art. Amistad National Recreation Area has two major rock art sites open for public viewing. Panther Cave, jointly managed with Seminole Canyon State Park, contains a rear wall covered, floor-to-ceiling, with hundreds of motifs that collectively form an uninterrupted panel more than 80 feet in length. The namesake of the site, a giant, red-painted mountain lion or panther, is more than ten feet long from nose to the tip of the tail. An on-site museum at Amistad houses more than 1.4 million prehistoric artifacts, the third largest collection in the National Park Service.

Upriver several miles from Amistad is Seminole Canyon State Park and Historical Site. Located on the lower Pecos River, it contains 2,172 acres of rough canyonlands. The park opened in 1980. Its rough and arid land-scape is populated by diverse flora and fauna, including white-tailed deer, raccoons, armadillos, and squirrels. People who inhabited the area some 7,000 years ago painted pictographs in rock shelters along the Pecos, Rio Grande, and Devils rivers. More than 200 pictograph sites exist, containing examples of art ranging from single paintings to murals 100 feet long. One site, Fate Bell Shelter, contains some of the oldest Indian pictographs in North America. The exact meanings of these paintings are lost, but their fascination for the viewer endures.

The Devils River State Natural Area, encompassing almost 20,000 acres north of Del Rio, was acquired in 1988. It contains many archeological sites. The park is very large and very remote: the nearest full service gas station is sixty-five miles away. Potable water is not available, and restroom facilities and campsites are limited. But the park is unmatched for a rugged river experience. Stretches of long, deep pools turn to wide shallows and relatively deep, turbulent rapids. The river is generally inaccessible and is essentially primitive and unpolluted. The area includes large, dense stands of live oak and pecan trees near the river, plus semidesert grasslands on ridges and slopes away from the stream.

Also in the area is Devil's Sinkhole State Natural Area, first known to Anglo settlers in 1867. The 1,859-acre site, in Edwards County, opened in 1992. The sinkhole is a vertical cavern, the opening at surface level measures 40 by 60 feet,. The circular abyss reaches a total depth of 350 to 400 feet and is accessible only by guided tour. Walls of the vertical shaft of the cavern support a Mexican fern species found in few other locations in the United States, and freshwater lakes ringing the perimeter of the sinkhole support two unique crustaceans: an endemic amphipod and a rare aquatic isopod.

Some 200 miles to the northwest lies Monahans Sandhills State Park, dominated by shining white sand dunes, many of which are as much as 70 feet high. The 3,840-acre park is located near Monahans along Interstate Highway 20. It opened as a state park in 1957. The park is a small portion of a large dune field that extends about 200 from south of Monahans north and westward into New Mexico. Indians camped in the area for hundreds of years, and early Spanish explorers noted the dunes in the sixteenth century. Abundant water lies beneath the dunes, providing sustenance for the willows and shinoak (*Quercus havardii*), plants that in turn stabilize the dunes. Shinoak, or shinnery oak, stands less than four feet at maturity but bears acorns like its taller relatives. Farther east, in the southwestern Hill County, is Kickapoo Cavern State Park. Located north of Brackettville, it encompasses almost 6,400 acres. The park opened to the public on a limited basis in 1991. Tours at the park showcase the area's birds, a primitive cave experience, and the viewing of thousands of Mexican free-tailed bats as they emerge near dusk. The park has fifteen known caverns plus biking, hiking, and birding trails.

Nearby is Lost Maples State Natural Area. Opened in 1979, it includes 2,174 acres on the Sabinal River. Archeological evidence indicates the park area has seen human use for centuries, but it is the combination of rugged canyons, grasslands, wooded slopes, and clear streams that draws most visitors. A large stand of Uvalde bigtooth maples (*Acer grandidentatum*) gives the park its name and provides spectacular fall foliage in the last weeks of October and early November. The rare green kingfisher can be spotted here year round, and other endangered birds can be seen in spring and early summer.

Garner State Park, with its deep canyons, crystal-clear streams, high mesas, and carved limestone cliffs, draws more than 300,000 visitors each year. The park's 1,419 acres were acquired in the mid-1930s and named for John Nance Garner of Uvalde, who served as Vice-President of the United States from 1933 to 1941. Visitors swim in the clear, cold, waters of the Frio River, scoot across its rapids on inner tubes, rent pedal boats, and hike its nature trails. The park's wildlife includes deer, turkeys, mourning doves, bluebirds, warblers, squirrels, and raccoons.

The 524-acre South Llano River State Park near Junction was donated to the Texas Parks and Wildlife System in 1990. Two miles of the Llano River front the parklands. The park contains a large pecan bottom, which is home to one of the oldest winter turkey roosts in the Hill Country. Other animals include wood ducks, white-tailed deer, squirrels, jackrabbits, javelinas, fox, beaver, bobcats, rabbits, and armadillos. Activities include camping, canoeing, swimming, fishing, hiking, bike riding, and bird and nature study.

The Trans-Pecos country contains the only national parks in West Texas: Big Bend and Guadalupe Mountains. The movement for a large park in the Big Bend began in 1933, and that year the Texas legislature created Texas Canyons State Park, consisting of 9,600 acres. Later the park was enlarged by 15,000 acres and renamed Big Bend State Park. In 1944 the state of Texas deeded the park to the federal government. The National Park Service acquired more land, bringing the total acreage to 801,163. The land is managed as natural zones and, except for a few structures and some remnants of abandoned buildings, remains largely unaltered by humans.

The southern border of Big Bend National Park is the Rio Grande, which flows through scenic Santa Elena, Boquillas, and Mariscal canyons. The park also includes the Chisos Mountains, the southernmost range in the United States. The mountains rise to 7,800 feet in elevation, with the Chisos Mountain Basin, an oasis in the Chihuahuan Desert, at their heart. Many of park's hiking trails begin near the basin. The park contains a wide variety of habitats, from river and desert in the lowlands to relict forests of ponderosa pine, douglas fir, Arizona cypress, quaking aspen, and bigtooth maple. The variety of plant life provides habitat for a multitude of animals, including some endangered species that can only be found in the Big Bend. The area is littered with archaeological sites, some dating more than 10,000 years before present. Paleontological sites, hot springs, the abandoned Mariscal quicksilver mine, and river rafting are further attractions. The park is one of the country's primary birding sites, with more than 450 species reported. In 1978 a 191-mile stretch of the

Rio Grande was designated a National Wild and Scenic River, 69 miles of which lie within the park.

Guadalupe Mountains National Park preserves some exposed remnants of the Capitan Reef, the most extensive fossil reef of the Permian period. on record. The park's 80,000 acres include the four highest peaks in Texas and beautiful McKittrick Canyon, known for its fantastic fall colors. The park contains pictographs from 12,000 years ago. Established in 1972, the park has eighty miles of trails for hiking and horseback riding. The trails provide access to the park's high peaks, deep canyons, and various springs.

Just west of Big Bend National Park is Big Bend Ranch State Park, the largest state park in Texas, encompassing more than 300,000 acres. Its rugged canyons, extinct volcanoes, and remote waterfalls include two mountain ranges. Fewer than 20,000 people visit the park annually, leaving it uncrowded, primitive, and pristine. The park features some of the most rugged terrain in the Southwest. Its most unusual feature is Solitario, a collapsed volcanic caldera nine miles in diameter.

North of the Big Bend National Park is Davis Mountains State Park and Indian Lodge. The Davis Mountains are the state's largest mountain range. The park, one of the state's first, opened in 1933 and covers 2,709 acres with piñon, juniper, and oak trees, and it is liberally sprinkled with wildflowers in the spring. The most recognized feature of the park is the pueblo-style Indian Lodge, built by the Civilian Conservation Corps in the 1930s. It includes twenty-four rooms, a meeting facility, a heated swimming pool, and a restaurant. The park offers birding, nature study, scenic drives, camping, and hiking, including a four-mile trail linking it to nearby Fort Davis National Historic Site.

Fort Davis was a key post in the defense of West Texas. The fort operated from 1854 through 1891, protecting settlers and travelers on the San Antonio–El Paso Road. Soldiers, including Buffalo Soldiers (black troopers), stationed at the post patrolled the Big Bend region; engaged Comanches, Kiowas, and Apaches; and served various civilian duties, such as building roads and telegraph lines. The fort became a national historic site in 1961.

North of Fort Davis, the area around Balmorhea State Park with its San Solomon Springs has long been an important oasis in the desert. The springs provided water for Indians, pioneers, ranchers, and farmers. The focal point of the 42-acre park is the natural-bottomed swimming pool, 77,053 square feet in area and 25 feet deep, built by the Civilian Conservation Corps in the 1930s. More than 20 million gallons of water flow through the spring-fed swimming pool each day. The temperature is a constant 72 degrees Fahrenheit, and the pool hosts the Mexican tetra, which (although a relative of the piranha), will eat tidbits offered from a diver's hands. Scuba divers often practice in the pool's clear waters.

Franklin Mountains State Park and Weyler Aerial Tramway are in El Paso County in Far West Texas. Local residents sought a park in the Franklin Mountains from as early as 1925, although their efforts failed until 1979. The Franklin Mountains form a rugged backdrop to the city of El Paso and extend north–south for twenty-three miles. The park's 24,000 acres make it the largest urban park in the nation and the second largest state park in Texas. It features Precambrian rocks (estimated to be 1 billion years old) and flora and fauna common to the Chihuahuan Desert. Franklin Peak reaches an elevation of 7,192 feet, and Weyler Tramway, located on the east side of the mountains, runs to Ranger Peak from which visitors can view some 7,000 square miles in three states and two nations. The tramway offers a spectacular vista of the vastness and stark beauty of the Southwest.

The 860-acre Hueco Tanks State Historical Site is thirty-two miles northeast of El Paso. Opened in 1970, it is named for the large natural rock basins, or *huecos,* that trap rain water. Indians and travelers, including people on the Butterfield Overland Stage, used water from the huecos in this arid part of Texas. Of interest, the rock basins host seasonal hatches of tiny, translucent freshwater shrimp that attract gray foxes, bobcats, prairie falcons, golden eagles, lizards, and other predators. Chihuahuan Desert vegetation mingles with the rock cliffs that soar up to 400 feet high. Three different cultures of Native Americans drew mythological designs and animal and human figures on the rocks. The pictographs include more than 200 face designs left by people of the Jornado Mogollon culture. The site includes an interpretive center and the ruins of a stagecoach station, and the park's massive cliffs are extremely popular with rock climbers.

Clearly, state and regional leaders have adjusted park management through the last century to keep pace with challenges related to changing ideas and philosophies concerning parks and recreation. At the same time they have kept pace with the transformation of West Texas from frontier to modern life ways, which in turn has produced needs for additional recreational and natural areas. As a result, from the striking and brilliantly colored canyon lands of the Panhandle through the broken lands, wooded areas, and picturesque settings of the Hill Country to the rugged and monumental vistas of the Big Bend, West Texas has a plethora of parks and recreational areas that are meeting modern needs.


## FOR FURTHER READING

*Big Bend Ranch State Natural Area Visitor Guide.* Austin: Texas Parks and Wildlife Department, 1990.

Guy, Duane, ed. *The Story of Palo Duro Canyon.* Lubbock: Texas Tech University Press, 2001.

Hogan, William Ransom. *The Republic of Texas: A Social and Economic History.* Austin: Texas State Historical Association, 1946.

Jameson, John. *Big Bend National Park: The Formative Years.* El Paso: Texas Western Press, 1980.

Kegley, George. *Archeological Investigations at Hueco Tanks State Park.* Austin: Texas Parks and Wildlife Department, 1980.

Maxwell, Ross A. *Geologic and Historic Guide to the Texas State Parks.* Austin: Bureau of Economic Geology, University of Texas, 1970.

Miller, Ray. *Texas Parks.* Houston: Cordovan, 1984.

Steely, James Wright. *The Civilian Conservation Corps in Texas State Parks.* Austin: Texas Parks and Wildlife Department, 1986.

———. *Parks for Texas: Enduring Landscapes of the New Deal.* Austin: Texas Parks and Wildlife Department, 1999.

Tyler, Ronnie C. *The Big Bend.* Washington, D.C.: National Parks Service, 1975.

# Selected Bibliography

Abbe, Donald R., Paul H. Carlson, and David J. Murrah. *Lubbock and the South Plains: An Illustrated History*. Chatsworth, Calif.: Windsor Publications, 1989. 2d ed., Tarzana, Calif.: Preferred Marketing, 1995.

Alexander, Thomas E. *The One and Only Rattlesnake Bomber Base: Pyote Army Airfield in World War II*. Abilene, Tex.: State House Press, 2005.

Alter, Judy. *Elmer Kelton and West Texas: A Literary Relationship*. Denton: University of North Texas Press, 1988.

Anderson, Charles G. *Reflections, an Album of West Texas History*. Snyder: Snyder Publishing Company, 1990.

Anderson, Gary Clayton. *The Conquest of Texas: Ethnic Cleansing in the Promised Land, 1820–1875*. Norman: University of Oklahoma Press, 2005.

Aryain, Ed. *From Syria to Seminole: Memoir of a High Plains Merchant*. Edited by J'Nell Pate. Lubbock: Texas Tech University Press, 2006.

Aston, B. W., and Donathan Taylor. *Along the Texas Forts Trail*. Denton: University of North Texas Press, 1997.

Austerman, Wayne R. *Sharps Rifles and Spanish Mules: The San Antonio–El Paso Mail, 1851–1881*. College Station: Texas A&M University Press, 1985.

Baker, T. Lindsey, and Billy R. Harrison. *Adobe Walls: The History and Archeology of the 1874 Trading Post*. College Station: Texas A&M University Press, 1986.

Bates, Larry. "R. C. Crane and the Promotion of West Texas." Master's thesis, Texas Tech University, 1996.

Bender, Avram B. "Opening Routes across West Texas, 1848–1850." *Southwestern Historical Quarterly* 37 (October 1933), 116–35.

Betty, Gerald. *Comanche Society before the Reservation*. College Station: Texas A&M University Press, 2002.

Britten, Thomas A. *The Lipan Apaches: People of Wind and Lightning*. Albuquerque: University of New Mexico Press, 2009.

Caffey, David L. *The Old Home Place: Farming on the West Texas Frontier*. Austin: Eakin Press, 1981.

Carlson, Paul H. *Amarillo: The Story of a Western Town*. Lubbock: Texas Tech University Press, 2007.

———. *The Buffalo Soldier Tragedy of 1877*. College Station: Texas A&M University Press, 2003.

———. *The Centennial History of Lubbock: Hub City of the Plains*. Virginia Beach, Va.: Donning, 2008.

———. *Deep Time and the Texas High Plains: History and Geology*. Lubbock: Texas Tech University Press, 2005.

———. *Empire Builder in the Texas Panhandle: William Henry Bush*. College Station: Texas A&M University Press, 1996.

———. *"Pecos Bill": A Military Biography of William R. Shafter*. College Station: Texas A&M University Press, 1989.

———. *The Plains Indians*. College Station: Texas A&M University Press, 1998.

———. *Texas Woollybacks: The Range Sheep and Goat Industry*. College Station: Texas A&M University Press, 1982.

———, ed. *The Cowboy Way*. Lubbock: Texas Tech University Press, 2000.

———, and Tom Crum. *Myth, Memory, and Massacre: The Pease River Capture of Cynthia Ann Parker*. Lubbock: Texas Tech University Press, 2010.

Carr, Joe, and Alan Munde. *Prairie Nights to Neon Lights: The Story of Country Music in West Texas*. Lubbock: Texas Tech University Press, 1996.

Cashion, Ty. *A Texas Frontier: The Clear Fork Country and Fort Griffin, 1849–1887*. Norman: University of Oklahoma Press, 1996.

Cook, John R. *The Border and the Buffalo*. 1907. Reprinted, Abilene, Tex.: State House Press, 1989.

Cool, Paul. *Salt Warriors: Insurgency on the Rio Grande*. College Station: Texas A&M University Press, 2008.

Cooper, Ralph. *First Methodist Church, Aspermont, Texas: A History of Methodism in Stonewall County, 1890–1967*. N.p.: n.p., 1968.

Cunningham, Mary S. *The Women's Club of El Paso: Its First Thirty Years*. El Paso: Texas Western Press, 1978.

Dale, Edward Everett. *The Range Cattle Industry: Ranching on the Great Plains, 1865 to 1925*. Norman: University of Oklahoma Press, 1960.

Dawidoff, Nicholas. *In the Country of Country: People and Places in American Music*. New York: Pantheon Books, 1997.

De León, Arnoldo. *San Angeleños: Mexican Americans in San Angelo, Texas*. San Angelo: Fort Concho Museum Press, 1985.

Dewlen, Al. *The Bone Pickers*. New York: McGraw-Hill, 1958. Reprinted, Lubbock: Texas Tech University Press, 2002.

Downs, Fane, ed. *The Future Great City of West Texas: Abilene, 1881–1981*. Abilene, Tex.: Rupert N. Richardson Press, 1981.

Duff, Kathryn. *Abilene on Catclaw Creek: A Profile of a West Texas Town*. Abilene, Tex.: Reporter, 1969.

Duncan, Dayton. "Below the Irreducible Minimum (Loving County)." In *Miles from Nowhere: Tales from America's Contemporary Frontier*, 173–87. New York: Viking Penguin, 1993.

———. "*El Despoblado*." In *Miles from Nowhere: Tales from America's Contemporary Frontier*, 217–38. New York: Viking Penguin, 1993.

Duty, Michael. *Wichita Falls: A Century in Photographs*. Wichita Falls: Midwestern State University Press, 1982.

Egan, Timothy. *The Worst Hard Time: The Untold Story of Those Who Survived the Great American Dust Bowl*. New York: Houghton Mifflin, 2007.

Elam, Earl H. *Kitiditi'sh: The Wichita Indians and Associated Tribes in Texas, 1757–1859*. Hillsboro, Tex.: Hill College Press, 2008.

Ely, Glen Sample. *Where the West Begins: Debating Texas Identity*. Lubbock: Texas Tech University Press, 2011.

Fink, Rob, and Tiffany M. Fink. *Love Unbounded: The Influence of First Baptist Church on Abilene, Texas*. Buffalo Gap, Tex.: State House Press, 2008.

Flores, Dan. *Caprock Canyonlands: Journeys into the Heart of the Southern Plains*. Austin: University of Texas Press, 1990.

Foppe, Regina E. "Response of the Roman Catholic Church to the Mexican Americans in West Texas." Master's thesis, Texas Tech University, 1976.

Fowler, Arlen L. *The Black Infantry in the West, 1861–1891*. Westport, Conn.: Greenwood, 1971.

Garcia, Mario T. *Desert Immigrants: The Mexicans of El Paso, 1880–1920*. New Haven: Yale University Press, 1981.

Glasrud, Bruce A., and Charles A. Braithwaite, eds. *African Americans on the Great Plains: An Anthology*. Lincoln: University of Nebraska Press, 2009.

———, and James M. Smallwood, eds. *The African American Experience in Texas: An Anthology*. Lubbock: Texas Tech University Press, 2007.

———, and Merline Pitre, eds. *Black Women in Texas History*. College Station: Texas A&M University Press, 2008.

———, and Michael N. Searles, eds. *Buffalo Soldiers in the West: A Black Soldiers Anthology*. College Station: Texas A&M University Press, 2007.

———, and Paul H. Carlson, with Tai Kreidler, eds. *Slavery to Integration: Black Americans in West Texas*. Abilene, Tex.: State House Press, 2007.

———, and Robert J. Mallouf, eds. *The Big Bend's Ancient and Modern Past*. College Station: Texas A&M University Press, 2013.

Godwin, Truman Dayon. *Tinker Carlen: An Original Cricket*. Denver, Colo.: Outskirts Press, 2007.

Gracy, David B., II. *Littlefield Lands: Colonization on the Texas Plains, 1912–1920*. Austin: University of Texas Press, 1968.

Graves, Lawrence L., ed. *History of Lubbock*. Lubbock: West Texas Museum Association, 1962.

——, ed. *Lubbock: From Town to City*. Lubbock: West Texas Museum Association, 1986.

Green, Donald E. *Land of the Underground Rain: Irrigation on the Texas High Plains, 1910–70*. 1973. Austin: University of Texas Press, 1981.

Griswold, J. T. *From Dugout to Steeple*. Nashville, Tex.: Parthenon Press, 1949.

Guy, Duane, ed. *The Story of Palo Duro Canyon*. Canyon: Panhandle–Plains Historical Society, 1979. Reprinted, Lubbock: Texas Tech University Press, 2001.

Haley, J. Evetts. *The XIT Ranch of Texas and the Early Days of the Llano Estacado*. Chicago: Lakeside Press, 1929. Reprinted, Norman: University of Oklahoma Press, 1977.

——, and William Curry Holden, eds., *The Flamboyant Judge: James D. Hamlin*. Canyon: Palo Duro Press, 1972.

Haley, James L. *The Buffalo War: The History of the Red River Indian Uprising of 1874*. Abilene, Tex.: State House Press, 1976.

Hamalainen, Pekka. *The Comanche Empire*. New Haven: Yale University Press, 2008.

Hancock, Tommy. *Zen and the Art of the Texas Two-Step: The Book on Dancing*. Austin: World Wide, 1998.

Haywood, C. Robert. *Trails South: The Wagon-Road Economy in the Dodge City–Panhandle Region*. Norman: University of Oklahoma Press, 1986.

Hickerson, Nancy. *The Jumanos: Hunters and Traders of the South Plains*. Austin: University of Texas Press, 1994.

Hofsommer, Don L. *The Quanah Route: A History of the Quanah, Acme & Pacific Railway*. College Station: Texas A&M University Press, 1991.

Holden, Francis Mayhugh. *Lambshead before Interwoven: A Texas Range Chronicle, 1848–1878*. College Station: Texas A&M University Press, 1982.

Holden, William Curry. *Alkali Trails: Or, Social and Economic Movements of the Texas Frontier, 1846–1900*. Dallas: Southwest Press, 1930. Reprinted, Lubbock: Texas Tech University Press, 1998.

——. *The Espuela Land and Cattle Company: A Study of a Foreign-Owned Ranch in Texas*. Austin: Texas State Historical Association, 1970.

Holliday, Vance T. *Paleoindian Geoarchaeology of the Southern High Plains*. Austin: University of Texas Press, 1997.

Isenberg, Andrew C. *The Destruction of the Bison: An Environmental History, 1750–1920*. Cambridge: Cambridge University Press, 2000.

Jordan, Terry G. *North American Cattle Ranching Frontiers: Origins, Diffusion and Differentiation.* Albuquerque: University of New Mexico Press, 1993.

Kavanagh, Thomas W. *Comanche Political History: An Ethnohistorical Perspective, 1706–1875.* Lincoln: University of Nebraska Press, 1996.

Keller, David J. *Below the Escondido Rim: A History of the O2 Ranch in the Texas Big Bend.* Alpine: Center for Big Bend Studies, 2005.

Kelton, Elmer. *The Day the Cowboys Quit.* New York: Forge Books, 2008.

———. *The Time It Never Rained.* New York: Forge Books, 2008.

———. *Wagontongue.* New York: Ballantine, 1972. Reprinted, New York: Bantam Books, 1996.

———. *The Wolf and the Buffalo.* Garden City, N.Y.: Doubleday, 1980. Reprinted, Fort Worth: Texas Christian University Press, 1986.

Kenner, Charles L. *Buffalo Soldiers and Officers of the Ninth Cavalry, 1867–1898: Black and White Together.* Norman: University of Oklahoma Press, 1999.

———. *The Comanchero Frontier: A History of New Mexican–Plains Indian Relations.* Norman: University of Oklahoma Press, 1969. Reprinted, 1994.

King, C. Richard. *Wagons East: The Drought of 1886.* Austin: School of Journalism, University of Texas, 1965.

Kupper, Winifred. *The Golden Hoof: The Story of the Sheep of the Southwest.* New York: Alfred A. Knopf, 1945.

Lack, Paul D. *The History of Abilene: Facts and Sources.* Abilene, Tex.: McMurry College, 1981.

Leckie, William H., and Shirley A. Leckie. *The Buffalo Soldiers: A Narrative of the Black Cavalry in the West.* Norman: University of Oklahoma Press, 1967. 2d ed., with Shirley A. Leckie. Norman: University of Oklahoma Press, 2003.

Lee, Mary Antoine. "A Historical Survey of the American Smelting and Refining Company in El Paso, 1887–1950." Master's thesis, Texas Western College, 1950.

Longo, Peter J., and David W. Yoskowitz, eds. *Water on the Great Plains: Issues and Policies.* Lubbock: Texas Tech University Press, 2002.

Malone, Ann Patton. *Women on the Texas Frontier: A Cross-Cultural Perspective.* El Paso: Texas Western Press, 1985.

Mann, Alan. *Elvis and Buddy: Linked Lives.* York, U.K.: Music Mentor Books, 2002.

Martin, Robert L. *The City Moves West: Economic and Industrial Growth in Central West Texas.* Austin: University of Texas Press, 1969.

Matthews, James T. *Fort Concho: A History and a Guide.* Austin: Texas State Historical Association, 2005.

McConnell, Joseph. *The West Texas Frontier; Or, A Descriptive History of Early Times in Western Texas.* Jacksboro, Tex.: Gazette Print, 1933.

Metz, Leon Claire. *City at the Pass: An Illustrated History of El Paso.* Woodland, Calif.: Windsor, 1980.

Moore, Richard R. *West Texas after the Discovery of Oil: A Modern Frontier.* Austin: Jenkins, 1973.

Morgan, Jonnie. *The History of Wichita Falls.* Wichita Falls: Nortex, 1980.

Morris, John Miller. *El Llano Estacado: Exploration and Imagination on the High Plains of Texas and New Mexico, 1536–1860.* Austin: Texas State Historical Association, 1997. Reprinted, 2003.

Murrah, David J. *"Are We Yet Alive?" The Centennial History of the Northwest Texas Conference of the United Methodist Church.* Abilene, Tex.: State House Press, 2009.

———. *C. C. Slaughter: Rancher, Banker, Baptist.* Austin: University of Texas Press, 1981.

———. *Oil, Taxes, and Cats: A History of the Devitt Family and the Mallet Ranch.* Lubbock: Texas Tech University Press, 2001.

———. *The Pitchfork Land and Cattle Company: The First Century.* Lubbock: Texas Tech University Press, 1983.

Nail, David L. *One Short Sleep Past: A Profile of Amarillo in the Thirties.* Canyon, Tex.: Staked Plains Press, 1973.

Neighbours, Kenneth F. *Robert Simpson Neighbors and the Texas Frontier, 1836–1850.* Waco: Texian Press, 1975.

Neugebaeuer, Janet, ed. *Plains Farmer: The Diary of William G. DeLoach, 1914–1964.* College Station: Texas A&M University Press, 1991.

Olien, Roger, and Diana Olien. *Oil Booms: Social Change in Five Texas Towns.* Lincoln: University of Nebraska Press, 1984.

Overton, Richard C. *Gulf to Rockies: The Heritage of the Fort Worth and Denver-Colorado Southern Railways, 1861–1989.* Austin: University of Texas Press, 1953.

Pace, Robert F., and Donald S. Frazier. *Frontier Texas: History of a Borderland to 1880.* Abilene, Tex.: State House Press, 2004.

Paddock, B. B., ed. *A Twentieth-Century History and Biographical Record of North and West Texas.* New York: Leois, 1906.

Pearce, William M. *The Matador Land and Cattle Company.* Norman: University of Oklahoma Press, 1964.

Perttula, Timothy K., ed. *The Prehistory of Texas.* College Station: Texas A&M University Press, 2004.

Porter, Millie Jones. *Memory Cups of Panhandle Pioneers.* Clarendon, Tex.: Clarendon Press, 1945.

Price, B. Byron, and Frederick W. Rathjen. *The Golden Spread: An Illustrated History of Amarillo and the Texas Panhandle.* Northridge, Calif.: Windsor, 1986.

Ragsdale, Kenneth B. *Quicksilver: Terlingua and the Chisos Mining Company.* College Station: Texas A&M University Press, 1976.

Rath, Ida Ellen. *The Rath Trail.* Wichita, Kans.: McCormick-Armstrong, 1961.

Rathjen, Frederick W. *The Texas Panhandle Frontier*. Austin: University of Texas Press, 1973. 2d ed., Lubbock: Texas Tech University Press, 1998.

Richardson, Rupert N. *The Frontier of Northwest Texas, 1846 to 1876*. Glendale, Calif.: Arthur H. Clark, 1963.

Rister, Carl Coke. *Oil! Titan of the Southwest*. Norman: University of Oklahoma Press, 1949.

Rodenberger, Lou Halsell. *Jane Gilmore Rushing: A West Texas Writer and Her Work*. Lubbock: Texas Tech University Press, 2006.

————, Laura Payne Butler, and Jacqueline Kolosov, eds. *Writing on the Wind: An Anthology of West Texas Women Writers*. Lubbock: Texas Tech University Press, 2005.

Rundel, Walter, Jr. *Oil in West Texas and New Mexico: A Photographic History of the Permian Basin*. College Station: Texas A&M University Press, 1982.

Rushing, Jane Gilmore. *Against the Moon*. Garden City, N.Y.: Doubleday, 1968.

————. *The Rainbow*. Garden City, N.Y.: Doubleday, 1977.

Scarborough, Dorothy. *The Wind*. New York: Harper & Bros., 1925. Reprinted, Austin: University of Texas Press, 1979.

Sheffy, L. F. *The Franklyn Land and Cattle Company: A Panhandle Enterprise, 1882–1957*. Austin: University of Texas Press, 1963.

Sherburn, Anne. *The Flavor of Odessa, 1891–1991*. Odessa, Tex.: Heritage of Odessa Foundation, 1991.

Skaggs, Jimmy. *The Cattle Trailing Industry: Between Supply and Demand, 1868–1890*. Norman: University of Oklahoma Press, 1973.

Smallwood, James M. *The Great Recovery: The New Deal in Texas*. Boston: American Press, 1983.

Smith, F. Todd. *The Wichita Indians: Traders of Texas and the Southern Plains, 1540–1842*. College Station: Texas A&M University Press, 2000.

Smith, Thomas T. *The Old Army in Texas: A Research Guide to the United States Army in Nineteenth-Century Texas*. Austin: Texas State Historical Association, 2000.

Sonnichsen, Charles L. *The Mescalero Apaches*. Norman: University of Oklahoma Press, 1973.

————. *Pass of the North: Four Centuries on the Rio Grande*. 2 vols. El Paso: Texas Western Press, 1968, 1980.

Spratt, John S., Jr. *Thurber, Texas: The Life and Death of a Company Coal Town*. Edited by Harwood P. Hinton. College Station: Texas A&M University Press, 1986.

Stuart, Claudia, and Jean Stuntz. *African Americans in Amarillo*. Charleston, S.C.: Arcadia, 2009.

Timmons, W. H. *El Paso: A Borderlands History*. El Paso: Texas Western Press, 1990.

Townsend, Charles R. *San Antonio Rose: The Life and Music of Bob Wills*. Chicago: Charles R. Townsend, 1976.

Tyler, Ron C. *The Big Bend: A History of the Last Texas Frontier*. Washington, D.C.: National Park Service, 1975. College Station: Texas A&M University Press, 1996.

Utley, Robert M. *Frontier Regulars: The United States Army and the Indian, 1866–1890*. New York: Macmillan, 1973.

Vigil, Ralph H., Frances W. Kaye, and John R. Wunder, eds. *Spain and the Plains: Myths and Realities of Spanish Exploration and Settlement on the Great Plains*. Boulder: University Press of Colorado, 1994.

Wade, Maria de Fatima, Don E. Wade, and Thomas R. Hester. *The Native Americans of the Texas Edwards Plateau, 1582–1799*. Austin: University of Texas Press, 2002.

Wallace, Ernest. *Ranald S. Mackenzie on the Texas Frontier*. Lubbock: West Texas Museum Association, 1964.

———, and E. Adamson Hoebel. *The Comanches: Lords of the South Plains*. Norman: University of Oklahoma Press, 1952.

Weaver, Bobby D., ed. *Panhandle Petroleum*. Canyon, Tex.: Panhandle–Plains Historical Society, 1982.

Weber, David J. *The Spanish Frontier in North America*. New Haven: Yale University Press, 1992.

Weddle, Robert S. *The San Saba Mission: Spanish Pivot in Texas*. Austin: University of Texas Press, 1964.

Whisenhunt, Donald W. *The Depression in Texas: The Hoover Years*. Boston: American Press, 1983.

Whitlock, V. H. "Ol' Waddy." *Cowboy Life on the Llano Estacado*. Norman: University of Oklahoma Press, 1970.

Willeford, Glenn P., and Gerald G. Raun. *Cemeteries and Funerary Practices in the Big Bend of Texas, 1850 to the Present*. Alpine, Tex.: Johnson's Ranch and Trading Post Press, 2006.

Williams, Clayton W. *Texas' Last Frontier: Fort Stockton and the Trans-Pecos, 1861–1895*. College Station: Texas A&M University Press, 1982.

Williams, J. W. *The Big Ranch Country*. Wichita Falls: Terry Brothers, 1954. Reprinted, Lubbock: Texas Tech University Press, 1999.

Wooster, Robert. *Fort Davis: Outpost on the Texas Frontier*. Austin: Texas State Historical Association, 1994.

———. *Frontier Crossroads: Fort Davis and the West*. College Station: Texas A&M University Press, 2006.

Zachry, Juanita Daniel. *This Man David—A Southern Planter*. Abilene, Tex.: Quality Printing, 1971.

# Contributors

**John T. "Jack" Becker** is an associate librarian at the Texas Tech University Library in Lubbock, where he works closely with the History Department. He has written several articles, book chapters, and book reviews on the American West and has published two books: *Georgia O'Keeffe in Texas: A Guide* (2012) and *Cotton on the South Plains* (2012).

**Sharon Morris Bogener** holds a Ph.D. from Texas Tech University. She is a professor of history at South Plains College in Levelland, where she has taught for the past fifteen years. Her publications on the Texas Parks System are among the most comprehensive such studies available.

**Stephen Bogener** is an assistant professor of history at West Texas A&M University in Canyon. He has published numerous articles and three books: *Ditches across the Desert: Irrigation in the Lower Pecos Valley* (2003), *Lubbock: Gem of the South Plains* (2003), and, with William Tydeman, *Llano Estacado: An Island in the Sky* (2011). Most of his publications focus on the confluence of environment, history, and culture in the American West.

**Thomas A. Britten** earned a Ph.D. in history from Texas Tech University in Lubbock with a research focus in Native American history. He is the author of *American Indians in World War One* (1998) and *The Lipan Apaches: People of Wind and Lightning* (2011), as well as several articles relating to Native American history and federal Indian policy. He is an associate professor at the University of Texas at Brownsville.

**Paul H. Carlson**, Professor Emeritus of History at Texas Tech University, lives near Lubbock with his wife, Ellen. He is a fellow of the Texas State Historical Association and a member of the Texas Institute of Letters and the Philosophical Society of Texas. He has written several books and articles. One of the articles and two of the books were also published in Europe, and one was a History Book of the Month Club selection in 1999.

**Sean P. Cunningham** is an assistant professor of history at Texas Tech University in Lubbock and the author of *Cowboy Conservatism: Texas and the Rise of the Modern Right* (2010). A native of West Texas, Cunningham also holds undergraduate and graduate degrees from Texas Tech University; he received his Ph.D. from the University of Florida in 2007. He lives in Lubbock with his wife, Laura, and daughter, Caitlin.

**Arnoldo De León** is the C. J. "Red" Davidson Professor of History at Angelo State University. His many books include *Mexican Americans in Texas: A Brief History* (2009) and *The History of Texas* (2007), the latter co-authored with Robert A. Calvert and Gregg Cantrell. He has taught at Angelo State University since 1973.

**Tiffany M. Fink** is an associate professor of history at Hardin-Simmons University in Abilene, where she lives with her husband, Rob, and their children. She is a native of Fort Worth and holds a Ph.D. in history from Texas Tech University in Lubbock. She enjoys the study of human attachment to place in the American West.

**Bruce A. Glasrud** is Professor Emeritus of History, California State University, East Bay, and retired dean of the School of Arts and Sciences, Sul Ross State University in Alpine. A specialist in the history of blacks in the West, his publications include *African Americans on the Great Plains* (with Charles Braithwaite) (2009), *Black Women in Texas History* (with Merline Pitre) (2008), and *The African American Experience in Texas* (with James Smallwood) (2007).

**Miguel A. Levario** is an assistant professor of history at Texas Tech University in Lubbock. His research focuses on the transnational context of immigration, militarization, and race in the U.S. West and northern Mexico, and his book *Militarizing the Border: When Mexicans Became the Enemy* was published in 2012.

**James T. Matthews** is employed by the San Antonio Area Boy Scouts of America. He is interested in nineteenth-century military history and has published articles on the black cavalry in West Texas as well as his award-winning book *Fort Concho: A History and a Guide* (2005). He and his wife, Becky, are editors of *The Cyclone*, the newsletter of the West Texas Historical Association.

**Monte L. Monroe,** is archivist for the Southwest Collections/Special Collections Library as well as adjunct professor of history at Texas Tech University in Lubbock. He is editor of the *West Texas Historical Review* and a former board member of the Texas Map Society. His book-length study "American Environmentalist: Ralph Yarborough of Texas" is awaiting publication. He was general editor of *The Centennial History of Lubbock: Hub City of the Plains* (2008).

**David J. Murrah** is Senior Historian for Southwest Museum Services, located in Houston. Previously, he was university archivist and director of the Southwest Collection at Texas Tech University in Lubbock. He has authored six books, all related to the history of West Texas. He and his wife, Ann, live on the Texas coast at Rockport.

**Curtis Peoples** is the archivist for the Crossroads of Music Archive at the Southwest Collection/Special Collections Library, Texas Tech University, in Lubbock. He holds a doctorate in history from Texas Tech, and having spent most of his life working with music, he remains an active musician, producer, and engineer.

**Gene B. Preuss,** a native of New Braunfels, took his B.A. and M.A. at Texas State University–San Marcos and earned his Ph.D. in History from Texas Tech University in Lubbock. He writes on the history of public education in Texas and is the author of *To Get a Better School System: One Hundred Years of Education Reform in Texas* (2009). He is currently an assistant professor of history at the University of Houston–Downtown.

**James M. Smallwood,** Professor Emeritus of History at Oklahoma State University, is the author or editor of thirty-five books and more than forty-five articles. He has twice received the prestigious Coral Horton Tullis Award, first for *Time of Hope, Time of Despair: Black Texans during Reconstruction* (1981) and again for *The Feud that Wasn't* (2008), a story of violence in Reconstruction Texas. He is a fellow of the East Texas Historical Association and the Texas State Historical Association.

**M. Scott Sosebee** is an associate professor of history at Stephen F. Austin State University in Nacogdoches, executive director of the East Texas Historical Association, and editor of the *East Texas Historical Journal.* He has published articles on Blanco Canyon rancher Hank Smith, on Hispanic people in West Texas, and on numerous topics related to East Texas.

**Leland K. Turner** is an associate professor of history at Midwestern State University in Wichita Falls. He has published several articles related to West Texas agriculture, and as a Fulbright Fellow is working on a book that compares cattle raising in the Australian Outback with similar activities in the American Southwest.

**Andy Wilkinson**, a poet, songwriter, singer, and playwright, has recorded eight albums of original music and has written seven plays. His work has received several awards, including the Texas Historical Foundation's John Ben Shepperd, Jr. Craftsmanship Award and five National Western Heritage "Wrangler" Awards. In addition, he is artist in residence at the Southwest Collection at Texas Tech University in Lubbock, where he is also visiting assistant professor in the School of Music and in the Honors College.

**Richard B. Wright** teaches the history of art and architecture at Texas A&M International University in Laredo. He holds degrees in art history from Wesleyan University (B.A.) and the University of Virginia (M.A., Ph.D.). Currently his primary research interest is the architectural history of Texas and the South Central United States from ca. 1900 to 1975.

# Index

Littlefield Lands Company, 51, 188

Livestock industry: cattle feeding, 21, 38–39, 112, 182, 190; goat raising, 4, 182–83, 209–10; and postwar economy, 208–209; sheep ranching, 4, 69, 71, 182, 200–201. *See also* Cattle ranching

Llano Estacado: agriculture in, 20–21; archaeological sites, 7; cultural traditions, 2; described, 16–17, 29–30, 185–86; economy, 185–90; geology, 14; Paleo-Indian occupation of, 15; parks and recreation areas in, 270–71; Spanish exploration, 16–17, 95. *See also* West Texas Plains

London, Nig, 124–25

"London Homesick Blues" (song), 228

*Lone Star Chapters: The Story of Texas Literary Clubs* (Wiesepape), 139

Los Lonely Boys, 227

Lost Maples State Natural Area, 274

Loving, Oliver, 187

LS Ranch, 32, 190

Lubbock: colleges and universities in, 263; as cotton growing center, 189; cultural achievement in, 155, 156, 224, 235; economy of, 45, 55, 129, 191–92; environmental problems, 21, 23; ethnic composition, 105, 109, 113, 116, 128, 130, 255; and New Deal programs, 174; population of, 23, 55, 56, 152, 153; public education in, 240, 241, 243–44; and railroads, 202; religious culture, 254, 255, 259, 260–63; school desegregation in, 246; songs written about, 230–31; as urban center, 5, 153, 159–60, 161, 162

Lubbock County, 52, 55–56, 110

"Lubbock Tornado, The" (song), 230–31

Lutheran groups, 258–59, 262

Lyle, Martha, 70

Mackenzie, Murdo, 49, 200

Mackenzie, Ranald S., 18, 31–32, 66, 121, 123, 198, 270

Mackenzie State Park, 267, 270–71

Maher, Peter, 81

Mahon, George, 175–77

Manso Indians, 75–76

Manuscript Club, Wichita Falls, 138–39

Marfa, 82, 85–86, 109

Mariscal quicksilver mine, 275

Massey, Sara, 136

Matador Land and Cattle Company, 48, 187, 188, 197, 199–200

Matthews, Lucinda Elizabeth. *See* Reynolds, Bettie Matthews

Matthews, Sallie Reynolds, 135

McCartt, Debra, 145

McComb, David, 152

McCullough County, 109, 110

McDonald, Walt, 220

McMurtry, Larry, 220

Megachurches, 262–63

Meinzer, Wyman, 218

Mendoza, Juan Dominguez de, 60–61

Mennonite colonies, 258

Mescalero Apaches, 30, 96, 98

Mesozoic era, 13, 14

Methodist Episcopal Church, 252–53, 255

Methodists, 252, 254–55, 257, 259–60, 262–63

Mexican American Legal Defense and Education Fund (MALDEF), 114

Mexican Americans: civil rights activism of, 113–14; cultural

historiography (7) -

Made in the USA
Columbia, SC
18 May 2023

16892698R00193